Breaking the Ashes

Breaking the Ashes

The Culture of Illicit Liquor in Sri Lanka

Michele Ruth Gamburd

Cornell University Press *Ithaca and London*

First published 2008 by Cornell University Press

Printed in the United States of America
First printing, Cornell Paperbacks, 2008

Library of Congress Cataloging-in-Publication Data

Gamburd, Michele Ruth, 1965–
    Breaking the ashes : the culture of illicit liquor in Sri Lanka / Michele Ruth Gamburd.
      p. cm.
    Includes bibliographical references and index.
    ISBN 978-0-8014-4660-3 (cloth : alk. paper)—ISBN 978-0-8014-7432-3
(pbk.: alk. Paper)
    1. Drinking of alcoholic beverages—Sri Lanka—Naeaegama. 2. Alcoholism—
Sri Lanka—Naeaegama. 3. Drinking customs—Sri Lanka—Naeaegama.
4. Naeaegama (Sri Lanka)—Social life and customs. I. Title.
HV5585.8G36 2008
362.292095493—dc22   2008020474

Cornell University Press strives to use environmentally responsible suppliers and materials to the fullest extent possible in the publishing of its books. Such materials include vegetable-based, low-VOC inks and acid-free papers that are recycled, totally chlorine-free, or partly composed of nonwood fibers. For further information, visit our website at www.cornellpress.cornell.edu.

Cloth printing   10 9 8 7 6 5 4 3 2 1

Paperback printing   10 9 8 7 6 5 4 3 2 1

In memory of
K. Sita Perera and
Christine De Nering Colvard

Contents

Acknowledgments		ix
	Introduction	1
1	Context: Religious, Historical, and Political Frameworks	25
2	Without One's Right Mind: Agency, Intoxication, and Addiction	46
3	We Don't Say No: Drinking and Identity	68
4	Jolly Drinking: Events and Taverns	87
5	Home Wars: Gendered Consumption Struggles	109
6	*Kasippu:* The Political Economics of Illicit Liquor	131
7	Over the Red Line: Social Rules for Drunken Comportment	156
8	Too Much Is Good for Nothing: Alcohol Dependence	176
9	A Goddess of Wrath: Treatments	201
	Conclusion	229

Appendixes:
	1. *Glossary*	237
	2. *Village and National Statistics on Alcohol Use*	240
	3. *Calculating Inflation in Sri Lanka*	244

Bibliography		247
Index		261

Acknowledgments

Writing is never a solitary activity, and I owe thanks to a number of people for the assistance I received in completing this book. First I want to thank my research associate, R. B. H. "Siri" de Zoysa. Siri is my guide, my mentor, and my protector. I rely continually on his enthusiasm and meticulous eye for detail. On the topic of alcohol, Siri is my local expert, without whom I would not have thought to write this book, and without whose vast insight I would never have completed it. He is a keen observer of humanity, with a gift for explaining unspoken social rules. Our relationship has not been without struggles and conflict, but it has stood the test of time. I am deeply grateful to him for his help over the years, for his unfailing good will, his dedication, his loyalty, and his full support. I hope that he will be pleased with the product of our labor.

Thanks also to D. Telsie Karunaratne, my good friend and source of pragmatic council and encouragement. Telsie welcomed me to her home, where I wrote the bulk of this book between April and August 2006. At her prompting, I have chosen a topic for "the next one."

R. Justin de Zoysa at the local Divisional Secretariat, Oliver R. Jansen at the Government Publications Bureau, and Dilrukshi Handunetti helped me procure Excise information and provided many other valuable insights. The staff at the Alcohol and Drug Information Centre, especially Rasika Manohari, made available to me the valuable assets in their library. Thanks to Dr. Manoj Fernando for speaking with me about the Mel Medura treatment modality, and to Swarna Kanthi Rajapakse for her eloquent translations. I wish also to acknowledge the Naeaegama residents who spoke with me at length about alcohol consumption. I appreciate the openness with which people welcomed me to the village and shared their experiences and feelings about this sometimes difficult topic.

For generous financial support and practical assistance I am grateful to the American Institute for Sri Lankan Studies and its representatives in the United States and Sri Lanka. Portland State University also provided funding for this research.

A number of people read drafts and chapters of this manuscript, including Sharon Carstens, Nancy Coleman, William Cornett, Peter Franklin, Geraldine Gamburd, Gavin Hymes, and Robert Willenbring. Many thanks for all of your comments and encouragement. I am particularly grateful to David Suggs and an anonymous reviewer at Cornell University Press for their trenchant questions and suggestions. Your insights have made this a better book; I alone am responsible for the remaining flaws.

Breaking the Ashes

Introduction

On Four Legs in the Evening

One afternoon in 2004, a neighbor came by with her son to visit the family I live with in Sri Lanka. I am a cultural anthropologist. When I do my ethnographic field work, I stay with my research associate Siri and his family in a village I call Naeaegama.[1] That afternoon, our neighbor brought Siri's father Martin a small gift. Siri walked through the spacious house to tell his father they had guests. Leaning on his cane, Martin made his way to the living room. He saw Siri's wife Telsie seated in the dining area. Martin, ninety-three years old, with failing hearing and eyesight, did not recognize his daughter-in-law. "Who is this pious lady (*upaasakamma*)?" he asked politely, trying to identify his visitor. The rest of us smiled.

Telsie said, "It's me!" several times, but Martin, striving to match her faintly heard words with a name he knew, could not understand. Coming to his father's rescue, Siri yelled in his ear, "She's *my* pious lady!" The rest of us chuckled.

The real guests identified and greeted, Martin settled gingerly into a comfortable chair and launched into poetry to comment on why he had not recognized his daughter-in-law of over thirty years. "When you get old

---

1. "Naeaegama" ("the village of relatives") is pronounced like the English word "nag" + ah + mah, with the vowel in "nag" slightly exaggerated. See the orthography provided in *The Kitchen Spoon's Handle: Transnationalism and Sri Lanka's Migrant Housemaids* (M. Gamburd 2000) for further details on Sinhala pronunciation. I use pseudonyms for local people and places to protect the privacy of my informants. In this book, I call only Siri's immediate family by their real names.

you can't see or hear well. Your friends avoid you when they see you coming," his humorous verses suggested.

Then Martin posed us a riddle: "What kind of creature walks on four legs in the morning, two legs at midday, and three legs in the afternoon?" We all knew this one: a man. Martin explained the answer anyway, waving his walking stick as the afternoon's extra leg.

Telsie then suggested an additional transformation: "In the evening, this creature goes on four legs again!" She referred implicitly to a man who drank so much he could only crawl. Everyone howled with laugher. Even Martin followed the joke. Siri, our resident drinker, smiled good-humoredly.

Martin's riddle and Telsie's addendum commented on the time- and alcohol-related changes undergone by the men of the household. Martin grouchily endured the slow transformations of age. Siri's substance-induced metamorphoses were swifter and less permanent, but disturbingly regular.

Theoretical Perspectives

"I'm going to break the ashes (*daella kaDaaganDa yanawaa*)," called one daily drinker to another as their paths crossed early in the morning on the road to the junction. The drinker's cryptic comment compared the warming power of alcohol—in the form of his first shot of *kasippu*, the local moonshine—with the rekindled heat of a kitchen fire. Why was this man drinking hard liquor before breakfast, and how did his family, friends, and neighbors react? In this book, I provide the background and context within which to understand this and many other drinking behaviors in the village of Naeaegama.

Anthropology strives to present a holistic view of social behaviors. One type of holism addresses the embodied, bio-cultural nature of human life. The study of mood-altering substances fundamentally debunks the possibility of splitting body from mind. Geoffrey Hunt and Judith Barker discuss "the inextricably intertwined bio-physical processes of the body and the socio-cultural phenomenological experiences of…the person" (2001, 176). Like all people, a drinker cycling to "break the ashes" is thoroughly embedded in material realities such as the potholes in the road, the rain clouds on the horizon, and the alcohol in his blood stream. But the cyclist also moves fluidly through the symbolic realm of language and culture, amusing his friend with a witty comment and keeping a wary eye out for the local police. Biological regularities ensure that alcohol has predictable chemical effects on a body. But cultural specificities mean that drinking behaviors differ; they differ between cultures in different places, within the same culture at different historical moments, between different individuals in the same community, and even within the same individual at different points in time and space. Mac Marshall, Genevieve Ames, and Linda Bennett point out the intricate relationships between "human beings as biological organisms, pharmacologically active substances…, and the sociocultural environments and historical settings within which those interactions occur" (2001, 159). In this holistic study of alcohol use, I explore the interaction between the physical effects of ethanol and the social contexts and meanings of its consumption.

People are what they eat—and drink—in both a physical and a social sense. One analytic theme that runs throughout this book is the relationship between consumption and identity. Recognizing the theoretical parallels between the study of food and alcohol, Hunt and Barker call for an integrated study: an "anthropology of ingested substances" (2001, 178). In addition to supporting basic life functions, the everyday practices of eating and drinking convey a great deal of symbolic meaning. Michael Dietler notes that food is "a special kind of material culture created specifically to be destroyed, but destroyed through the transformative process of ingestion into the human body" (2006, 232). Because we incorporate food by eating it, food takes on "an unusually close relationship to the person" (232). This close relationship between substance and self allows people to make symbolic statements through their choice of food and drink. Meaning imbues what someone drinks, and where, when, how, and with whom he or she consumes it (Douglas 1987). The morning drinker entrusts his bike to the guard at the railway gate, chats with the regulars lingering by the side of the road, and learns the latest gossip from a fellow drinker in the *kasippu* tavern's back room. By consuming particular substances, people make statements about their individual social position and the groups to which they belong. Thomas Wilson writes, "Drinking practices are active elements in individual and group identifications" (2005, 10). Through alcohol use, like other forms of consumption, individuals and groups in Naeaegama perform their identity.

As drinking creates social cohesion within a group, it also constructs boundaries between groups—boundaries with attendant relations of hierarchy and oppression. Compare, for example, the bicyclist peddling back from the tavern after his hurried gulp of morning *kasippu* with another local man—a gentleman climbing into an air-conditioned, chauffeur-driven car that afternoon after sipping foreign liquor in a hotel bar. Anthropologists retain the basic understanding of alcohol's integrative role in society, but also look closely at issues of power and politics. Hunt and Barker suggest, "Recent theoretical developments in anthropology have attempted to push the focus away from closed, static, taken-for-granted functionalist social systems and cultural orders into open, fluid, emergent relationships based on understanding access to, control over, and manipulation of power in relationships" (2001, 175). In Naeaegama, complex power dynamics permeate village society. For example, the cyclist's cryptic greeting reaffirms his place in the male drinking community but also earns the disapproval of the respectable housewife who overhears him while sweeping up leaves in front of her gate. In this way, alcohol use can simultaneously create solidarity within a group and set groups at odds with each other. As a contribution toward an anthropology of ingested substances, this book examines what and where people drink, and what their drinking says about their place in society.

Understanding the role of alcohol use in systems of power and inequality requires the analysis of both ideology and economics. In parallel with a discussion of symbolism and identity, this book presents a second analytic theme: an investigation of political economy. Economic studies consider the production, distribution, and consumption of goods and services. Who made this batch of *kasippu*, and how did it arrive at the junction tavern? Dietler (2006, 232) notes the usefulness of considering alcohol a commodity, examining the land and labor necessary to produce the raw materials; turn them into beer, wine, or hard liquor; and give or sell the alcohol to those who drink it. A political economic perspective examines what these exchanges mean not only in terms of profit but also in terms of power and prestige. Once manufactured, "Alcohol is deployed in the micropolitics and microstrategies of the manipulation of power and the construction of authority" (Dietler 2006, 237). Ethnographic and archaeological studies show that individuals and groups claim leadership by hosting feasts. Throwing a good party requires serving plentiful alcohol (J. Smart 2005; Wilson and Rathje 2001). This is certainly true of celebrations and informal drinking in Naeaegama, where by providing and consuming alcohol, people negotiate their standing in social networks of family and friends. Furthermore, what status does the rich but disreputable *kasippu* manufacturer hold in the community, and how does he relate with local notables, politicians, and policemen? Studying the economic and political aspects of alcohol consumption forms a key element in this holistic ethnography of ingested substances.

Politics is the study of power in human relationships. Power permeates all levels of social structures, starting with the household. After "breaking the ashes," the Naeaegama cyclist will return to his home, bringing a loaf of bread for breakfast. Paul Spicer cautions that "We can no longer base our theories simply on the public drinking behavior that is evident at the tavern and the ceremonial—settings that lead us toward findings of function and integration. We must understand as well the implications of drinking for hearth and home. For it is here...that many of the most troubling aspects of alcohol use are manifest" (1997, 318). In this ethnography, I examine political economics at the family level, exploring gender relations and household dynamics. Feminist anthropologists studying alcohol use around the world consider the micro-politics of household decision making, domestic violence, and women's organizing against problem drinking (Eber 2001; Harvey 1994). But to understand family dynamics requires attention to wider contexts. Frustration over local and international inequalities, social hierarchies, and lack of economic opportunities often provide the foundation for gendered struggles and domestic violence (Singer et al. 1998, 295). Caught up in Sri Lanka's ongoing economic problems, the morning drinker cannot support his family on a workman's wages, and his wife plans to get a job as a domestic servant in Saudi Arabia in order to earn enough money to buy land and build a house. The wide-ranging effects of transnational politics and the emerging neoliberal capitalist economy mean that scholars cannot study the household in isolation from wider national and global influences.

A related level of political-economic analysis focuses on how large-scale contexts and dynamics affect alcohol use. Noting the value of a historical perspective, Dietler writes, "Alcohol has come to be seen as an important component of the political economy and a commodity centrally implicated in strategies of colonialism and postcolonial struggles over state power" (2006, 229). For example, during the colonial period, government regulation of the alcohol industry fundamentally affected class and caste hierarchies in Ceylon, as Sri Lanka was then known (Jayawardena 2000; Peebles 1995; Roberts 1982). In the contemporary era, Merrill Singer (1986) emphasizes the importance of placing drinking practices within a context of global capitalism and national and international class relations. Singer also urges scholars to examine the role of government and industry in shaping consumption patterns (1986). Worries over corruption in Sri Lanka mirror international trends toward accountability and transparency (Sampson 2005). Currently, Sri Lankan laws govern the liquor industry, and law enforcement personnel deal with violations, particularly the manufacture and sale of illicit distillates. The morning drinker vividly recalls a two-month police crackdown on *kasippu* that shut down all but the largest village tavern. Now as in the past, government officials balance the importance of revenue earned from taxing the liquor industry against the value of reducing alcohol consumption to safeguard public health and social order. Government policies and police strategies reverberate through village society.

In discussing ingested substances, it is vital to separate use from abuse. A third analytic theme running through this ethnography examines how Naeaegama villagers distinguish normal from problematic drinking and how they handle destructive behaviors. Dwight Heath (2000) emphasizes the rich diversity of normal drinking patterns around the world. Cross-culturally, most drinkers do not drink to excess or become dependent on liquor, and alcohol use serves valuable integrative functions in society. Using the classifications of the cultures they study, anthropologists distinguish between normal use and problematic abuse—classifications that vary from place to place. In some contexts, only abstinence is acceptable. In other places, moderate social drinking or binge drinking may be the norm. People distinguish between allowable and problematic drunkenness, and many societies recognize heavy drinking and alcohol dependence as problematic. Although most people drink within socially accepted limits, cases of inappropriate drunkenness and addiction do occur.

As an ego-altering substance, alcohol raises interesting issues for anthropological theories of personhood and agency. In religious and social contexts around the world, people use substances to achieve transformations of self. These chemically induced states can enhance communication with the divine or diminish accountability for choices and actions. And yet drinkers maintain a degree of volition in their actions. As psychologist Craig Mac-Andrew and anthropologist Robert Edgerton wrote nearly forty years ago, alcohol is not "the solvent of the superego" it sometimes seems in Euro-American contexts (2003 [1969], 85). In every society, rules govern drunken comportment. Despite the influence of alcohol, most drinkers follow these rules. Lapses result in diminished respect and authority. Like intoxication, addiction also raises questions of personhood, as craving for a substance supposedly supersedes free will (Valverde 1998). Some scholarly and lay discourses tend to portray drug addicts and alcoholics as isolated, passive "others"—dangerous, different, diseased (Hunt and Barker 2001, 182, 169). But these individuals remain fully embedded in society. Ethnographic methods can provide data about the rules of drinking and the worldviews of drinkers. By putting people in context and understanding their choices, an anthropological analysis challenges stereotyped views about drunkards and addicts. As I hope to show in this book, ethnographic findings can prove useful in crafting treatments and public health initiatives.

I now return to the Naeaegama drinker riding his bike to go "break the ashes" early in the morning. To provide a holistic context for his behavior, one needs to consider the symbolism behind it and examine how the drinker and his fellow villagers construct his identity based on his consumption choices. One has also to understand his drinking in light of a series of political and economic backgrounds, including household and village relations, national policies, colonial history, and transnational capitalism.

To understand how his neighbors judge this drinker's early morning trip to the *kasippu* tavern, one should also consider norms governing alcohol use in the village, local definitions of problem drinking, physical issues of addiction and withdrawal, and available avenues for treatment. The best way to gather data on these issues is to engage in long-term ethnographic field work.

About the Author, Sri Lanka, and Naeaegama

My experience with the village of Naeaegama goes back to 1968. As a three-year-old, I accompanied my mother and father when my mother, anthropologist Geraldine Gamburd, began the research for her doctoral dissertation (G. Gamburd 1972). When I returned to Naeaegama in 1992 to start research for my own dissertation, I stayed with Siri's family, which had hosted my mother and father twenty-four years earlier. Since my initial year and a half of field work, I have returned to Sri Lanka on five different occasions for another two years. My research on alcohol grew out of a prior focus on transnational labor migration (M. Gamburd 2000, 2005) and the military (M. Gamburd 1999, 2004b), since some service men and husbands of migrant women drink heavily, and even more are perceived by outsiders to have this habit. During interviews, numerous Naeaegama women and men spoke passionately about problem drinking. To the topic of alcohol use I brought my interest in changing gender roles, the local effects of the country's civil war, and Sri Lanka's growing integration into the international division of labor.

Choice of a research topic depends on the fortuitous conjunction of available data and curiosity. My personal interest in alcohol stems from several sources. First, I must credit my trusted research associate, Siri. Siri drinks *kasippu* (the local moonshine), sometimes to excess. Life in Siri's household has given me, along with many other rich cross-cultural insights, some firsthand experience with heavy drinking. As anyone who has lived with a drinker can guess, our relationship has had its share of struggles and animosity. Nevertheless, it has withstood the test of time. I could not have written on this topic without my key informant and expert witness. A well-known and well-liked member of the village community, Siri has helped me develop a solid rapport with people in Naeaegama. As a social drinker, Siri had access to male drinking groups with whom I, as a woman and a non-drinker, could not socialize alone. He facilitated my entry into *kasippu* taverns and arranged interviews with both drinking and non-drinking villagers. He remained remarkably patient when our interviewees made personal comments about his drinking. A keen observer of humanity, Siri has a gift for explaining unspoken social rules. Between Siri's local knowledge

Fig. 1. The ethnographic team: Siri de Zoysa and Michele Gamburd. Photograph by J. Varuni de Silva.

and the openness with which men and women raised issues related to alcohol in his presence, I feel I have acquired a multidimensional picture of local drinking norms and habits. Siri's drinking habit provided both impetus and data for the book. I hope he will be pleased with the product.

Sensitized to alcohol issues by my research in Sri Lanka, I began to see them in many contexts in the United States as well. The struggles of several friends and relatives (though none in my immediate family) provided a second impulse for this research. The themes that emerged in my work with migrant women and military men provided a third impulse, leading me to consider alcohol not just from an angle of personal interest but also from a scholarly perspective. In-depth qualitative research in Naeaegama has enabled me to think critically about drinking patterns both at home and abroad and to begin to understand the complex mix of chemistry and cultural logic that governs alcohol use in these disparate social contexts.

Because my own views about alcohol color my research and my writing, let me position myself clearly from the outset of the book. I do not drink, but neither do I hold a strong moral, religious, or ideological stance against alcoholic beverages. I recognize the potentially positive effects of alcohol consumption, and I sympathize with the various reasons that Naeaegama men drink. Despite this, my deeper empathy lies with the women and families who suffer from alcohol's adverse social effects, and I worry about the physical consequences of heavy drinking for men. I have never been employed by or held any financial interest in an alcohol-related business. Nor do I have personal or professional experience with alcohol addiction and its treatment beyond what I present in this book. I bring to this research the academic training of a cultural anthropologist and over a decade of field work experience in the village of Naeaegama and the country of Sri Lanka.

In 2004 the island of Sri Lanka was home to approximately 19.5 million people (Institute of Policy Studies 2005, viii), the majority of whom live in the fertile wet zone in the southwest of the country. About 70 percent of the population follows Theravada Buddhism, with Hindus, Muslims, and Christians making up the remainder. The Buddhists and many of the Christians speak Sinhala—an Indo-Aryan language, while the Hindus, many of the Muslims, and some of the Christians speak Tamil—a Dravidian language (Eller 1999, 96). Over 90 percent of the population can read (Department of Census and Statistics 2001), and the country has long had the highest standard of living in South Asia (Central Intelligence Agency 2006).

Despite these social advantages, like many former colonies Sri Lanka carries a high debt burden. The International Monetary Fund, which reviews government fiscal policies, has advised Structural Adjustment Programs to help Sri Lanka pay back its debt. These programs have adversely affected the poorer portions of the population, among whom unemployment and underemployment remain high (Institute of Policy Studies 2003, 63–65; Ruwanpura 2000, 3). Although the market expanded after the February 2002 ceasefire in Sri Lanka's twenty-year-old civil war, "Major economic problems such as widespread poverty, a low per capita income, high structural unemployment, high inflation, a rising public debt burden, continued exchange rate depreciation and vulnerability to external shocks have continued" (Central Bank 2003, 3). The gradual renewal of hostilities culminating in the breakdown of the ceasefire in 2006 have further damaged the economy. The Central Bank reports that 25–39 percent of Sri Lanka's population can be classified as poor (2003, 9). Sri Lanka pays back its international debts using foreign exchange earned through the export of tea and manufactured garments and the remittances of migrant workers. All three sources hinge on the labor of women. Sri Lanka's foreign exchange earnings reflect the feminization of the international working class.

The Sinhala-Buddhist village of Naeaegama sits near the highway that runs along the south coast, about fifty miles south of the capital, Colombo. One's first impression of the village includes a crowded market at the junction, and a gradual decrease of traffic as one travels down a narrow road

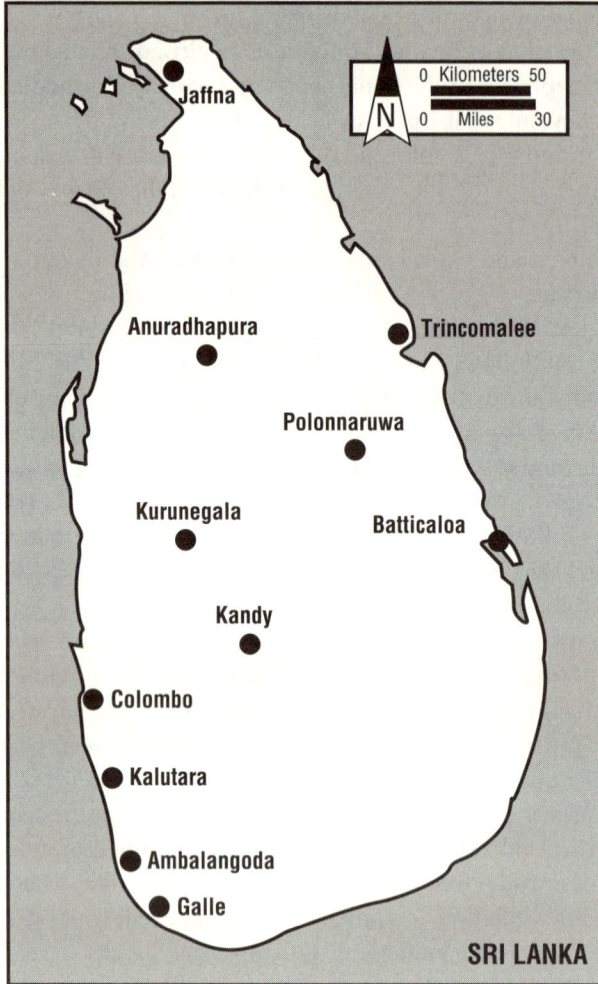

shaded by tall trees. Birds sing, children laugh in the school playground, and hand-operated bike-wheel machines clatter as women make coconut fiber rope. A mile from the coast, the village of Naeaegama narrowly escaped the waves of the Indian Ocean Tsunami in December 2004. That year the village had a population of roughly 1,100 individuals. Although a few villagers hold significant acreage, most people rent or own small plots of land that cannot support a family's agricultural needs. Local employment opportunities for men include work in the armed services or the tourism industry, civil service jobs, daily manual labor jobs, and self-employment as cinnamon peelers or makers and peddlers of coconut fiber brooms. Work opportunities for women include making coconut fiber rope, teaching, working in local garment factories, and laboring as migrant housemaids in the Middle East. In recent years, rampant un- and underemployment have assured that many families subsist at or below the poverty line.

Research Methodology

Research that I undertook in Naeaegama in 2004–6 generated information on local drinking habits. My methods for data collection included interviews, participant-observation at festive occasions, and analysis of statistical, historical, and media sources.

Interviews with more than a hundred villagers and other expert informants provided the bulk of the data used in this book. Although I speak passable Sinhala, Siri, who had studied English and used it frequently in a variety of jobs, accompanied me at all interviews to translate. In Naeaegama, I held interviews and informal focus groups with drinkers, their family members, and non-drinkers. I asked questions about drinking norms, the history of drinking in the village area, health consequences, alcohol-related accidents and fights, domestic harmony, household financial strategies, and definitions of normal and problem drinking. These interviews provided information on intra-family consumption struggles, particularly related to international female labor migration and masculine drinking prerogatives.

I recorded information with pen and paper, and I tried to write down particularly evocative Sinhala statements verbatim. I have inevitably missed a word or phrase here and there, but to the best of my ability I present what my informants said in interviews. In several cases to preserve the colloquial sense of the Sinhala utterances I have deliberately strayed from word-for-word translations, but I have retained the flow of the conversation and the gist of the meaning. I entered notes into my computer immediately after each interview, while the details were fresh in my mind. Unless otherwise marked, all quotes are Siri's and/or my translations from Sinhala. I have indicated in the text when informants spoke in English. I have also included some important Sinhala words and phrases. (See Appendix 1 for a glossary of terms.)

Alcohol plays a major role in Sri Lankan ceremonies, where people gather to negotiate social status and reinforce social bonds. As they occurred during my time in Naeaegama, I attended over a dozen ceremonies, including coming-of-age ceremonies, weddings, funerals, and other occasions where the hosts served alcohol. I noted behaviors of drinking and non-drinking guests and tried to ascertain the rituals, customs, and gender roles surrounding alcohol use. To understand social networks, I paid particular attention to which friends and relatives attended, and who drank together. Because self-reporting of alcohol consumption is notoriously unreliable (Abeyasinghe 2002; Pernanen 1991), my observations at events, holidays, and celebrations provided a crosscheck for behaviors reported during interviews. Through these observations, I determined what sorts of behavior are expected and witnessed after drinking, and which among these are judged deviant.

In and out of the village, I talked with law enforcement officials and politicians. I also visited several *kasippu* taverns and learned about the production of illicit liquor. On the topic of problem drinking, I interviewed western doctors, native healers, and practitioners at Buddhist temples, other religious institutions, and non-governmental organizations that run formal and informal therapeutic programs. In addition, to acquire a national-level context for local alcohol consumption data, I consulted material from governmental institutions regarding changing policies on alcohol, and gathered statistical material regarding trends in alcohol consumption. By collecting data through a variety of methods from a diverse array of sources, I have tried to present multiple perspectives on alcohol use in Naeaegama.

Methodological Challenges and Ethical Questions

The study of alcohol poses a number of methodological and ethical challenges. These issues are both inherent to the general study of alcohol use and particular to my research in the village of Naeaegama. The first challenge, a perennial one for anthropologists, consists of understanding things that happen in another language and culture. Time, experience, and expert translation greatly facilitate comprehension. In the three and a half years that I spent in Sri Lanka between October 1992 and August 2006, with Siri's able assistance I interviewed members of all the Naeaegama households about one topic or another. My in-depth, holistic research provides a longitudinal perspective on events in the area. Although as a foreigner I will always remain a stranger to a certain degree, my outsider status grants certain advantages—it allows me to ask questions on topics that natives might not bring up, and I am struck by the newness and difference of Naeaegama practices that natives might take for granted.

The more I learned of the local drinking culture, the clearer the second challenge grew. Most anthropologists rely heavily on participant observation, but in Naeaegama respectable women do not drink. Local norms thus forbade my participation in the activity I chose to study. This posed no personal hardship, but greatly limited my access to an important source of data. Luckily Siri provided endless colorful details about all-male drinking activities. I would have little understanding of what goes on among drinkers at ceremonies or in drinking establishments were it not for Siri's gracious generosity with his knowledge and experience. Siri also facilitated interviews with drinkers, who spoke freely in his presence. In some cases both the drinker and I hesitated to start talking about alcohol, but Siri easily broke the ice, sparking open and relaxed discussions.

Although it limited me in some ways, my gender proved advantageous in talking with women and other non-drinkers, who spoke unreservedly with me about alcohol. Villagers' assumptions that all westerners drink must inevitably have colored our conversations, perhaps prompting people to speak more or less harshly about alcohol than they would have otherwise. Here Siri's presence as a male drinker posed a third challenge to the research. At first I worried that women and non-drinkers might feel inhibited and self-censor in Siri's presence. But interviewees seemed to speak their opinions freely. Some took an "if the shoe fits, wear it" attitude when talking about alcohol use in front of Siri; others politely stated that they excluded him from the categories and behaviors they discussed. Occasionally Siri got into lively discussions with people critical of and even hostile toward alcohol use, but the debates did not grow angry or heated. Instead, these interviews provided a venue for a type of discussion that would not have occurred otherwise. These informal focus groups generated some of the most valuable data I gathered.

Sociologist Robin Room (1984) discusses a fourth challenge, this one to qualitative field work in general. Room suggests that anthropologists often miss the types of data garnered through epidemiological and other quantitative studies. For example, statistical data could accurately present information on recorded rates of alcohol-related health problems, accidents, and violence. I agree that quantitative research done throughout Sri Lanka, in both rural and urban areas, would reveal valuable information. Acknowledging the importance of quantitative data, to shed light on what I learned in Naeaegama and to place the village data in a wider context I provide some statistical information in this chapter and in Appendix 2. But as Heath points out, ethnographers recognize the importance of studies that emphasize depth rather than breadth (1987, 41). Without strong background from qualitative data, quantitative researchers have little basis for designing surveys or interpreting statistics. To understand another culture and learn about local theories and interpretations, long-term, in-depth, ethnographic methods have no equal. With few exceptions, the data in this study is unabashedly qualitative in nature.

The personal and particular nature of ethnographic work presents a fifth challenge. By sampling widely within the village population, I have tried to gather a representative range of views on alcohol use. But I may have missed or exaggerated various positions, for example neglecting or overemphasizing the problems or pleasures inherent in alcohol use. Room (1984, 172) suggests that anthropologists might easily see the public fun of the (usually male) drinking group, but not the private anguish of wives and children, especially if the researcher does not have access to the household. In my work I experienced the opposite problem, and I have struggled to give due hearing to male drinking because the majority of my female and non-drinking informants disapproved of alcohol use. Further, people find some topics difficult to discuss, and certain individuals speak more eloquently and voluminously than others. Even more challenging are those who do not speak at all. Ethnography, based on stories and interviews, struggles to deal with silences (Das 1997). Feminist anthropology has grappled with the thorny issue of multiple perspectives and subaltern narratives for several decades (Spivak 1985). By presenting many voices in my work, I strive to preserve the diversity of local opinions and avoid imposing a single authoritative interpretation (Clifford and Marcus 1986; Foucault 1994).

Thornier still on both the conceptual and ethical levels is a sixth challenge—how to do ethnography on altered states of consciousness. A researcher who became intoxicated while participating in and observing drinking behaviors might have difficulties understanding, remembering, and recording the experience. Personal preference and local gender norms kept this from becoming an issue for me in Naeaegama. But several of my alcohol-dependent informants always had some liquor in their system, making it impossible for me to interview them while they were sober. This raised a question of utmost ethical importance: can a drunken individual give informed consent for an interview? If people seemed coherent, I talked with them. I did not interview obviously intoxicated individuals; they made little sense to me and probably did not understand or care when I told them who I was, why I wanted to speak with them, and what I would do with the data I collected. Although I have no regrets about avoiding overtly drunken informants, Kai Pernanen (1991) sees a shortcoming in the fact that researchers never take intoxicated people's ideas into account. He writes, "The points of reference have been exclusively from a sober viewpoint" (Pernanen 1991, 211). I have tried to compensate for this bias by talking with drinkers uncritically about their memories of alcohol-induced highs, withdrawal symptoms, and other drinking experiences.

Issues presenting a seventh challenge arise when researching and writing about the production, distribution, and consumption of an illegal substance. On the methodological front, difficulties come up in estimating countrywide alcohol consumption, because drinkers may prefer not to admit to researchers that they drink illicit liquor, and its sales go unreported

(R. Smart 1998). Because women rarely drink at all and many men drink cheap illicit liquor in Sri Lanka, the official per capita rate does not reflect actual consumption (Hettige 1991). "To write of average individual consumption in a country where most of the alcohol consumed is probably illicit and unrecorded...has little meaning," notes Diyanath Samarasinghe, a leading Sri Lankan expert on alcohol (2006, 626). Nevertheless, scholars propose best-guess estimates of consumption. The Alcohol and Drug Information Center (ADIC) estimates that only half of the liquor consumed in Sri Lanka is legal (1999, 5); Bergljot Baklien and Samarasinghe (2003, 13) suggest that 50–70 percent of the alcohol consumed in Sri Lanka is illicit; Ranil Abeyasinghe (2002, 125) gives a similar estimate of 60 percent; and the World Health Organization (WHO) places the figure as high as 90 percent (2004b, 3). Siri felt that the illicit distillate *kasippu* accounted for most of the liquor consumed in the Naeaegama area, with men indulging in arrack (legally distilled palm liquor) only on special occasions. In this instance, qualitative field work usefully informs quantitative estimates.

On the ethical front, Abeyasinghe (2002, 18) suggests that talking or writing indiscreetly about *kasippu* can get drinkers, sellers, manufacturers, and researchers into trouble. Nevertheless, a number of scholars and local media sources have discussed this well-known problem (Baklien and Samarasinghe 2003). In Naeaegama, most people accepted (although they did not necessarily condone) the consumption of *kasippu* and discussed this illicit distillate freely. To protect individuals from potential problems with *kasippu* manufacturers or law enforcement officers, throughout this book I use pseudonyms for people and places, and I take care to disguise identities of those involved with the illicit liquor trade.

An eighth and final challenge concerns writing about alcohol use of any type, either legal or illicit, in a Buddhist context where the production and consumption of intoxicating substances violates fundamental religious dictates. By publishing on this topic, I draw attention to an aspect of local culture that respectable teetotalers, local women, ordinary Buddhists, and Sinhala-Buddhist nationalists may find shameful. Although I have not chosen this topic to denigrate the country, critics may feel I have exposed an ugly underbelly of society best left hidden.[2] They may also suggest that as a foreigner I have no right to "blame" Sri Lankans for a habit introduced by other foreigners—the colonists of prior centuries.

2. The impulse to silence unpleasant news ties into a larger social pattern where the powers that be censor reporting on a variety of topics. As the editor of the *Sunday Times* (an English-language newspaper in Sri Lanka) remarked about past restrictions on press freedoms, "Their credo seemed to be 'if it was not reported it never happened'" ("Censorship and Cacophony" 2006, 10).

I answer these anticipated criticisms as follows. First, this book does not pass judgment on alcohol or its users. I neither support nor condemn alcohol consumption, though I present local opinions that do both. Most Naeaegama drinkers consume alcohol in socially accepted ways. A small percentage becomes dependent on alcohol. Alcohol addiction, like drug addiction and the spread of HIV/AIDS (also blamed on foreigners in Sri Lanka), are serious public health issues that, whatever their origin, require attention, beginning with research into the nature of the problem in the local context. Epidemiologists note that the worst thing one can do in the case of the HIV/ AIDS epidemic is to remain silent about the topic, keep people in ignorance, and thus facilitate the spread of the disease. Alcohol use affects many more people in Sri Lanka than do HIV/AIDS and illicit drugs. While most drinkers use alcohol responsibly, alcohol use does cause problems. My own concerns on this score echo those voiced by community members in Naeaegama and by local scholars (Abeyasinghe 2002; Samarasinghe 2005, 2006). This book on alcohol fits into an extensive corpus of anthropological literature on Sri Lanka covering a wide variety of topics. Using a holistic approach and accepted ethnographic methodologies, I have investigated the role of alcohol in a village community, considering both moderate social drinking and problem drinking. If critics find the situation I describe bad, shameful, or in need of change, I hope that my research will provide a useful stepping-off point for remedies. My silence would not change the evidence, and "shooting the messenger" will have no ameliorating effect on the state of affairs.

Village Drinking

Despite Buddhist prohibitions on the consumption of mind-altering substances, many men in Naeaegama regularly drank liquor, known as *mat paen* in Sinhala. The verb *bonDa* means "to drink," and covers the consumption of water, juice, and tea, as well as alcoholic beverages. One also "drinks" medicine and cigarettes. According to widely accepted village norms, men could smoke and drink alcohol, but respectable women could not. Smoking cigarettes correlated closely with liquor consumption. While some men smoked without drinking, few who drank failed to smoke. No women drank in the local area (with one notable exception whom I will discuss in chapter 3), so I use the pronoun "he" for drinkers throughout the book.

While both nicotine and alcohol are addictive substances, cigarette smoking does not significantly alter people's moods and cognition. In addition, although Naeaegama men found both cigarettes and alcohol expensive, smoking was much less likely than drinking to damage social relations and household budgets. In 2004 (the year to which I have standardized all rupee [Rs.] figures to take account of rapid inflation), a beedie cost Rs. 1 and the highest quality of cigarette cost Rs. 10.³ A quarter bottle of *kasippu* (155 ml. of 67 proof liquor) cost Rs. 25, and a bottle cost Rs. 100.⁴ For these reasons, although local people thought of smoking and alcohol consumption in tandem, cigarettes play only a minor role in my discussion of "drinking."⁵

Cross-culturally, proportionally few people have problems with addiction (Heath 1998a). WHO suggests that worldwide, two billion people drink. Of these, 76.3 million have diagnosable alcohol disorders—a large number, but less than 4 percent of the total (World Health Organization 2004a, 1). Because people in Naeaegama did not hold a disease concept of addiction, I use the phrase "alcohol dependent" instead of "alcoholic" to refer to addicted individuals. The phenomena described by these two terms share many physical and social symptoms. Nevertheless, as the concept of "alcoholism" comes laden with many Euro-American assumptions, I eschew its use in the Sri Lankan context.

History of Drinking in the Naeaegama Area

Although it is difficult to figure out exactly what sort of drinking took place in the past in Naeaegama, collecting people's accounts of past drinking proved relatively easy. Most of the people I interviewed think that drinking has increased over the past several decades. Every person's account is told from a particular perspective, often with the aim to make a point or affect a current situation. For example, Gilbert Quintero examines Navajo

3. A beedie is a cheap smoke made of tobacco rolled in the leaf of the *diospyros melanoxylon* or *diospyros ebinum* tree. Cigars are rolled in tobacco leaves, and tobacco wrapped in anything else is called a cigarette (Tobacco Tax Act No. 8 of 1999, 13).

4. Rampant inflation in Sri Lanka makes comparing prices from different years difficult. Throughout most of the book, unless otherwise noted, monetary figures have been adjusted for inflation, and are stated in 2004 rupees. Occasionally I give both nominal values (rupee values informants report) and real values (equivalents in 2004 figures, adjusted for inflation) to show how dramatically inflation has affected prices. In other instances, particularly when quoting informants, I have left nominal values in the text to preserve the flow of the narrative, especially if modifying a round figure would seem awkward and presenting the real value serves little analytic purpose. In cases where exact figures matter to the argument and the interview did not take place in 2004, I mention 2004 values in square brackets in the sentence. More information about standardizing monetary figures to adjust for inflation is presented in Appendix 3.

5. In addition to the study of alcohol, a holistic approach to the anthropology of ingested substances in Naeaegama might include a study of foods of all sorts (e.g., imported fast food, traditional curries), beverages (e.g., the colonial legacy drinks tea and coffee; soft drinks; and hygienic groundwater), and local pleasure substances (e.g., the relatively benign betel, tobacco, and marijuana, and the more recent import, heroin).

narratives about abusive drinking, which is seen as a sign of cultural and moral decay (2002, 14). Directed at youth and heavy drinkers, "Narratives of degeneration provide an idiom for recollecting, organizing, and reflecting on transformations taking place in Navajo culture" and evaluating widespread and fundamental cultural changes (Quintero 2002, 14). At the same time, Quintero hypothesizes that this sort of story may also reflect a long-standing form of discourse used to discipline young people (2002, 16). Using the idiom of alcohol, adults can compare an idealized (perhaps also fictionalized) cultural past with the unsatisfactory present.

Whatever motives shape elders' narratives about drinking, the underlying fact remains that societies all over the world have undergone significant economic changes in the past half century, and that these changes can and often do affect how people drink. In his inspiring review of anthropological literature on alcohol, Dietler notes, "A frequent long-term result of commercialization has been the recruitment of new categories of drinkers…, an increase in the overall quantities of alcohol available, and an increase in the proportion of the population involved in heavy drinking" (2006, 241). Around the world, anthropologists have noted that economic relations affect patterns in alcohol use. For example, writing of Botswana, David Suggs (1996, 2001) considers the shift from a family-based, redistributive, agricultural economy to a class-based, wage-labor, capitalist economy. Formerly, elder men held power based on their control over people, labor, and herds. But currently people derive power from money, resources, education, and jobs. In the older context, alcohol served socially and economically integrative functions, and drinking of home-brewed sorghum beer did not seem to lead to alcohol dependence. With the introduction of a cash economy, alcohol continues to serve integrative functions, but people drink more frequently in contexts beyond their elders' control. Similarly, Stephen Kunitz suggests that among the Navajo, initiation into drinking has moved from a family context to one dominated by schoolmates and peers. Alcoholic beverages are readily available in local towns, and youth now drink with less supervision from adult relatives. He writes, "The restraints imposed by isolation and obligations to kin are far less common than they once were, and…the pervasiveness of drinking has itself become a risk factor for alcohol misuse" (Kunitz 2006, 294). In these cases, social and economic changes have altered drinking patterns, particularly among the youth. Danny Wilcox (1998, 115) suggests that as the market economy atomizes and depersonalizes relationships, alcohol use in many cultures becomes more asocial and pathological.

Over the past forty years, Sri Lanka has grown more integrated into the global economy. Simultaneously, both villagers and scholars have observed some alarming changes in alcohol consumption patterns (Abeyasinghe 2002; Samarasinghe 2006). Most villagers I spoke with felt that drinking had increased in the past twenty to forty years, and that men currently drank at younger ages than in the past. Lalith, a tall and imposing retired police constable, and his cheerful wife Janaki, a retired school principal, were often willing to talk with Siri and me on the wide veranda in front of their house. They claimed that in the old days, people drank legal liquor instead of *kasippu*. At that time arrack was Rs. 8 a bottle, and people made about Rs. 220 a month.[6] Janaki and Lalith recalled that drinkers in the past were ashamed to be seen drunk. Only the older men drank. Now, they joked, boys started drinking "as soon as they are born!" More seriously, Janaki thought that boys as young as fifteen drank liquor. Lalith attributed this to social pressure: "If they don't drink, they don't feel they have a place in the community. If you drink and yell, then everyone knows about you. You get publicity from drinking." This family credited changes in drinking patterns to peer pressure and the quest for social recognition.

Several other villagers confirmed the change in amounts of alcohol consumed and the age of the drinkers. Indrani, a dynamic and outspoken women in her fifties who had spent over a decade working in the Middle East, lived in a house near Siri's. I often spoke with her informally, and we had several formal interviews as well. When I asked her if she had seen a change in drinking behavior over the past twenty years, Indrani replied, "Now is worse. Even kids are drinking now. Those days, people started when they were older, maybe thirty or forty. Now kids drink at twenty, or maybe even younger than that." Bandula, a slender and quiet man with family ties to the village, often visited Siri's house. During a conversation with Siri and me, Bandula answered a similar question this way: "There was less drinking then. Hosts would have only one or two bottles at a wedding. They were hidden, not public. People would drink and come back and not show that they were drunk. They weren't staggering. They would have been ashamed to be drunk in front of their male elders. But now sons drink in front of their fathers. Also, people used to start drinking when they were mature, thirty or thirty-five. Now they start at sixteen or eighteen." Siri topped Bandula's statement by saying, "What eighteen?! They start at fourteen! And they start with cigarettes at eight!" Like Bandula and Siri, most villagers placed the onset of drinking in a man's late teens.

---

6. Although rupee values have changed dramatically, the percentage of monthly salary spent for a bottle of arrack (3.6 percent) is nearly the same in the past as prices current at the time of the interview, Rs. 285 for a bottle out of a monthly salary of Rs. 8,000 (3.5 percent).

Edward was a handsome, well-spoken retired army Sergeant with a large family and a heavy drinking habit. Siri and I interviewed him several times on Siri's breezy front porch. Edward pinned the start of drinking age between eighteen and twenty. He, like many others interviewed, felt drinking had increased over the past twenty to forty years. Edward claimed, "In the past, not even ten men in the village drank; now half of them probably do. In the past, men only drank occasionally, and they didn't come home shouting." But in contrast to Edward's claim that past drinkers had not caused trouble, one elderly woman told me about repeated incidents of domestic violence perpetrated by her inebriated husband. She added that the family turned up their radio so that outsiders could not hear the arguments. She might not have been alone in this experience. Whatever the real instance of past alcohol-related disputes, local narratives suggested a sharp increase in liquor consumption over the past four decades. People also uniformly asserted that boys started drinking at younger ages, and that drinking behaviors were now more open and less respectful than in the past. Regardless of the accuracy of these assertions, the perception of a change for the worse forms an important social fact in its own right.

Local Statistics

This study provides a snapshot of drinking behavior in the early twenty-first century as a baseline against which to measure future changes in the village. Most of this book is based on qualitative data, but numerical information provides important context regarding drinking in the village of Naeaegama and in Sri Lanka more generally. WHO ranks Sri Lanka as a country with one of the lowest rates of recorded alcohol consumption, with a per capita consumption of 0.18 liters of pure alcohol per adult per year in 2000 (2004a, 11). Even including the WHO estimate of a further 0.5 liters of pure alcohol per adult per year in "unrecorded" or illicit consumption, Sri Lanka still falls well below the global average of roughly 5 liters per adult per year (2004a, 9, 16). But ethnographic data about illicit consumption suggest that actual alcohol intake may be much higher, particularly for men.

When pressed into figures, Naeaegama residents estimated that 80 percent of men drank. In search of collaborating quantitative data, Siri and I did a rough count of drinking men in the immediate village area in 2006. I discuss our methods and present detailed results in Appendix 2. We found that less than half of the men (45 percent) drank (see appendix table 2.1). In comparison, ADIC's bi-annual "spot survey" for July 2005 found that in the Galle District (which encompasses the village of Naeaegama), 60.1 percent of the men surveyed used alcohol at least occasionally (compared to

61 percent nationally) (ADIC 2005). Both sets of numbers challenge Nae-aegama residents' estimate of 80 percent.

Villagers estimated that roughly 20 percent of drinkers drank on a daily basis. The ADIC 2005 Spot Survey found that among drinkers nationally, 60.6 percent drank on special occasions, 28.0 percent drank a few times a month, and only 11.4 percent drank daily (2005, 7). In the Naeaegama data, out of the 126 drinkers, 34.9 percent drank occasionally, 27.8 percent drank at least once a month, and 37.3 percent drank more than four times a week (see appendix table 2.2). Interestingly, the ADIC survey found a higher proportion of daily drinkers in the Galle district (21.6 percent) than in the nation on average (11.4 percent) (2005, 7). The discrepancy in these figures suggests the need for further quantitative investigation.

Despite the disparities, the ADIC and the Naeaegama surveys concur in their general assumption of female abstinence (with ADIC not even bothering to survey women and Siri assuming no village women drank). They also show a consistent pattern of male alcohol consumption, and a small but significant number of daily drinkers. Other sources also reveal high numbers of daily drinking and/or alcohol-dependent men in Sri Lanka. For example, WHO reports that a 2002 study among 1,027 individuals revealed heavy episodic drinking (13.3 percent) and heavy and hazardous drinking (15.6 percent) among males, with no instances of such drinking among females (World Health Organization 2004b, 2). Abeyasinghe (2002, 32) claims that in the Colombo slum where he did his research, 15 to 20 percent of men were dependent on alcohol, only 1 or 2 percent abstained totally from liquor, and the rest were social drinkers. He also found that 4 or 5 percent of the women were dependent on alcohol and 10 percent drank socially, numbers much higher than reported by ADIC or found in Naeaegama. Drinking habits clearly vary from place to place, with identity factors influencing consumption patterns.

New Year 2006 and Overview of the Book

I first put finger to keyboard on this book while staying at Siri's and Telsie's house in Naeaegama. In early April 2006, revelry commenced for the Sinhala and Tamil New Year, a season for family gatherings and a period of high liquor consumption in Sri Lanka. As I started to write, I witnessed the dramatic duality of formal tradition and equally traditional but formless descent into altered states of consciousness.

Around 7:00 in the evening on 13 April, New Year's Eve, a young man and his wife had a fight in their house on the road to the junction. Siri, reporting on the swearing and destruction, speculated that the man wanted more money to gamble. Siri and I had spotted this same man that afternoon among the enthralled gamblers crouching on a mat playing Donkey (*buuruwaa*, a card game). As Siri related the village news, the temple played an hour-long tape of *pirith* (Buddhist teachings) on the loud speaker. Outlasting the religious display, gambling and drinking went on late into the night.

At the astrologically significant time of 6:47 in the morning on New Year's Day (14 April), noise shattered the morning quiet. The temple bell rang and every household lit firecrackers. Howling, local dogs joined the hubbub. At 7:14 Telsie lit a new fire in the hearth and cooked milk rice (*kiribath*) in a new clay pot for the first meal of the year. In our new, colorful clothing, facing the south, Siri, Telsie, and I took turns lighting a coconut oil lamp at the auspicious time of 8:24; Siri's father Martin begged off the oily task, saying his failing eyes could not see the matchbox and cloth wick. Then Telsie distributed milk rice and an array of traditional sweets to everyone, beginning with Martin, the eldest. As she handed me my plate, she told me to stay healthy and to come share the next New Year with them. Her genuine kindness moved me to tears.

In the background, the television, counting down minutes and seconds in the upper right hand corner, showed people engaged in traditional New Year activities. Guided by this electronic window on the nation, people all over the country coordinated their ritual undertakings with astrologically auspicious moments. My mouth full of oil cake (*kaewum*), I watched dignitaries many miles away load their plates with the same foods that graced our table. I marveled at the complexity of the moment—that astrologers had found order and meaning from the spinning of stars, sun, and planet to choose significant times, and that people in households all over the country prepared so similarly to celebrate the event so elaborately. Telsie too commented on the sense of solidarity created by the roar of neighborhood fireworks and the scenes on the TV.

While the New Year ceremonies emphasized togetherness, the traditions also highlighted hierarchy. In homes, family members performed rituals according to age and status. Workers came to patrons' houses, bringing sweets and receiving presents of money carefully wrapped in betel leaves. Friends and family also exchanged New Year foods. After we ate, Telsie put our remaining sweets in plastic tins, which she stacked in a cake pan filled with water to keep out ants. By afternoon, visitors had brought us so many treats that precariously placed containers towered five layers deep.

Alongside the order of elaborately scripted activities with auspicious times, visits to the temple, traditional recipes, and synchronized fireworks, ran a pattern of chaos and carnival, as men celebrated the New Year by drinking and gambling. Despite the closure of legal liquor shops, drunken revelry prevailed. *Kasippu* sellers had stocked up on illicit liquor, which flowed in abundance. For a few days before and after New Year, gossip circulated about who got drunk and shouted, who lost his sarong, and who passed out from too much liquor. In houses hosting illegal gambling, men hovered over cards on mats while people placing side bets looked on intently and sentries kept an eye out for police uniforms. Sums as large as a month's salary changed hands repeatedly, and the size of games increased as the days went by. In Donkey games with Rs. 100 minimum entry fees, Rs. 20,000 or Rs. 40,000 circled until someone won it all and ended the game. Several days after New Year, Siri reported a game among *kasippu* sellers for Rs. 100,000 [Rs. 82,700 in 2004 figures, or about US$827]. The chaotic side of the New Year celebrations began about a week before and stretched a week after the official holiday, finally reined in by the Buddhist festival of Vesak in mid-May.

Although anthropologists find the orderly side easier to analyze, the carnival and chaos also form a key part of the New Year festival. The orderly tradition emphasizes food; the disorderly one emphasizes drink. On both sides, money changes hands, but on the orderly side it passes along firmly established lines in premeditated amounts. On the disorderly side, it passes in a flurry of excitement as men place bets on card games, often drinking and sometimes fighting at the same time. The orderly side reaffirms community solidarity and maps out factions using a well-established social pattern. The disorderly side readjusts relationships less systematically, as abundant alcohol and heavy gambling losses exacerbate festering disputes or create new factions within the community. The solidarity of family relationships established with the New Year rituals clashes with the tensions built between husbands and wives, as losers seek money to reenter the Donkey games and men seek money for alcohol. But despite the frenzy, the disorder has its own recognizable, even predictable, pattern and logic.

In this book I hope to give a sense of the order and the randomness, the ritual and the carnival associated with alcohol, not only during the holiday season but throughout the year in Naeaegama. In chapter 1, I present some background information on religion, colonial history, and current government policies on alcohol. The rest of the book falls into three informal sections. The three chapters in the first section explore issues of consumption and identity formation, examining how alcohol drinking shapes and is shaped by identity. Chapter 2 considers the Naeaegama concept of being without one's right mind (*sihiya naetuwa*), a complex notion that includes but is not limited to intoxication. I reflect on issues of agency and altered states of consciousness. In chapter 3 I delve into the issues of gender identity and age as they relate to alcohol consumption. In chapter 4 I assess the events and contexts in which men drink for fun, examining in particular the social networks maintained and transformed by communal consumption at ceremonies and in *kasippu* taverns.

In the second section of the book, two chapters explore issues of political economics. In chapter 5 I consider gendered consumption struggles, as men and women negotiate different agendas surrounding household finances. While examining the relationship between female migration and male alcohol use, this chapter also illuminates issues of household economics, gendered rights and obligations, domestic violence, and divorce. In chapter 6 I examine the production, distribution, and sale of *kasippu,* the most common illicit liquor in the Naeaegama area. Manufacturing and selling *kasippu* provides employment to many village men and women and forms a major part of the local economy. I also analyze the ambivalent position held in the community by rich but disreputable *kasippu* businesspeople.

People everywhere strike a balance between pleasure and pathology when discussing alcohol use. The three chapters in the third section of the book investigate village assessment of problem drinking, alcohol dependence, and available local treatments. In chapter 7 I deduce Naeaegama rules for drunken comportment by examining stories about funny and tragic events that have happened to people under the influence of liquor. I include a discussion of narratives about intoxication and an analysis of accidents, suicide attempts, fights, and alcohol-related deaths. In chapter 8 I consider local assessments of alcohol dependence and related social and physical illnesses. Finally, in chapter 9 I examine community-administered correctives for excess alcohol consumption, in addition to treatments offered by western and indigenous medical practitioners, rehabilitation centers, and local ritual specialists.

This book provides a holistic anthropological analysis of the social dynamics surrounding alcohol use. Each section provides a concentrically broadening examination, situating changing drinking practices within wider economic, political, and religious dynamics in the village, country, and global context. Together, these three sections present the economics and identity politics of alcohol consumption and sketch out the cultural logic of illicit liquor in Naeaegama.

1 Context: Religious, Historical, and Political Frameworks

In this chapter I discuss the wider context in which I situate Naeaegama area drinking. I first examine issues of religious prohibition on the use of intoxicants. Theravada Buddhism requires people to stay mindful at all times—a state at odds with the consumption of alcohol, marijuana, opiates, and other drugs. Despite widespread approval for social alcohol use, particularly at celebrations and ceremonies, the general religious context condemns intoxication. Next I consider the history of alcohol production and consumption in Sri Lanka. Though alcohol has been known in South Asia for at least three millennia, people in Sri Lanka began to drink heavily only during the colonial period. The practice came from and was associated with the foreign colonizers and the local elite who supported them. While some local families profited from the government-supported alcohol industry, a number of others used temperance movements as a vehicle to protest colonial rule. Today, Naeaegama residents still see alcohol as a foreign import and vestige of colonial oppression.

Moving to the present, I examine the government's dilemma in regulating alcohol production and consumption. Ninety percent of the price of legal liquor consists of government surcharges, and revenue from alcohol constitutes around 4 percent of government income. The government thus has a large stake in the continued prosperity of the liquor industry. At the same time the government bears responsibility for public health and safety. Alcohol-related illnesses and accidents drain public funds by burdening the health-care system, and work absences due to hangovers and alcohol-related domestic violence decrease productivity in both the public and private spheres. I examine current Excise Department policies governing the licensing and policing of liquor production, and the new legislation to establish a National Authority on Tobacco and Alcohol.

Buddhism: Right Livelihood and the Fifth Precept

A variety of human practices govern links between alcohol and religion. Some religions associate particular deities with liquor, for example, the Greek god Dionysus and the Roman god Bacchus (Heath 1998a). In many settings around the world, alcohol plays a role in religious rituals. For example, Beatrice Medicine suggests that the Apache used intoxicants in ceremonial contexts (2007, 21). Similarly, Christine Eber (2000) suggests that in Chiapas, Mexico, rum distilled from corn beer is used in some Christian rituals. In the local cosmology, rum is equated with God's blood and exchanged in rituals of reciprocity. It is also sprinkled on tree branches during shamanistic curing rites and distributed to helpers and attendees at festivals. Ritual regulations govern how much and when to drink. Certain religious factions use rum while others favor its prohibition. Recognizing the problems caused by excess alcohol consumption, some people in Chiapas substitute soda for rum in rituals, or raise their cup to their lips without drinking (Crump 1987; Eber 2000).[1] In Chiapas, as elsewhere in the world, alcohol consumption is a part of devotion.

Although in some instances alcohol can provide a shortcut to the divine and a way to communicate with spirits, in other instances religions forbid drinking. In South Asia, the predominant religions prohibit, or at least frown upon, alcohol use. Islam and many sects of Buddhism strongly discourage consumption of intoxicating substances, while Hindus identify abstinence with high social status (Mohan and Sharma 1995, 131; Rahula 1959; Rogers 1989, 323; Saxena 1999, 38). Ritual healing ceremonies in southwestern Sri Lanka that invoke supernatural entities may involve the use of alcohol, but only when practitioners deal with low-status spirits, ghosts, and demons (Kapferer 1983). Although the formal religious teachings powerful in Sri Lanka forbid alcohol and animal sacrifice, local ritual specialists see a role for its use in certain practices (Feddema 1997). Traditions in the Naeaegama area allow ritual uses of alcohol depending on the status and power of the supernatural entities involved.

In Theravada Buddhism, the Five Precepts (*pancha silaya* or, informally, *pansil*) set out basic rules for conduct. Akin to the Ten Commandments in Christianity, the Five Precepts direct lay devotees not to kill, steal, be

---

1. Since the Zapatista rebellion, many people in Chiapas have given up alcohol as part of the anti-colonial revitalization movement (Eber 2001, 257–58).

unchaste, tell lies, and take intoxicating substances. Ananda Thero, the energetic and charismatic chief monk at a Naeaegama area temple, gave me a sheet printed in Sinhala that discussed the benefits of following the Five Precepts.[2] The sheet suggested that by abstaining from mind-altering substances, a Buddhist will always act mindfully and avoid becoming a crazy or lazy person in the next life. According to Mahanama Thero, the chief monk at another local temple, observing the Fifth Precept will allow a Buddhist to follow the other Precepts more easily. Desires and cravings lead to perpetual suffering. Avoiding intoxication helps with meditation and the development of wisdom, two key factors in a person's mental and spiritual development. In practical terms, avoiding alcohol will improve the devotee's health and household economics, and keep him out of fights. The Lord Buddha expressly forbade alcohol, saying that it would lead people to womanizing, gambling, and other crimes.

Livelihoods dependent on producing and selling liquor are also against the religion. Right Livelihood, one of the principles of ethical conduct that makes up the Noble Eightfold Path of Buddhism, suggests that Buddhists should not make their living through professions that harm others, including trading of weapons, poisons, or alcohol; killing animals; and cheating others (Rahula 1959, 47). Mahanama Thero explained that making illicit liquor might lead to short-term profits, but in the end such manufacturers would get caught by the police or suffer other setbacks. Other villagers echoed these sentiments, suggesting that money earned disreputably or dishonestly would not bring prosperity for the individual or his family (M. Gamburd 2004a). The universe's ethical principle of karma would eventually punish wrongdoers.

Despite religious prohibitions on making, selling, or drinking alcohol, many people drank regularly in Naeaegama. Perera, a wiry laborer who lived in a humble, two-room wood-plank house with his wife and daughters, spoke openly with me about alcohol on a number of occasions. Discussing religion, Perera said, "The priests say not to drink alcohol, but no one listens. No one even goes to the temple!"

"What about the government," I asked. "Do they put up sign boards?"

"Yes, they have an alcohol awareness week where they give advice." Perera joked, "During that week people drink more than ever!"

Drinkers who wished to find religious justification for their habit sometimes punned on the Pali verse of the Fifth Precept.[3] The real Pali verse of

2. "Thero" is the Sinhala equivalent of "Reverend."

3. Pali, the language in which Theravada Buddhist texts are preserved, is related to Sinhala much as Latin is related to French. Few besides Buddhist monks and devout lay people

the Fifth Precept reads: "Do not take even a little bit of an intoxicating sub-stance (*Suraa meraya majja pamaadaThanaa weeramanii sikkhaapadam sa-maaDhiyaami*)." The new interpretation of the first half of the Fifth Precept became: "Taking alcohol to a medium level will be most beautiful (*Suraa meraya mada pamanin gat pasu wee ramaniya*)."[4] This sort of joking im-plicitly acknowledged the power of Pali verse and Buddhist teachings, but simultaneously used them to undermine the actual text of the Precept and support an alternate, pro-alcohol interpretation. The joking framework set around this interpretation assured drinkers and others that the real author-ity of the Buddhist teachings endured despite the challenge. Whatever his or her position on drinking, a Buddhist in Sri Lanka knows the official reli-gious prohibition on alcohol and other mind-altering substances.

The Colonial History of Alcohol

The natural process of fermentation makes alcohol easy to obtain. Archae-ologists speculate that beer and wine arrived on the scene early in human prehistory (Heath 1987, 20). People strive to provide desirable, high-status foodstuffs for entertaining family and friends. In the past, as in the present, alcohol played a role in social gatherings. Scholars suggest that alcohol pro-duction might have spurred the domestication of certain grains and tubers ten thousand years ago. In order to provide large amounts of alcohol at the competitive feasts that indicated social standing, status-conscious leaders may have encouraged the cultivation of these crops (Fernandez-Armesto 2002). Alcohol has played a long-standing and influential role in social or-ganization and subsistence strategies.

Various sources provide a glimpse of the history of alcohol use in South Asia. Archaeological research reveals some of the earliest surviving chemical traces of alcohol to come from the Middle East (Dietler 2006, 233), an area of the world long linked to the Indian subcontinent through trade. Textual

---

understand the language, but they do know the meaning of these particular verses. Children learn the Five Precepts in school and people repeat them at the beginning of most official func-tions at temples and other venues.

4. Phrase by phrase, here is how Naeaegama drinkers transform the Fifth Precept. The original verse reads: *Suraa meraya majja pamaadaThanaa weeramanii sikkaapadam samaaDhi-yaami*, meaning "Do not take even a little bit of an intoxicating substance." Naeaegama drink-ers preserved the meaning of *Suraa meraya* (liquor or other intoxicant). Then they suggested that *majja pamaa* meant *mada pamanin*, "to a medium level." They substituted for *daThanaa* the phrase *gat pasu*, "after taking." They concluded the joke by changing *weeramanii* to *wee ramaniya*, "will become most beautiful." The new verse reads: *Suraa meraya mada pamanin gat pasu wee ramaniya*, which means: "Taking alcohol to a medium level will be most beautiful."

records suggest that South Asians drank beer during the Vedic period (second millennium BCE) (Dietler 2006, 234). Two epic poems composed around 1000 BCE denounce alcohol use: the *Ramayana* brands drinkers as bad and abstainers as good, and the *Mahabharata* asserts that one warrior dynasty in the tale disintegrated due to "fighting among themselves while inebriated" (Mohan and Sharma 1995, 131). But South Asian texts have not always condemned alcohol. Sutras written between 800–300 BCE portray bureaucrats supervising alcohol sales (Mohan and Sharma 1995, 131). Known in what is now Nepal at the time the Buddha taught, alcohol and its manufacturing techniques could have spread with the merchants who brought the religion to South India and Sri Lanka around 300 BCE. A millennium later (700–1100 CE), South Asian texts discuss the art of alcohol making, especially homebrews and wine (Mohan and Sharma 1995, 132). Soldiers, emperors, and common people reportedly drank during the Islamic period (Saxena 1999, 38). Arrack, hard liquor distilled from the fermented sap of the coconut blossom, was likely made and widely exchanged in Sri Lanka's coastal areas at least as far back as the 1400s (Roberts 1982, 88), and was probably an item valued by merchants plying their trade across the subcontinent and around the Indian Ocean.

Although written records suggest use of intoxicants in South Asia for over three millennia, many people credit European colonizers with introducing high levels of alcohol manufacture and use. During colonial rule, the British set up a brewery in India, and then taxed alcohol sales to stop great increases in consumption (Mohan and Sharma 1995, 132). Colonial powers balanced the use of alcohol for mobilizing workers against their worries about alcohol's role in "producing an unruly subject population and disrupting work discipline" (Dietler 2006, 240). In Sri Lanka, the colonial government discourse touched on both the dangers of alcohol to society and the importance of the revenues generated from the state monopoly on taxing liquor and licensing liquor outlets. Historian John Rogers (1989) suggests that the government leaders wanted to strike a balance between licensing too many outlets (thus encouraging drinking) and licensing too few or taxing too much (thus encouraging illicit manufacture). A lively debate raged on this topic in the Sinhala press in the late 1800s (John Rogers personal communication, 10 August 2004).

The alcohol industry played a crucial function in the relationship between colonists and local elites in Sri Lanka. Many prominent Sinhala families, particularly Christians of the Karaava caste, made their fortunes in the mid-nineteenth century by entering the arrack business (Peebles 1995, 162; K. M. de Silva 1981, 350). According to historian Patrick Peebles,

Dutch and later British colonial authorities "rented" to local middlemen the right to distill, distribute, and trade in liquor in Ceylon, as the colony was then known (1986, 65). By commissioning knowledgeable indigenous people to collect taxes, the British reduced their administrative costs (Roberts 1982, 82). The British set up "rents" or "tax farms" not only for liquor but also for fisheries, ferries, tolls, and rice cultivation (Roberts 1982, 82). In exchange for a sum of money decided at auction, arrack "renters" obtained the right to sell liquor under certain government regulations in particular taverns or, later, in large administrative districts. Although they derived their livelihood from their association with the government, strong local business networks strove to circumvent administrative controls (Peebles 1986, 74). Arrack renting allowed local entrepreneurs to amass fortunes during the British colonial period, and was one of the main sources of government income, generating 10 to 15 percent of British revenues in the late 1800s (Jayawardena 2000, 126; Rogers 1989). Both the colonial powers and local businessmen profited substantially from the liquor trade.

Liquor consumption increased dramatically with colonial rule. The large working class created by the economic transformations brought by merchant capitalism, and later plantation capitalism, formed a ready-made market for arrack. As the colonial economy underwent transformations during the 1800s, the working class grew, consisting of migrant laborers from India working on the coffee and tea plantations, urban workers (particularly laborers at the harbor), construction workers on railways and other infrastructural projects, and peasant farmers (Jayawardena 2000, 87). Political scientist Kumari Jayawardena argues that the wretched conditions endured by workers led them to drink: "Where conditions of misery were created by direct exploitation by plantation, factory and mine owners, the liquor traders moved in to provide an 'escape' from these harsh conditions. Liquor was par excellence the 'opiate' of sections of 'the masses'" (2000, 102). Furthermore, workers would often "forgo food for liquor since it provided a much-needed and quicker stimulant" (Jayawardena 2000, 101). In this view Jayawardena joins Sydney Mintz, who examines items of common consumption among the emerging working class in Europe's industrial revolution. Mintz calls substances such as sugar, tea, coffee, rum, and tobacco "proletarian hunger-killers" (1997, 360). He analyzes the political-economic links between labor on colonial plantations and the urban proletariat in Europe. The products of oppressed laborers on West Indian sugar plantations and Sri Lankan coffee estates (1830s–1880s) and later tea estates (1880s–present) provided cheap, quick energy to industrial workers. Jayawardena's evidence suggests that these same plantation workers as well as urban proletarians and rural peasants in the British empire also provided a market for cheap stimulants, either food or drink.

In South Asia, a widespread temperance movement formed part of the subcontinent's drive for independence (Mohan and Sharma 1995, 132; Samarasinghe 1995, 271; Saxena 1999, 39). Ceylon's temperance movement of the early 1900s accompanied a revival of Buddhism in the late 1800s. Temperance rhetoric suggested that through alcohol use, the colonizers were converting people to the lifestyle of the conquerors (Samarasinghe 1995, 271). Begun by Christians, the temperance movement in Ceylon gradually shifted to Buddhist leaders, who "linked consumption of liquor with westernization and 'Christianization'"—characteristics shared by the colonial government (K. M. de Silva 1981, 374). Although most of the colonial bourgeoisie, particularly those involved in the liquor trade, supported British rule (Jayawardena 2000, 303–4), a few (including members of some of the same families who had profited through the arrack trade) supported this movement. Rural elites also asserted their right to leadership though this cause (Rogers 1989, 332). The movement sought to spread middle class ideas, raise moral standards, and promote thrift. In addition to tapping Buddhist anti-alcohol values, the local movement drew on middle class Protestant values and used British temperance group arguments (Rogers 1989, 340). By imposing these values on the lower classes, and calling the values "Sinhala," the temperance movement made alcohol an issue of Sinhala-Buddhist cultural identity.

Although it commented critically on the colonial government and created a nascent Sinhala-Buddhist nationalist identity, the temperance movement did not promote as much nationalist activity in Ceylon as it did elsewhere in South Asia. One reason for this was the movement's growing association with the Sinhala-Buddhist rural elites. Non-Buddhist elites in the capital city did not join, fearing that temperance could serve as a vehicle for religious nationalism (K. M. de Silva 1981, 377). In addition, leaders of the Buddhist Revival and the temperance movement did not see eye to eye, so the two organizations did not mesh closely, thus blunting the movement's appeal and stunting its growth (K. M. de Silva 1981, 377). During the early 1900s, the movement went through cycles of effervescence and decline. For example, after several months of popular activity in 1904, the movement weakened due to social discontent, clashes over leadership, and steps taken by the alcohol industry (Rogers 1989, 338). Despite its nationalist and anticolonial aspects, the temperance movement's potential for activism never fully blossomed in Ceylon.

Drinking patterns and attitudes toward alcohol established during the colonial period persist into the present. For example, the British military formed a large market for alcohol (Jayawardena 2000, 41, 91), and plantations all over the British empire that employed migrant labor from South India reported drinking problems (Chatterjee 2003, 192). To this day, Sri Lankans continue to expect heavy drinking among military personnel (M. Gamburd 2004b), estate workers (Bass 2004, 245), and manual laborers. Although Christian missionaries supported temperance, Christian colonists were stereotyped as heavy drinkers. Historically, as they imitated colonial lifestyles, local elites developed a taste for imported alcohol, particularly "malt liquor, spirits of all kinds (brandy and gin heading the list) and wines from Europe and Australia" (Jayawardena 2000, 131). This same valuation of foreign liquor persists into the present (Baklien and Samarasinghe 2003, 68). Both the colonial rulers and the leading Sinhala-Buddhist families of the time played a role in popularizing particular styles of alcohol consumption in Sri Lanka.

Village Views on Colonialism and Drinking

Nationalist beliefs about colonialism, Buddhism, and alcohol use extend from the nineteenth and twentieth centuries into the present. Padma was an elderly and well-educated Naeaegama lady whose husband had drunk heavily toward the end of his life. When I asked her whether there had been an increase in village alcohol consumption, she responded with a narrative presenting clear-cut distinctions between past and present, pure and impure, locals and foreigners, Buddhists and non-Buddhists, Sinhala and Tamil ethnic identities, high and low caste statuses, and vegetarian and meat-eating diets. In this framework, consumption choices clearly indexed distinctions between "us" and "them." Ingesting meat and alcohol indicated moral turpitude and the decline of political legitimacy; abstinence denoted merit. Padma's narrative linked details about her own family life with a discussion of the colonial period and the current political situation in the country:

> There has been an increase in alcohol consumption. When I was small, there was just one person in the village who drank. He didn't cause any trouble. After drinking he would recite some poetry and go to sleep. People just laughed at him.
>
> Those days people didn't have their ceremonies in hotels, they had them at home. They didn't give alcohol. In my home we didn't even have eggs or chicken, let alone alcohol. Once when my grandfather got sick, the *vedamahattayaa* [Ayurvedic doctor] said to take a medicine with brandy. My

grandfather said, "No. Even if I die, I don't want that medicine." He said he wouldn't take any more medicine from that doctor. This was because of Buddhism, Sinhala Buddhism.

I didn't even feed my kids eggs when they were young. In the past thirty years I have not eaten meat or fish. I don't even bring that [non-vegetarian] food into the house. There was a saying years ago that eating beef was something that the RoDii [untouchable caste people] did.

The Portuguese came here and ate bread and drank alcohol. The local people called bread "white stones." They thought the wine was blood. They only knew that the Portuguese were eating something white and drinking something red.

The ancient kings drank, but only toddy. The normal people didn't drink. This is what the history books say. Then the last king, who was a Tamil, was a drunkard. He was caught and taken to Bangalore in India, where he died.

Now boys who are only fourteen are drinking *kasippu*. I have heard that in Jaffna [a Tamil-majority city], kids are given toddy for breakfast. They are so poor that they can't give their children a meal. So the kids come to school sleepy. I heard this from a Sinhala teacher who went to Jaffna, and a school inspector also said this.

A close reading of Padma's story reveals her masterful use of symbolic dichotomies. She associates purity with vegetarianism, abstinence, Sinhala Buddhism, and people of her own family, caste, and ethnicity; she associates impurity with eating meat, drinking alcohol or blood, and being from an untouchable caste. On the impure side of the scale fall the Portuguese colonists, Sri Lanka's last (Tamil) kings, and the caretakers of the Tamil schoolchildren who drink toddy for breakfast in Jaffna—the Tamil heartland. For Padma, alcohol carried negative associations at both personal and political levels.

Padma was not the only villager to associate alcohol use with the negative influence of Sri Lanka's colonial past. Ananda Thero also saw alcohol consumption as a habit that came from outside the Sinhala-Buddhist tradition. Like Padma, this local monk linked alcohol use and meat eating with foreigners and uncivilized others, using two examples. At one point during an interview he said, "The English government started the fashion of alcohol. The English and Portuguese ate beef and said 'cheers' with alcohol, so it became a style." Soon thereafter, he suggested a different origin for local alcohol use. He claimed, "The habit of drinking is something that came from the *veaddo* [Veddas, autochthonous hunter-gatherers viewed as the original inhabitants of Sri Lanka]." Ananda Thero attributed the origin of drinking in Sri Lanka to cultural "others"—either colonists from foreign countries or the uncivilized, pagan foragers who predate the rice-cultivating Sinhala-Buddhist agriculturalists.

Like Padma, Ananda Thero associated alcohol consumption with eating meat. His narrative suggested the following about how the *vaeddo* invented alcohol: "They were hunting and found a big water cavity. Animals had come to drink the water collected in there. They slipped in and drowned. The *vaeddo* found this water and drank it. They got a kick and got used to drinking it." This assertion suggests a double source of impurity: the *vaeddo* consumed not merely meat and alcohol, but rotten carrion. Contrary to Ananda Thero's suggestion, meat products are not used to make alcohol, although they may be added later for flavoring, as the remainder of the narrative suggests. Ananda Thero continued, "Now people drink animal wine in different places. They drink gecko [chameleon] wine on the border near Laos and Cambodia. They use geckos as bites [snacks to eat while drinking]! And they have snake wine in Africa and Thailand." By suggesting that foreigners made alcoholic drinks with creatures deemed inedible in Sinhala culture, Ananda Thero strengthened the association between vegetarianism, abstinence, and local Buddhist values. He concluded by saying, "Our *kasippu* has the same recipe: all sorts of rotten things." Concluding a lengthy diatribe against alcohol, this last statement associates the popular local distillate with impurity, meat eating, and disturbing foreign customs.

These Naeaegama narratives illustrate how ideas about alcohol, colonialism, and ethnic identity have percolated into and been preserved by local knowledge. According to both Ananda Thero and Padma, alcohol originated from outside Sinhala-Buddhist culture. Expunging the dangerous, foreign influence of alcohol consumption would improve health, morality, and the state of society (Brodie and Redfield 2002). This position echoes those taken by other colonized peoples (Eber 2001; Medicine 2007; Quintero 2002; but also see McKnight 2002). In conjunction with the colonial history related above, these two narratives suggest that abstinence and alcohol consumption play a large role in Sinhala-Buddhist identity construction, and have for at least a century.

Current Context

In subsequent chapters, I delve into details of alcohol consumption in Naeaegama, including local drinking habits and mores and the economics of illicit distillation. Here I sketch out the economic and regulatory background against which local situations unfold.

Local Beverage Choices

Around the world, people drink different substances in different styles. Heath (1998a) summarizes the imperfect and impermanent but nonetheless useful categories of beer, wine, and spirits cultures. In wine cultures with "French" or "Mediterranean" styles of drinking, men and women frequently consume liquor in moderate quantities, often with food. Such societies have low rates of drinking problems. In contrast, in spirits cultures such as those in the Nordic countries, drinking often takes place in all-male drinking sessions, without food. Drinkers show less concern for moderation, have a higher instance of intoxication, and sometimes use drunkenness as an excuse for anti-social behavior. The rest of society sees such activities as unhealthy but deems them a necessary escape. Beer cultures often have high rates of accidents and gang violence, but display few of the lasting psychological and social problems found in spirit cultures. Though far from the Nordic countries geographically, Sri Lanka follows the drinking patterns found in spirit cultures.

In Sri Lanka, men drink a number of alcoholic beverages, including foreign liquor, locally bottled beer and arrack, locally produced toddy, and illegally manufactured *kasippu*. People mark their class status by their choice of drinks, with more costly drinks carrying higher levels of prestige. The combined influence of taxes (which regulate affordability) and advertising (which influences desires) help shape consumer choices (Abeyasinghe 2002, 66; Marshall and Riley 1999).

In Sri Lanka, foreign liquor costs more than locally produced liquor. Foreign liquor is available from local "wine shops," bars, and tourist hotels. For example, the beverage list of the four-star Bentota Beach Hotel (run by the John Keells Company) includes Harvey's Bristol Cream, Johnny Walker Black Label Whiskey, Beefeater Gin, Smirnoff Vodka, and Bacardi Rum. Local arrack, as well as locally produced whisky, gin, vodka, rum, and brandy are also available. The imported liquor sells for 30 to 300 percent more than the local liquor. Although most locals do not drink wine, tourist hotels provide it for their guests. The assistant food and beverage manager for a five-star hotel informed me that three quarters of the liquor his hotel serves is imported and the remaining 25 percent is locally made. Both local and foreign guests drinking at prestigious hotels prefer foreign liquor.

While foreign liquors hold high status in Sri Lanka, local drinks pique the interests of foreign visitors. The *Travel Lanka* tourist magazine recommends that tourists sample local liquors. The editor notes, "The two traditional Sri Lankan drinks that cheer and very easily inebriate, are arrak [*sic*] and toddy. Toddy is the fermented sap of the coconut flower. Arrack is the distilled essence of toddy. VSOA (Very Special Old Arrack), 7 year Arrack, and double distilled Arrack are served in most hotels, but the best toddy is found at wayside taverns. The local beers—lager, pilsner, three coins & stout, are also very popular" (*Travel Lanka* 2003, 45, irregular punctuation and spelling in the original). Prominent local manufacturers of hard liquor include the Distilleries Company of Sri Lanka, International Distillers Limited, and Rockland Distilleries, while Lion Brewery produces most of the local beer (Commissioner General of Excise 2005, 10–13).

Among varieties of locally produced alcohol, legal products cost more than illegal ones. More readily available and much less prestigious than legal liquor, the illicit distillate *kasippu* occupies a proud place in the thriving black market trade. The World Health Organization reports, "On a regional basis, unrecorded alcohol consumption is estimated to be at least two thirds of all alcohol consumption in the Indian subcontinent" (2004a, 15). Researchers suggest that in Sri Lanka an estimated 50 to 90 percent of the alcohol consumed is illicit (Abeyasinghe 2002, 125; Baklien and Samarasinghe 2003, 13; World Health Organization 2004b, 2–3). No formal quality controls regulate the *kasippu* made by an unknown number of small manufacturers, and people often speculate on possible irregular ingredients and production procedures. But while its alcohol percentage varies, the small amount of available scientific data suggests that *kasippu* is actually quite pure (Abeyasinghe 2002, 92). *Kasippu* dealers and their customers risk arrest by the police, but few people in the local area see *kasippu* consumption as criminal behavior. Nevertheless some villagers, especially women, would like the government to challenge the trade in illicit alcohol. Potentially adulterated, stigmatized as illegal, but cheap and readily available, *kasippu* is a perennial favorite among working class and even some middle class drinkers.

Government Policies

Like all governments, the Sri Lankan administration must strike a balance between government finances and public health. During a conversation at a Naeaegama temple, Mahanama Thero suggested, "Making alcohol is a major industry in Sri Lanka. The government also doesn't want to ban legal liquor because they make an income on it through taxes and licenses." Virasena, a tall, lanky, silver-haired man who worked for the temple, agreed with the chief monk. He said, "If the government prohibited liquor, people would just make it illegally. Plus the government makes a lot of money from liquor licenses, so they are not going to stop it. But the government might want to stop *kasippu* to make people drink more arrack." In another context, Suddhamma Thero—a chief priest, former temperance worker, and drug-rehabilitation program organizer—addressed similar issues. When I asked about the dilemma between gaining revenue through taxes and spending money on medical services (Room 1999), Suddhamma Thero laughed and said, "Yes, that's the problem!" Then he opined, "They are spending more on health than they make in taxes." These local views cover many of the main issues faced by the Sri Lankan government in its regulation of alcohol.

Governments can control alcohol consumption in a number of ways by placing limits on availability and restrictions on use. Such policies include price regulation, taxation, licensing, limiting operation hours, rationing, and prohibition (Whitehead 1998). Restrictions can cover every element of the alcohol business, including types and placements of advertisements; who can manufacture and sell alcohol; and who can buy how much of what substances, when, and where. States often regulate the distances to be maintained between places where alcohol is sold and consumed and places like schools and religious institutions. Additional restrictions that may cover physical aspects of a drinking establishment include whether it is visible from the street, whether it serves food, and whether it provides warnings on alcohol containers (Heath and Rosovsky 1998). In addition, states often regulate alcohol consumers' practices through medical initiatives, educational measures, and legal interventions (such as drunken driving legislation) (Babor et al. 2003). Commenting on the ad hoc mix of policies put in place to regulate alcohol in Canada, Mariana Valverde notes, "Despite the fact that alcohol controls intersect with the concerns of law, psychology, sociology, fiscal policy, and several branches of medicine, the administrative law of liquor control and licencing has not been guided by any of these experts" (1998, 148). Instead, she contends that a hybrid, historically emergent nexus of practices govern drinking establishments and, to a lesser extent, individual drinkers with the intent of minimizing harm and risks. A similarly emergent system exists in Sri Lanka.

The Excise Department

Price manipulation through taxation is a major governmental instrument for regulating alcohol consumption in Sri Lanka and elsewhere in the world. This strategy also generates considerable revenue for the government. Excise duties, often based on strength of the liquor, are levied on legal alcohol at a number of points. Passed on to the consumer, these charges raise the price of legal liquor above the cost of production and may create incentives for tax evasion (Thurman 2000). Thus the taxing and policing of alcohol often go hand in hand.

In Sri Lanka, the Excise Department is in charge of supervision, revenue collection, and law enforcement around several types of products. First, it administers the liquor industry. The Excise Ordinance regulates "the import, export, transport, manufacture, sale, and possession of intoxicating liquor" (Excise Ordinance 1956, 269). The Department administers duties, taxes, fines, and licensing fees for the manufacture and sale of liquor in Sri Lanka and covers law enforcement for the industry. Second, the Excise Department also regulates tobacco and intoxicating drugs, and enforces the Poisons, Opium and Dangerous Drugs Ordinance (Commissioner General of Excise 2005, 1). Fees on locally manufactured alcohol and tobacco are referred to as Excise (Ordinance) Duty. In addition to Excise (Ordinance) Duty, which covers locally manufactured goods, the government charges Excise (Special Provisions) Duty on items imported from abroad. The Excise (Special Provisions) Duty covers cigarettes, petroleum products, motor vehicles, and various electrical goods (*Government Gazette* 2005b; "Tax Information at a Glance" 2005, 7–8). Administration of fees and fines surrounding imported items is done by the Excise (Special Provisions) Unit of the Department of Customs.

Excise (Ordinance) Duties generate a great deal of money. A duty is imposed on each liter of liquor legally manufactured in Sri Lanka. For example, in 2004 a duty of Rs. 351 was imposed for each proof liter of arrack (including molasses, palmyrah, coconut, and processed arrack), of which over 32 million liters were produced. A duty of Rs. 38.50 per bulk liter was charged for beer of 5 percent alcohol content and above, of which nearly 18 million liters were produced (Commissioner General of Excise 2005, 4, 11–13). In addition to duties levied on liters of manufactured alcohol, the Excise Department also charges licensing fees for the manufacture, wholesale, and retail sale of alcohol. Hotels, bars, and restaurants need licenses to sell and serve liquor. The government regulates the number of licenses issued, taking into account "the population, pattern of consumption of liquor and other social requirements of the area" (*Government Gazette* 1997, 2A). Premises for which licenses are sought must meet certain criteria. For example, in 1997 the government dictated that retail outlets should have a minimum floor area of 250 square feet. Locations selling alcohol for consumption on and off site should be 500 and 100 meters away, respectively, from schools and places of public religious worship (*Government Gazette* 1997, 3A). In 2004, the government garnered over Rs. 200 million in foreign liquor licenses (Commissioner General of Excise 2005, appendix F). An additional Rs. 88 million came in from fines for alcohol-related offenses such as the unlawful manufacture or possession of spirits (Commissioner General of Excise 2005, appendix H). According to Commissioner General of Excise (2005, 16), the Excise Department collected revenue totaling Rs. 13.5 billion in Excise (Ordinance) Duties from duties, fees, and fines levied on alcohol and tobacco manufacturers in 2004.

Excise duties form a major source of government revenue. The combination of Excise (Ordinance) and Excise (Special Provisions) Duties composed about 20 percent of all government revenue in 2004 (Rs. 311.8 billion) (Central Bank 2006, 105). For 2004, the Central Bank reports revenue from excise duties as Rs. 65.8 billion (about US$ 658 million) (Central Bank 2006, 105). Of that, Rs. 13.5 billion or 20.5 percent came from charges and fees related to alcohol and tobacco. This suggests that in 2004, one-fifth of the government's excise duty revenue, or about 4 percent of the government's total revenue, came from alcohol- and tobacco-related charges and fees.

Both the 2005 and the 2006 government budgets increased excise duty on hard liquor and beer. In addition to generating revenue, these measures were intended to "reduce alcohol and tobacco use with a view to improving health[,] decreasing poverty and improving productivity of the labor force" (Budget Speech 2005 Part II, 32). The 2006 Budget Speech asserts, "Tax [on] alcohol and tobacco should be increased regularly to discourage consumption. It is also necessary to tighten combating operations to eradicate the usage of illicit drugs and manufacturing of illicit liquor" (2006, 48). The speech suggests that the government balances issues of public health and crime control with those of revenue generation. It should be noted, however, that most fee increases do little more than keep pace with inflation. As with duties on manufactured liquor, the nominal figures for license fees have risen dramatically over the past dozen years, but the real values have held relatively steady.[5] By raising taxes and fees, the government keeps its revenues in line with inflation, and politicians can present themselves as tough on the sale of intoxicating substances when reporting these changes to the public.

The National Authority on Tobacco and Alcohol

Sri Lanka has recently commenced a major initiative for the regulation of tobacco and alcohol use. In May 2006, Parliament passed an act

---

5. Double-digit inflation drastically affects the real values of excise duties. In December of 2005, for example, the duty on a proof liter of molasses, palmyrah, coconut, and processed arrack rose from Rs. 351 to Rs. 369, a nominal increase of Rs. 17 that represents a drop of Rs. 46 to Rs. 305 in real value when standardized to 2004 values. The nominal duty on a bulk liter of beer of 5 percent alcohol content and above increased to Rs. 53.50 [Rs. 44.30], a real increase of less than Rs. 6 (*Government Gazette* 2005a, 2A–3A). Changes in license fees also illustrate the effects of inflation. For example, in 1995 a hotel with over 250 rooms paid Rs. 200,000 [Rs. 323,800] for a license to sell foreign and local liquor (*Government Gazette* 1995, 1A). In 1998, the license fee rose to Rs. 250,000 [Rs. 335,058] (*Government Gazette* 1998, 2A), and by 2005 the fee stood at Rs. 375,000, which represented a real value drop to Rs. 317,886 (*Government Gazette* 2005c, 2A). See Appendix 3 for more information on adjusting monetary figures for inflation.

establishing the National Authority on Tobacco and Alcohol. When fully implemented, the organization will consist of staff from various government ministries with expertise in health, justice, education, media, trade, and youth affairs. In addition, professional representatives and individuals from the National Dangerous Drugs Control Board, the Excise Department, and the police will be included (*Government Gazette* 2006, 1–2). The new organization will be charged with "identifying the policy on protecting public health;…the elimination of tobacco and alcohol related harm though the assessment and monitoring of the production, marketing and consumption of tobacco products and alcohol products; [and] discouraging persons especially children from smoking or consuming alcohol, by curtailing their access to tobacco products and alcohol products" (*Government Gazette* 2006, cover). The Authority will perform research, formulate and implement policies, and evaluate the impact of actions taken. It will also advise the government on policy decisions and liaise with local communities as well as regional and national organizations on issues related to alcohol and tobacco use. This organization will have the power to make and enforce laws as it sees fit. In addition, the bill itself includes several major dictates. It establishes a minimum drinking age of twenty-one, requires warning labels on tobacco products, restricts advertisements for tobacco and alcohol products, and prohibits smoking in public places (*Government Gazette* 2006, 15–21).

Passage of the Act establishing the National Authority on Tobacco and Alcohol elicited mixed public reactions. The director of a Colombo-based alcohol rehabilitation program spoke glowingly of the government's enactment, particularly its restrictions on promotions (M. Fernando, personal communication, 29 June 2006). But a bitingly sarcastic letter to the editor of an English daily newspaper notes that in the midst of an escalating civil war, "The government has taken a sudden interest in the health and welfare of its citizens by passing legislation to appoint a National Authority to regulate the fag and the tot [British slang for cigarettes and servings of alcohol]" (Frederick 2006, A10). The letter then suggests that the government should also protect the citizens by regulating their consumption of sweets, fatty and oily foods, and salt, and by policing political corruption and the indiscriminant use of loudspeakers. The author asserts that with these changes, tourists will rush to Sri Lanka and "live happily thereafter unless they perish by the bullet or the bomb" (2006, A10). The letter writer's juxtaposition of the trivial (sweets) with the tragic (twenty years of ethnic conflict) places the regulation of alcohol and tobacco use on the inconsequential end of the

scale and denigrates the importance of the Act. The letter mocks government priorities and dismisses the seriousness of alcohol-related problems.

Falling between the two positions mentioned above, an editorial in an
English Sunday newspaper comments favorably on the establishment of
the new National Authority, but then notes that a concurrent reduction of
the duty on brown sugar will provide a boon for the *kasippu* industry. The
editorial implicitly supports the regulation of legal addictive substances,
stating, "Nobody in his/her proper sense will dispute the immense harm
alcohol and tobacco causes their consumers as well as their families. The
evidence is irrefutable that cancer and cardiac disease are directly linked to
smoking. Immoderate drinking causes liver disease and quite apart from
that the social consequences of drunken husbands beating their wives and
children are too well known to require elaboration" (*"Sugar, Booze and
Fags"* 2006, 8). The writer then condemns government hypocrisy:

> But what boggles the mind is that while the legal tax paying liquor and to-
> bacco industries, massively enriching state coffers because over 90% of what
> consumers pay for their bottle of arrack or cigarette goes to the government
> as taxes, are sanctimoniously loaded with ever-growing restrictions, the il-
> licit producers are given a free run. Despite the government wielding price
> stick and the widespread knowledge of the harm that liquor and cigarettes
> cause, people continue to drink and smoke regardless and the legitimate
> manufacturing industries continue to thrive. But the illicits do better thanks
> to governmental lethargy plus, undoubtedly, the nexus between politics and
> the underworld. (*Sunday Island* 2006, 8)

While praising government initiative on one front, the editor suggests that
corruption and criminal connections force other government policies to
favor illegal liquor production. Future research will fruitfully explore how
the National Authority confronts these forces as it implements its duties.

Conundrums and Debates

The regulation of drinking through public policy has spurred a number
of debates. Scholars and policy makers have to consider how best to control public health issues around alcohol consumption. One debate concerns
whether it is better to reduce alcohol consumption across the board or to
target risky drinking practices instead. Eric Single and Victor Leino (1998)
suggest the need to modify the prevailing public policy stance of controlling availability of alcohol for all as opposed to controlling binge drinking and excess consumption, the behaviors that the authors believe cause

the most problems.[6] Increasing taxes might reduce drinking, but more so among moderate social drinkers (who would lose alcohol's protective cardiovascular health benefits) than among the heaviest drinkers (who cause the majority of traffic fatalities and suffer the most alcohol-related health problems) (Heath 1998b, 166–67). In contrast, economist Donald Kenkel suggests that "When alcohol taxes go up, heavy drinking, drunk driving, cirrhosis, and traffic fatalities fall" (1998, 162). Speaking from a Sri Lankan perspective, Samarasinghe similarly argues, "If fewer people drink alcohol there will be fewer problems. And if each drinker drinks less alcohol there will be fewer problems. Alcohol-related problems in a society decline when the average individual consumption of alcohol in that society comes down" (2005, 27). Samarasinghe continues by observing that suggestions to target risky drinking often stem from the alcohol beverage industry, which hopes to install "interventions…that do not reduce overall alcohol consumption" (2005, 93). This complex and multifaceted issue deserves consideration beyond the scope of the present ethnography.

Another debate concerns the effects of taxation and prohibition. One position suggests that high taxes increase prices, bringing about various socially undesirable activities such as smuggling, illicit distillation, and accidental poisonings from drinking homemade or non-beverage alcohol (Heath and Rosovsky 1998, 208). Samarasinghe sees little trouble in increasing taxes, except that "a significant part of the increased revenue may come from those less able to afford it" (2005, 19). He counters arguments that increasing taxes may increase the manufacture of illegal liquor by pointing out that reducing taxes could lead to increased alcohol consumption across the board (Samarasinghe 2005, 43). Samarasinghe also suggests that the legal manufacturers in Sri Lanka could increase their market share by supporting the government in its actions against illicit manufacturing and smuggling (2005, 119). While debate goes on over the effects of taxes, history clearly suggests that in situations of considerable public demand for liquor, prohibition creates a vibrant black market in which organized crime can flourish (Saunders and de Burgh 1998; Schneider and Schneider 2005).

A third debate concerns the diversity of community opinions about government efforts to regulate alcohol consumption. Heath and Rosovsky

---

6. One of the contributors to the volume in which the Single and Leino (1998) article appears, Stephen Whitehead, was at the time of publication with International Distillers and Vintners, London, UK. The volume as a whole (Grant and Litvak 1998) argues against policies that strive to reduce overall alcohol consumption, and has been copyrighted by the International Center for Alcohol Policies, a group largely funded by international alcohol companies (Hunt and Barker 2001, 172).

(1998) suggest that the effectiveness of policy depends on community reactions. Although in some instances people have called for restrictions, in
many cases resistance is widespread. Those who see alcohol as a harmless
avenue for social enjoyment feel needlessly penalized for the actions of the
small part of the population responsible for causing problems. Beverage
companies and other people object to some of these restrictions, seeing
them as puritanical infringements on individual rights. Heath and Rosovsky
argue, "Virtually any government initiative is suspect in those developing
countries whose population has become accustomed to official corruption,
especially when the initiative interferes with and increases the cost of those
few pleasures afforded to hard-working, low-paid members of society with
little voice in government" (1998, 212). Others see some benefits of restrictions but do not find the policies effective. Some people, particularly those
who follow religions with restrictive dictates, want stricter controls. As the
following interviews with Naeaegama residents illustrate, even a small percentage of population can hold a wide range of view on alcohol policies.

Villagers' Views of Government and Religious Initiatives

Villagers in Naeaegama held a diversity of views on government policies
and religious prohibitions. Moderate social drinkers had little to say about
the status quo, which suggests they found the situation tenable. The most
vocal opinions came from community members who, unable to control a
man's drinking through informal sanctions, had sought help from higher
authorities.

Misilin, mother of two substance-abusing sons, felt that Buddhism, particularly the Fifth Precept, provided a social and ethical framework to condemn consumption of intoxicants. If people refused to listen to the monks
and stop drinking, they would receive their karmic just desserts in the future. Misilin felt that a drinker's bad behavior would affect his own pros-
pects and those of his offspring as well. Describing the ills that befell Adalin
veda-mahattayaa, the first *kasippu* producer in the Naeaegama area, Misilin noted, "One of his sons was shot, and another ran off with Mangala's
wife. His granddaughters are going here and there [unsupervised];[7] they are
banned from good society. This is punishment for their father's and grandfather's deeds." But while belief in karmic justice might help non-drinkers

---

7. Many villagers find the unsupervised mobility of unmarried females disrespectable. Misilin's condemnation of these wandering young women echoes the pleas of daughters who beg
their fathers to stop drinking or selling liquor to save their reputations (see chapter 9).

come to terms with the devastation wrought by alcohol-dependent relatives, drinkers themselves did not seem to worry about Buddhist prohibitions or their own future rebirths. The Buddhist monks could do little more than provide advice.

Many people turned to the government to help solve drinking problems. Aravinda, a local politician, saw the problem of drinking as socially based and socially curable. Although he felt that *kasippu* drinkers should receive a prohibitively high fine or go to jail, Aravinda also thought that if the government trained unemployed people and found them jobs, they would not drink. He suggested other potential solutions, including sports clubs and youth groups. Experienced with the realities of political administration, Aravinda proposed moderate and realizable initiatives.

In contrast with Aravinda's suggestions for social programs, wives and mothers of alcohol-dependent men called for more drastic measures to control access to alcohol. For example, Misilin named successive government regimes that had not forbidden drinking despite voicing strong support for Buddhism. She wished that the monks were strong enough to force the government to outlaw liquor. Misilin said, "If the government could ban liquor forever, it would be good. In the Middle East there is no drinking. If you drink and get caught, it's all over." She spoke wistfully of Islamic nations as utopian societies where the governments stood behind religious injunctions not to drink. In a similar conversation, a woman whose husband passed away of an alcohol-related illness felt that the government should put a ban on alcohol and enforce it strictly. "But the government is making money from alcohol," she said. She then voiced the common village assumption that politicians and police at all levels of administration were complicit in the illicit liquor business and had no real desire to suppress it (Abeyasinghe 2002, 153). She grumbled, "The police raid, but the *kasippu* sellers don't stop." Then she admitted, "I myself once told a *kasippu* seller that the police were coming. She is a village person, you know?" This case suggests that ambivalence about controlling alcohol pervades all levels of society.

Conclusion

All three areas examined in this chapter—religion, colonial history, and government policies—reveal some ambivalence around the regulation of alcohol. Buddhism strictly prohibits the consumption of intoxicating substances, but many Sri Lankan men do not take this prohibition seriously. Historically, the Sinhala-Buddhist identity formed in opposition to colonial powers. Nationalists engaged in temperance movements took the colonists to task for introducing liquor to the country. At the same time, many prominent business families acquired their fortunes in the liquor industry. In current policy, the same tensions persist. Religious and medical voices argue for banning or reducing alcohol consumption, while the liquor industry pushes for greater freedom. The government, caught between these two forces, balances the need to promote public health and social well-being against its need for the revenues generated by taxes, duties, and license fees imposed on the legal manufacture and sale of liquor. Public opinion ranges widely on these issues. Having set the religious, historical, and political contexts surrounding the use of liquor in Sri Lanka, I now turn to the cultural logic of alcohol consumption in the village of Naeaegama.

2 Without One's Right Mind: Agency, Intoxication, and Addiction

"Alcohol causes a distortion or metamorphosis. The drinker changes into a different person," Indrani commented. As this dynamic mother of five who had spent over a decade working in the Middle East suggests, observers often feel that ingesting alcohol alters people's physical responses, cognition, and affective state. Intoxicated people all over the world display similar observable behavioral changes. Despite—and because of—these biological commonalities, drinkers act in socially shaped ways and their behaviors take on culturally specific meanings. In this chapter I examine issues of personhood, agency, and self-control that underlie the discourse on altered states of consciousness in Naeaegama.

A number of questions arise when discussing alcohol-induced transformations. One question concerns what sorts of behaviors alcohol affects. Most scientists and laypeople agree that consuming sufficient quantities of alcohol can impair motor control. Drinking can cause visible and audible changes in people's physical behavior—staggering and slurred speech, for example. More controversially, many people see alcohol as an ego-altering substance. Describing Alaskan bar patrons, novelist Dana Stabenow evocatively suggests, "They were all drinking their misery away, and their good sense with it" (2002, 29). This leads to a second question: whether alcohol's perceived mental effects are learned or biologically caused. Research indicates that alcohol consumption can lead to "heightened affectivity" and emotional fluctuations (Pernanen 1991, 208). But some scholars suggest that in social drinking contexts, the mood may come more from the setting and one's expectations of enjoyment than from a chemical effect (Fekjaer 1993). Arguing against a purely associational influence on mental states,

Pernanen (1991, 212) points out that beverages such as tea, coffee, and milk never acquire the same reputation as alcohol does. Whatever the operating mechanism, alcohol clearly influences behaviors. As MacAndrew and Edgerton assert, "Alcohol is *not* simply an inert placebo" (2003, 169). Herein lies its power to signify.

In the late 1960s, bucking a determinist mainstream, MacAndrew and Edgerton (2003 [1969]) made a strong and influential argument for the importance of learning in alcohol-related behavior. They state that alcohol provides a cheap, usually legal, fast-acting, controllable, relatively undamaging, and transient alteration in motor control. By drinking, individuals can induce physical impairments that show they have entered an altered state of consciousness. These easily recognizable signs cue bystanders that a person is intoxicated. Given this straightforward system of signals, MacAndrew and Edgerton suggest, "It remains for societies but to 'declare' that [alcohol's] ingestion produces an involuntary and thus an uncontrollable moral incompetence as well" (2003, 171). Cross-culturally, communities recognize special arenas of sociability for the inebriated. In these "time-out" settings, behavioral norms and accountability may be set aside—briefly and within publicly recognized limits (MacAndrew and Edgerton 2003, 168). Since behavioral patterns vary cross-culturally, MacAndrew and Edgerton argue that drinkers learn—and usually follow—social rules governing drunken comportment.

Incorporating new cultural and medical data, scholars continue to ask how much of drunken behavior can be attributed to the physical effects of alcohol, and how much is learned social behavior dependent on conditioning and context. Simply answered, both the substance and the situation play crucial roles in shaping the actions of drinkers and their interlocutors. Different circumstances show different degrees of chemical and cultural influence. For example, passing out from excess alcohol consumption is almost entirely biological. At the other extreme, rituals of swirling, sniffing, sipping, or gulping liquor depend largely on cultural norms. In the ambiguous middle ground, aggressive or tearful behavior may reflect both learned expectations and alcohol's physiological mood-altering power. Therefore understanding intoxicated actions requires a theoretical framework that recognizes the role of culturally guided behavior while simultaneously accounting for biology's part in altering mental states.

A third and related question around alcohol-induced transformations concerns the effect of altered states of consciousness on an individual's identity. Understanding a drinker who is not quite "himself" requires a theory that encompasses mind, body, and society. Gregory Bateson (1972, 315) suggests that starting from the occidental concept of self based in Cartesian dualism can cause problems for both drinkers and scientists. Cartesian dualism, which posits a sharp distinction between mind and matter, brain and body, self and environment, creates a lack of understanding of how the self is integrated into larger systems. The state of intoxication makes a mockery of the mind-body split. Analytically examining a Cartesian perspective on alcohol consumption and then moving beyond it, Pernanen (1991) asserts that alcohol-induced behavior is neither purely learned (of the mind) nor purely physiological (of the body). Drinking behavior simultaneously incorporates the physical effects of alcohol, individual choices made in light of social values, and the actions and expectations of interlocutors. This situation requires a relational, embodied, interactive view of the subject.

A fourth question concerns the relationship between "influence" and agency: How much volition and autonomy does a drinker have when acting under the influence of alcohol? Here again, an answer must critically challenge common assumptions that separate mind from body and free will from compulsion (Sedgwick 1993, 133–34). Although individual drinkers display considerable agency and volition, alcohol clearly affects some people's decisions. Does this influence negate an individual's agency? Answering this question requires an investigation of how much autonomy and free will any individual has, regardless of blood-alcohol level. Practice theorists argue that actors are heavily constrained by the material and social limits in their cultural habitat (Ortner 2006). Pierre Bourdieu suggests that we think of human agency as bounded innovation or "regulated improvisations" (1977, 78) within a restrictive framework. But the framework is constantly changing; the accumulation of individual actions reproduces and transforms the wider structure.

With its patterned but improvisational nature, intoxicated behavior mirrors all other human comportment. No one drinks in a social vacuum. People recognize connections between alcohol use and behavior; thereafter, cultural associations and expectations mediate the direct effects of alcohol consumption (Pernanen 1991, 213, 221). Because they expect particular behaviors from someone who has consumed alcohol, people interact with that person in a certain way, and their learned assumptions in turn shape the interaction. A paradigm that theorizes agency and practice within social constraints escapes the pitfalls of Cartesian dualism and provides a way to simultaneously analyze mind and body, culture and substance, individual and society.

The first half of this chapter explores issues of agency, volition, and identity as they pertain to altered states of consciousness. The second half examines in detail the continuum of transformations brought about by alcohol use. These culturally specific stages of intoxication and concepts of self-control reveal rules that govern drinking behaviors in Naeaegama.

Substance Use and Concepts of Agency

Explaining human behavior under the influence of alcohol requires an analysis of local models of agency (Ahearn 1999, 2001; Ortner 1989). In the next two sections, I focus on two cultural models concerning the loss of control. I first examine Euro-American perspectives on addiction, and then turn to the Sinhala concept of *sihiya naetuwa* (being without one's right mind or consciousness).

A good place to begin the search for agency is in a context where many presume there is none—the case of compulsive addiction. Euro-Americans pathologize the loss of self-control and self-discipline, associating them with the "diseases" of alcoholism and drug addiction (Wilcox 1998, 37). The loss of control and the divergence from normal drinking patterns, not the amount drunk, provide the crucial diagnostic factors (Room 1984, 175–76). Many views on addiction suggest that drugs destroy identity—a notion of identity dependent on an agent's free will (Brodie and Redfield 2002, 10). Addiction is seen as a defect or disease because individuals cannot act freely against their desires; they are not their own masters. Impulses disowned as alien, outside, or "not mine" usurp individuals' consciousness. In the discourse on addiction, Timothy Melley identifies what he terms an "agency panic," a "serious anxiety about the autonomy and individuality of persons" (2002, 39). The discourse suggests that "Individuals *ought to be* rational, motivated agents in full control of themselves," and should not be swayed by outside influence (Melley 2002, 39). Control is seen an all-or-nothing phenomenon, and any behavior resulting from external inducement threatens individual autonomy. Pushing this mindset to its logical conclusion, individuals who cannot control themselves are no longer considered complete persons (McKechnie and Cameron 2000, 51). Although Euro-American culture has since Freud acknowledged the role of the subconscious, the libido, and other non-rational motivations in determining how people act, the rational agent retains its hold on folk knowledge about identity.

The emerging role of consumption in shaping identity in Euro-American society sheds light on the value of rationality and free will and the concern over a less-than-self-controlled agent. By fulfilling their desires through consumption, subjects create their identity (Baudrillard 1981; Miller 1995). Based on the items that they acquire and use, people distinguish themselves from others and form cohesive social groups (Bourdieu 1984). In cases of addiction, desire continues to constitute the subject, but the need is obsessive, excessive, external, and dangerous. Formal economic theory, with its attendant agent "rational economic man," requires a self free from compulsion. Addiction—the uncontrolled desire to consume—compromises the rationality required of the ideal agent. In this worldview, strong self-discipline leads to morality, success, and self-respect. Addiction is seen as moral bankruptcy because the subject lets his or her will succumb to desire (Margolis 2002). For the addict, drugs are the ultimate product, offering pure satisfaction of need (Brodie and Redfield 2002, 7). The prevailing economic discourse condones urges acquired from advertisements, but condemns those stemming from addiction, deeming the addict's will "insufficiently free," his choice "insufficiently pure" (Sedgwick 1993, 132). Addiction disrupts the assumptions about desire, consumption, and identity vital to the ideal of the rational economic agent.

Although these assumptions correspond to Euro-American folk knowledge about addiction, a critical investigation into the area of free will and compulsion reveals troubling paradoxes. Referencing assumptions about Cartesian dualism and moral autonomy, Valverde writes, "The idea that there is a sphere of moral freedom that is quite opposed to the world of natural necessity is a fiction generated by the bad habit of thinking abstractly" (1998, 36). A critical analysis of common contrasts reveals internal contractions. For example, although Euro-American folk knowledge judges addicts to have weak wills, they often display nearly insurmountable determination to find their next fix (Royce and Scratchley 1996). Further, Eve Sedgwick sees slippage between choice and compulsion in discussions of alcoholism. She identifies a "deadly system of double binds where an assertion that one can act freely is always read in the damning light of the open secret that the behavior in question is utterly compelled—while one's assertion that one was, after all, compelled, shrivels in the equally stark light of the open secret that one might indeed at any given moment have chosen differently" (Sedgwick 1993, 134–35). In addition, Sedgwick suggests that people distinguish desires "between those considered natural, called 'needs,' and those considered artificial, called 'addictions'" (1993, 136). If certain substances "artificially" stimulate "natural" desires, how does one distinguish natural from artificial? Pushing the addiction argument to its extremes, Sedgwick questions the logic of suggesting that some people are "addicted" to eating or exercise, two basic human needs.

The way out of these abstract traps is through a discussion of habits, those "semi-conscious patterned acts that are neither fully willed nor completely automatic" (Valverde 1998, 36). Such habits are the shaping power of the social structure that bounds innovation and regulates improvisation. But through their everyday practice, people challenge and recreate social norms. Humans are, according to pragmatist C. S. Peirce, creatures with the unlikely habit of habit-change (Colapietro 1989). As a discipline that theorizes habit and firmly situates the individual within a cultural context, anthropology has much to offer to the discussion of agency, choice, and addiction.

Sihiya Naetuwa: Without One's Right Mind

Euro-American culture applauds consumption in general and the moderate consumption of alcohol specifically, but at the same time condemns addiction. In contrast, Theravada Buddhist philosophy denounces all consumption of mind-altering substances. In addition, Buddhism directs devotees to eschew desires for material possessions, because craving (*taanhaawa*) perpetuates the cycle of rebirth as people's psychic energies travel from life to life in endless suffering. Attachment and the illusion of ownership cause reincarnation (*sansaaraya*). Through mindful living and meditation, one can abolish cravings, disaggregate identity, reach nirvana (*nibbaana*), and escape suffering. Although Buddhism idealizes a self becoming non-self liberated from desire, consumer culture depends on the creation of identity through the consumption of goods and services. Euro-American ideology glorifies the fulfillment of desires but requires them to be "one's own" and subordinate to one's will. Although polar opposites in many ways, both worldviews require a rational agent with a self-conscious mind and assume that desire shapes identity.

While loss of "rational economic man" challenges concepts of proper agency and self-control in Euro-American fears of addiction, in Naeaegama people worry that problematic drunkenness will lead to the loss of "rational social man." Getting dizzy or high (*mat venawaa*) is a fairly straightforward and not very revealing concept in Sinhala. People can get intoxicated, sleepy, or lightheaded from drinking alcohol, taking drugs, smoking marijuana (*ganja*), breathing someone else's cigarette smoke, swinging on a swing, or twirling around in the living room. Without passing judgment on the subject's morality, agency, or identity, the term merely describes a physical state. To understand the complexity of village concepts of problematic drunkenness, one has to understand another Sinhala term, *sihiya naetuwa*. A person who is *sihiya naetuwa* is without (*naetuwa*) memory (*sihiya*, right mind, conscience, or consciousness)—the polar opposite of "rational social man." Use of this term entails a complex attribution of relational selfhood and agency.

The English language has separate concepts for problematic drunkenness, senility, preoccupation, absentmindedness, and unconsciousness (be it from anesthesia, a fainting spell, an epileptic fit, or an alcohol overdose). The Sinhala term *sihiya naetuwa* encompasses all of these concepts. At first I thought *sihiya naetuwa* referred to passing out, particularly from drinking excess alcohol. Then I heard it applied to drunkenness prior to loss of consciousness. I later heard the term used in several different and at first puzzling ways. For example, Indrani used the phrase to describe the state of mind of her increasingly senile mother-in-law. Telsie's elderly aunt, who had injured her head in a car accident, described herself as *sihiya madii* (having too little memory) when she had trouble recognizing the guests who came to visit her. The ability to recognize relatives and treat them properly is a major part of being a fully functional member of society. Although Telsie said her aunt was "like a baby," no one described young babies as *sihiya naetuwa*. Babies have nothing wrong with their mind or memory; they simply have not yet learned to move fluidly in their culture. That same lack of understanding in an older person causes a loss of full adult status.

With yet another use of the term, Telsie related a story about a school staff member. The teacher had put a heating coil into a plastic jug to boil water for tea. She then absentmindedly returned to her classroom, forgetting that she had started this endeavor. When someone finally switched off the coil, the jug had melted along with some plastic cups and saucers. Telsie referred to the teacher's state of mind as *sihiya naetuwa*. Another woman used the same term to describe her worry and preoccupation after learning that her husband needed medical treatment. The concept of *sihiya naetuwa* thus includes absentmindedness and preoccupation, both states in which one becomes heedless of ordinary social responsibilities.

An absence of "right-mindedness" or "memory" forms the commonality Sinhala speakers find between the disparate uses of the term *sihiya naetuwa*. In all the cases above, subjects have lost their rational social focus. The schoolteacher suffered a temporary lapse of mindfulness, the movement of a busy mind away from one project to another. The wife neglected other duties while preoccupied with worry over her husband's health. The elderly women lost their minds in a more permanent and tragic way. Reduced to a child-like state, they could not follow the day-to-day events of their families because of their lack of short-term memory. In all these cases, the term *sihiya naetuwa* refers to a lapse in full, adult, mindful social awareness—the absence or loss of rational social agency.

Somewhere between absentminded forgetfulness, preoccupation, and senility lies the concept of becoming excessively high or drunk by consuming ego- and mood-altering substances such as alcohol, drugs, and marijuana. Manori, Siri's forthright and talkative neighbor who was married to a heavy drinker, saw being *sihiya naetuwa* as exceeding a reasonable limit (*orottu denne naeae*) beyond which a drinker cannot control himself and does not know what he is doing. She explained that someone who is "good" when he is sober can become completely "different" after drinking too much. People in this state forget or ignore social norms for correct behavior.

Villagers often equated addiction and problematic drunken acts (particularly violence inflicted on innocent people) with craziness. Edward, a village drinker from a respectable family, associated being *sihiya naetuwa* with being "without thought" (*cheetanaawak naeae*), and likened both states, when caused by drinking, to being crazy (*pissu*). The temple monk, Mahanama Thero, made a similar statement when he compared addiction with the forgetfulness associated with insanity and lunacy (*unmaadiya,* a noun closely related to the word for memory). Perera said that his son-in-law's "head is not good" (*oluwa honda naeae*) when he drinks. Indrani asserted that "The drunk is like a crazy person until he sobers up (*veri hindenakan* [literally until the drunkenness reduces]). Until he gets to the hangover stage, he won't remember." Villagers also considered the mentally ill as *sihiya naetuwa,* but found problematic drunkenness less threatening because a drunken man would eventually sober up. Thus a conceptual continuum runs from sober to drunk to crazy.

Like a senile elder, a drinker who has sobered up is often described as "like a baby." One informant told me,

> An elder may wet the bed and need help eating and bathing. He or she may be emotional and moody. Like a baby, a drunkard may have smashed some cooking pots in a temper tantrum. In the morning, he will be gentle, innocent, and loving. He may have broken many social rules while drunk, but doesn't remember his bad behavior afterward. He knows he's done something wrong because people are angry at him. So in order to get back into the good graces of his family, he will work with his wife peeling onions and scraping coconuts to apologize for the broken plates. Relatives find it useless to hold him accountable for deeds he claims he doesn't remember.

Echoing this villager's view, Baklien and Samarasinghe (2003, 141) suggest that women see the connection between alcohol and violence clearly, but they blame the alcohol, not the man, for the problem. Several village women assured me that if they turned a drunken husband in to the police at night, they would have to bail out the sober man in the morning.[1] Although

---

1. Scholars of abusive drinking in Euro-American contexts assert that personality transformations characterize alcohol-dependent people (Royce and Scratchley 1996). Such transformations

forgetfulness provides a convenient absolution for the abusive drinker, it comes at the cost of being considered, at least for some time after waking, not quite fully or consistently adult.

In all of these cases, local people implicitly set forth an ideal of a "rational social person"—a concept of normal agency that requires a focused train of thought by a coherent and historically continuous subject who obeys commonly accepted social rules. Breaks in the stream of consciousness, whether from distraction, senility, or the excessive consumption of mind-altering substances, create the abnormal state of *sihiya naetuwa*. This irrational social state worries Naeaegama villagers in a way parallel to Euro-American fears of addiction.

The Continuum of Self-Control

If alcohol solely induced changes for the worse, no one would drink it or allow others to do so. People drink alcohol in moderate quantities to achieve a pleasurable state of mind. Increased quantities of alcohol result in transformations on a continuum from dubious to deviant and even deadly. The "right" amount of alcohol varies from person to person, depending on one's body size and metabolic capacity, how fast one drinks, what one has had to eat, the altitude, and cultural norms and social settings. But when does alcohol consumption become excessive or "wrong"? Pointing out the "toxic" in intoxication, Heath notes, "The poison is in the dose rather than in the substance" (2000, 125). Although communities uniformly seek to avoid alcohol poisoning, drinking people behave in a very wide variety of manners within and between societies. A growing body of ethnographic literature sheds light on the consumption of alcohol cross-culturally, allowing researchers to differentiate universal patterns from cultural elaborations.

Western researchers distinguish between intoxication, excessive regular consumption, and dependence (Ritson and Thorley 2000, 15). Intoxication or obvious drunkenness is often associated with issues of self-control. But one can regularly drink large quantities of alcohol without appearing intoxicated if one spaces out the drinks. This pattern of drinking can cause physical problems, and people can grow dependent on alcohol even if they never appear drunk and never display deviant behavior while drinking. But because dependence can lead to withdrawal symptoms, a dependent drinker

---

eventually undermine a drinker's full personhood. McKechnie and Cameron write, "Drinkers are…confronted with a system which initially does not take their utterances seriously when they are drunk but later proceeds not to take them seriously at any time, as if they have lost the right to a voice within the system" (2000, 50).

may find it difficult not to drink. Therefore in states of both intoxication and dependence, drinkers face issues of self-control. I will discuss addiction later on in this chapter and in subsequent chapters. In this section, I focus on stages of intoxication.

Alcohol's mood-altering property makes it a much sought-after social lubricant that facilitates communication, enhances laughter and liveliness, and creates fellowship. Taken in moderation in contexts where people expect drinking to lead to disinhibition, alcohol can help people "loosen up," relax, and enter a frame of leisure and play (Gusfield 1987). Languages often have many terms for the desired feeling. For instance, Heath writes that "In Danish, there is a word similar to 'coziness' that describes an ideal state to be achieved from 'just enough' drinking; this state carries no risk and is relaxing and welcome when achieved"; similarly, the term *ivresse* in French indicates "gaiety, spontaneity, and zest, the very antithesis of impairment" (2000, 125). Among the Lakota in North America, this stage is referred to as a "laughing spell" (Medicine 2007, 60). In Sinhala, local people say that men drink to feel "jolly," for the pleasurable feeling (*aaswaadaya*), and to have fun (*vinoodayak*, delight, joy). The Sinhala slang phrase *aatal eka* refers to a pleasurable high, whereas *somiya* covers enjoyment with friends. All these terms indicate an enjoyable state achieved by moderate social drinkers.

In some social circumstances, more intense drunkenness is expected and required. For example, Marshall writes about "weekend warriors" on Truk, young men who deliberately drink to intoxication to affirm their masculinity, aggressiveness, and assertiveness (1979). Similarly, at festivals in Malta held in honor of soccer victories and patron saints, men engage in raucous public drunkenness to affirm identity and assert local claims to space (Mitchell and Armstrong 2005). In cases such as these, loss of self-control is the intended effect, at least for the short term. In some cases, however, intoxication is not desired. For example, among the Lele of Kasai, "Drunkenness is socially disapproved of, for it indicates a lack of self-control and an egoistic lack of sharing; it indicates that one has drunk alone and too much" (Ngokwey 1987, 118). Lele social groups try to keep someone from drinking to intoxication by reminding him to share with others in the community. These cases show that the rules regulating drunken comportment vary from place to place. Below, I examine Naeaegama classifications of intoxication and the norms that govern associated behavior.

Stages of Intoxication in Naeaegama

In Naeaegama, the "right" amount of alcohol varies depending on gender; women should not drink at all, but men can, do, and sometimes *must* consume liquor. As the level of alcohol increases in his system, a drinker's behavior changes due to both physiological and cultural influences. Around the world, opinions differ on what constitutes a standard drink size. In Naeaegama, villagers categorize levels of intoxication according to behavior, and predict behaviors according to a widely accepted serving size: quarter units of a 625-milliliter bottle of *kasippu,* the local moonshine. Although dilution various, *kasippu* is usually 30 to 40 percent alcohol by volume. A "quarter" (156 milliliters) is the equivalent of three and a half 44-milliliter "shots" of hard liquor in the United States.

Sitting on Siri's front porch, Siri and I had a long interview with Somaratne, a short and energetic local carpenter and a heavy drinker. During a conversation that stretched well into the evening, Siri and Somaratne discussed categories of intoxication and associated behaviors. They agreed that without drinking, a man was sober. After a quarter bottle of *kasippu,* a man would eat and drink well, but talk and joke more than if he were sober. Perhaps drawing on his own experience of quarter-bottle drinks, Somaratne suggested, "Our man will not get involved in fights, even if his wife shouts at him. He can come home, sit in an easy chair and sing a small song." Never much of a singer himself, Siri modified the portrait, saying, "He will water the flower plants and sweep the compound."

"After a half bottle," Siri continued, "Our man is thinking how to afford another half bottle, and he is happy to reach into his shirt pocket to buy drinks for friends." After three-quarters of a bottle, a man's behavior changes visibly. He will start to boast (*pampooriya kiyenawaa*), listing his good deeds, his qualifications, and his important relatives. To provide an example, Siri recited his own claims to status: "I can speak English, I work with a white lady professor, I have a prestigious school certificate, and my father is a retired school principal and a justice of the peace!" Somaratne and I laughed at this rendition, imagining the excess emphasis and inappropriate contexts in which Siri might trot out his list. In an antagonistic setting, a drinker might instead recite embarrassing past actions of his enemies (*kula kiyenawaa*). Boasting about oneself and one's family and badmouthing others form two sides of the same conversational coin.

After drinking a full bottle, a man gets very drunk. "He walks weaving on the road," Siri suggested. "Or his friends have to drag him home," Somaratne concluded. This drinker causes problems, shouts, and swears. He might come home in a disrespectable way, "raising the sarong [and accidentally revealing his genitals]." Worse yet, he could pass out in the middle of the road.

Drinkers and non-drinkers differed over which of these stages qualified as being *sihiya naetuwa*. Non-drinkers used the term to refer to anyone whose social actions seemed negatively altered by alcohol. If someone became argumentative or boastful, raised his sarong too far, or begged indiscriminately for money, many non-drinkers deemed him *sihiya naetuwa*. Drinkers, however, felt that as long as a man had memory of himself, his relatives, and enemies, he was not yet *sihiya naetuwa*. Drinkers reserved the term *sihiya naetuwa* for more intense intoxication, the stage where a drinker urinated in his sarong, suffered a blackout, or passed out. They felt that if a man could boast, scold an enemy, or fight, then he might have lost his ability to hide his thoughts and feelings, but he had not yet lost his memory.

As the conversation above illustrates, communities note patterns in alcohol-related transformations. The Lakota Sioux recognize similar stages of inebriation. Medicine (2007, 60) suggests a four-way classification, starting with a "feeling good stage" with a great deal of talking, joking, and bragging; a stage of "maudlin reminiscences" that may include tears; a stage "in which bellicosity and belligerence dominate" and fights can take place; and finally a stage where drinkers become comatose. Naeaegama and Native American classifications display striking similarities, but show a high degree of cultural specificity as well.

Two Poems

Sinhalese people have a long history of dealing with drinkers, and folk culture has captured categories of intoxication in verse. In a gathering of several people that took place in their airy living room, Lal and his mother related the following poem. Although similar to the classification related by Siri and Somaratne above, the poem reveals a more extensive cultural elaboration and evaluation of drunkenness.

> *Kaalak biiwama, kaala kanniyaa*
> *bhaagayak biiwama, bhagya vantayaa*
> *tun kaalak biiwama, tun lookayaTama lokka*
> *bootalayak biiwama, boodhi satva.*

> When you've drunk a quarter, you're a time-eater
> When you've drunk a half, you're a lucky man
> When you've drunk three quarters, you're chief of the three worlds
> When you've drunk a bottle, you're a Bodhisattva.

Sinhala speakers say and spell the term for "a quarter" (*kaalak*) and the term for "time" (*kaalaya*) in the same way. In the first line of this verse, the term *kaala kanniyaa* (literally "time eater") refers to an idler who wastes time. The term *bhagya vantayaa* means "half [a bottle] lucky."

Siri glossed this as someone who intended to drink only a quarter bottle but got another quarter for free. The phrase *tun lookaya Tama lokka* (literally "chief of the three worlds") refers to the shouting and boasting of a man who has had three-quarters of a bottle of liquor and disregards everyone else's advice. By referring to the man who has drunk a whole bottle as a Bodhisattva (pre-incarnation of a Buddha), the final line of the poem implies the drinker is just about to pass out. Siri mimed a sleeping, folded-hand position and claimed that such a drinker could not talk, let alone shout. One of the women present objected to this line, saying, "That's a lie told by drunkards. The Lord Buddha never touched a drink!" The men acknowledged her theological point but stuck with their interpretation of the poem.

"What happens if someone has more than this amount of alcohol?" I asked in Sinhala.

"Knock out," replied Lal in English. He then joked in Sinhala, "That person will get a burnt liver and end up in the hospital, where the doctor will decide his post! But someone who has had that much liquor won't need any other medicine."

"And," Siri chimed in, "If the man dies, he is already embalmed!"

On another occasion in Siri's elderly relative Padma's spacious kitchen, Siri, Padma, Padma's daughter Kusuma, and I talked about the phases of drunkenness. When Padma started speaking in verse, I thought she had launched into one of her periodic lectures on Buddhism. But the humorous poem Padma recited only sounded formal. Kusuma, an English teacher by profession, suggested in English that this was "to make the irony more poignant." Kusuma translated the poem this way:

> One pint will keep you fine
> The second will be too bad
> The third will make you feel like a lion
> The fourth will make you a pig.
>
> Repeating each word
> Ten times or more
> Smoking little pieces of cigars
> Spitting all over constantly
>
> Moving limbs high and low
> Bellowing many a word
> Men who are sane
> Will of course disapprove of this.

These lines evoke the transformation in consciousness wrought by alcohol. Like Siri and Somaratne's conversational assessment of the stages of drinking and the first poem above, these verses see little harm in the first two servings of alcohol. But like the other sources, this poem notes a significant transformation after the third and fourth drink. The second stanza mentions repetition of statements, a behavior that Siri recognized as typical of local drinkers. He launched into a funny rendition, smiling goofily and stating: "I'm Siri. I'm *Siri*. I am indeed Siri. My name is Siri." Padma, Kusuma, and I laughed. Siri also acted out "moving limbs high and low" with great hilarity. Everyone seemed to find these harmless drunken behaviors funny. At a certain point, however, drunken comportment ceases to amuse. Siri explained the last two lines of the first stanza, saying that feeling like a "lion" meant starting to brag and boast because one thought one was an important person. Being a "pig" meant sleeping in a ditch. By non-drinkers' standards, the lion and pig states count as *sihiya naetuwa*. The animal references suggest that intoxicated individuals are in some sense no longer completely human.

The equation of excessive intoxication with madness and social irresponsibility occurs in numerous cultures. The last two lines of the poem's third stanza imply that visibly drunken behavior indicates lunacy—a loss of social sense that "sane" men would eschew. Similarly, an Al-Anon pamphlet suggests, "There is no one way all alcoholics act while intoxicated; but they are not rational or sensible; they are not responsible. They are apt to ignore the rules of social conduct, sometimes even to a criminal degree, of which driving under the influence is a clear example. If a sober person acted this way, we would consider him insane" (Al-Anon Family Groups 2003a, 5). Likewise, during the mid-1800s the British considered alcoholics to inhabit "the shadowy zone between sanity and insanity" (Valverde 1998, 46). Along these lines, Quintero (2002) looks at Navajo narratives of alcohol and drinking. Many Navajo elders see abusive alcohol use by youth and heavy drinkers as indicative of the degeneration of traditional values and practices. Those who drink are at risk of not acting morally or respecting the authorities. Quintero writes, "Drinking, as a form of mind loss and unsound thinking, is devalued since it threatens the integrity and stability of social relationships and undermines the basic precepts of the Navajo moral economy. This sentiment itself may be related to culturally important notions of control in Navajo philosophy, where thought is seen as fundamental to action and a lack of control in thinking would lead to lack of control in all aspects of life" (2002, 13). Like the Naeaegama, Al-Anon, and British perspectives, Navajo discourse likens problematic drunkenness to insanity. Intoxication undermines rational social agency.

Embarrassing Behaviors: Violating the "Within Limits" Clause

Learned standards and social environment play a large role in determining drinking behavior, governing who drinks what quantities of which sorts of liquor, at which time, for what occasions, in whose company, with which rituals and taboos (Single and Leino 1998). MacAndrew and Edgerton suggest that drinkers are allowed to break some of the rules that govern sober comportment, but that a different set of rules governs the "time out" context of intoxication. They write, "The *within-limits* character of drunken changes-for-the-worse constitutes an absolutely crucial puzzle with which any theory of the effects of alcohol on man must somehow come to terms" (2003, 82). Naeaegama knowledge of typical behaviors attributed to drinkers illustrates both within-limits drinking and patterns of out-of-bounds intoxication. For example, Sri Lankans expect men to drink at ceremonies, in which case they tolerate moderate intoxication. But by drinking to excess at celebrations or by drinking in inappropriate contexts, a man becomes *sihiya naetuwa*, strays from the ideal of rational social agency, and loses his status in the community.

Drinking in the wrong place implies that a man's need for alcohol has exceeded the bounds of socially responsible drinking. It is shameful to be intoxicated at a government office or a doctor's dispensary, and intoxicated people should not approach or enter Buddhist temple properties. Consider the following case, in which a major temple in the city of Kandy protested against a liquor shop: "This liquor shop, situated on land owned by a leading Kandy private school, is patronized by past pupils of that school. The liquor shop is open for business day and night and the indisciplined [*sic*] behaviour of the sports club members is a nuisance to the [monks], as the liquor shop is in close proximity to the [temple]" ("Liquor Shop" 2006, 1). The monks asked Sri Lanka's President to cancel the club's liquor license, seeking executive authority to protect the bounds of proper social conduct violated by heedless club clients.

Drinking the wrong substance can erode a man's status. Men who can afford to drink arrack and bottled beer have higher status than men who drink *kasippu*. But a bottle of legally manufactured arrack cost four times as much as a bottle of *kasippu*, which led Siri to suggest that arrack drinkers could not become addicted to liquor because they could not afford to drink enough to do so. Drinking *kasippu* marked a man as poor or alcohol-dependent. Siri said, "There's no shame in hanging around at a legal bar drinking legal things if you have plenty of money. If you've had too much, you ask the waiter to find you a three-wheeler [taxi], and give him your address. Drinking *kasippu* is not like that. You can't hang around. Sometimes the retailer gives a man his drink through the window and sends him off with a few bad words. You have to pay up front and come home on your own power." Because it is cheap and illegal to consume, *kasippu* carries much less prestige than arrack and other legal liquors, marking all its drinkers with social stigma.

Drinking to excess in public is more acceptable in a socially sanctioned venue such as a wedding or other celebration that at the locations discussed above. But when a man reaches the state of intoxication where he will swear, fight, and perhaps pass out, everyone recognizes him as drunk. Although men are expected to drink at weddings, exceeding certain behavioral limits still draws comment. For example, Indrani described the behavior of Manori's husband Wasantha at a wedding, saying, "He swore a lot. Oh, yes, he spoke 'beautiful Sinhala language' [in English]. He is of no use. He was yelling at the wedding. He was talking dirty stuff. He wasn't wearing his pants. He was dead drunk." Indrani's statement suggests that Wasantha lost control in several social spheres at once.

Fighting, either with the neighbors or with one's family, is an embarrassing but common consequence of drinking. Private fights damage reputations less than public ones do, but strain family bonds and finances. During one discussion, Siri admitted to fighting with his wife Telsie for no reason while intoxicated. "Pots were broken," Telsie scowled. Breaking clay pots, plates, chairs, and household fixtures such as lamps, doors, and windows is a common element of drunken domestic fights. The expensive destruction of household goods indexes the level of a man's loss of control.

Villagers condemn visible drunkenness, especially if the drinker cannot make his way home. I asked Indrani if passing out in public was shameful. "Isn't that for sure!? No woman likes it if her husband drinks a lot and then sleeps in the ditch. This causes problems for the household. Some people drink and then sleep. Some drink and then they don't remember the next day what they did. They don't remember what happened, whether they scolded someone or had a fight." Passing out correlates with other actions that villagers deem beyond a drinker's conscious choice but nonetheless condemn.

Being excessively intoxicated is less embarrassing in the privacy of one's own home than in public. Reiterating the categories discussed above,

Bandula described the different levels of shameful behavior: "The deepest shame is to pass out in a drainage ditch. Then there's the stage where you swear loudly, raise your sarong, and fight. Slightly less bad is when you stagger home on the road, dropping various vegetables from the shopping bag as you come. Even when someone brags, he is troublesome to his listeners. If people just drink to enjoy, sing a bit, come home, and play with their kids, that's okay. But only a few people are like that. Drinkers don't usually want to stop. First they have a little, then the next door neighbors know, and finally the whole village knows they've been drinking." The more social rules drinkers broke, the more exasperated and disdainful the social condemnation. Like Bandula, many villagers felt that if a man could not behave properly after drinking, he should limit the amount he consumed. This suggests that people in Naeaegama simultaneously recognized alcohol's power to alter behavior and the drinker's agency in choosing how much to drink.

Stigmatized Addiction: The Habitual Drunkard

Although many inappropriate drinking behaviors correlated with excess intoxication, the element of habitual drunkenness also entered into the assessment of status and agency. Occasional and regular intoxication set drinkers apart from more respectable sober men, with habitual drunkards (*beebaddoo*) accruing the most stigma.

Alcohol-dependent individuals often violated social rules about when to drink. Drinking in the afternoon was accepted, but drinking in the morning indicated dysfunction and addiction (see Samarasinghe 2005, 125). I asked Titus what time people started to drink. "Any time is tea time," Titus replied in English. But then he refined his statement, saying, "People who drink after 5:00 cause no trouble; they just come home and sleep. But some addicted people drink early in the day. They say that they can't work without a drink. Their hands are shivering. They talk about alcohol as if it is a medicine without which they can't start the day." But Manori disagreed, saying "It's not like taking medicine; there's no control over giving it and no special time to have it." Since addicted individuals drank to relieve painful withdrawal symptoms, alcohol did hold medicinal qualities, as Titus suggested. But Manori looked at medicine as something given in measured quantities at specific times. She felt that addicts did not moderate their intake, instead drinking as much as they could whenever they could get it. Recognizing these dual dynamics, Brodie and Redfield refer to addiction as "a sickness that strengthens itself in curing itself" (Brodie and Redfield 2002, 9). The twin aspects of dependence and lack of control put addicted drinkers, marked by morning drinking, into a shameful category.

Morning drinking has acquired a number of euphemisms in the village. Most Sri Lankans enjoy a hot cup of "bed tea" when they wake up. Playing on this, Siri jokingly referred to people who needed a shot of *kasippu* first thing in the morning as "bed tea fellows." Manori sarcastically remarked that morning drinkers went to the junction "to catch the Samudra," referring to the Samudra Devi office train that stops at the local station around 7:00 AM. Manori said with distaste, "You can see them at the side of the railroad tracks, near the *kasippu* taverns." Her barbed joke deliberately and unflatteringly juxtaposed morning drinkers with industrious, fully employed, presumably sober office workers. In contrast, Siri noted that after 4:00 in the afternoon, "The shops are busy and the streets are full. No one watches who's going in for a shot. People aren't as concerned about who's going where and why, unless someone is fighting or making trouble." Controlled afternoon drinking does not draw the same censure as an addict's first shot in the morning. Aware of the stigma surrounding their habit, morning drinkers employed terms of their own to disguise their habit, such as the phrase "breaking the ashes" that forms the title of this book. The elaborate euphemisms around the practice of morning drinking suggest both its prevalence and its low status.

Other characteristics also mark alcohol-addicted individuals. Siri, a daily drinker, was sensitive about definitions of "habitual drunkards" (*beebaddoo*), objecting particularly to criteria that would include him in the category. Indrani said she would call people who drank every day and could not be without alcohol *beebaddoo*. But Siri claimed that the term applied only if someone made noise and trouble when he drank, stating, "If someone takes up a knife and fights on the road after liquor, that person is a drunkard." Indrani and Siri then discussed a neighbor who drank every day but did not cause any trouble, and Indrani agreed that this man did not qualify as a *beebaddek* (a drunkard). Siri next suggested that a local man who occasionally passed out in the drainage ditch was a *beebaddek*. But Indrani countered by saying that this man did not cause any trouble. Indrani and Siri then settled on two other area drinkers who drank heavily and caused trouble, agreeing that those men unambiguously qualified as *beebaddoo*. In a separate conversation, Manori claimed that daily drinking did not make someone a *beebaddek* unless he also fought with his family. But given the prevalent unwillingness of outsiders to intervene in domestic disputes, such violence often goes unreported. Regular displays of antisocial or violent public excess, combined with visible daily drinking, seem the least contentious and most commonly agreed criteria for the *bee-baddoo* category.

Mindfulness and Discretion: Highs Leashed and Loosed

In Sri Lanka as in the West, people accept "drunken comportment that deviates—within limits—from usual norms of behavior" (Heath 1987, 37). Naeaegama villagers recognized alcohol's propensity to enhance emotions and exaggerate behaviors. Those interacting with the drinker often absolved him of breaking social rules, assigning responsibility to the physiological effects of the alcohol instead (Pernanen 1991, 15). At the same time, people also recognized that drinkers sometimes had more control over their behavior than at first appeared, and that they could use their drunken state to accomplish things they could not do while sober.

Although people acknowledged diminished mental capacity after alcohol consumption, in some contexts they suspected that the drinker had more control over his actions than he let on. Baklien and Samarasinghe suggest that Sri Lankan men shout to display that they have been drinking. In contexts where drunkenness is not appropriate, for example in front of a religious institution or an important person's house, they can and will fall silent (Baklien and Samarasinghe 2003, 131). Despite diminished capacity, respect for certain social rules remained.

Consciousness of social status can rein in drunken carelessness. Several Naeaegama villagers mentioned that drinkers seemed to sober up quickly in the presence of a respectable person. Lalith, the retired policeman, said that in general heavily intoxicated people were quite troublesome when one passed them on the road. "They joke, they swear, and they insult people," he opined. But his wife Janaki, the retired school principal, reported a different pattern: "They just say 'Buddha's blessings' (*Budu saranayi*) to me." In addition she asserted that if one of the neighborhood drinkers walked by her house while drunk, "He passes through as if he is sober." Shivanthi, a schoolteacher, similarly noted that even though many people in her neighborhood drank, they did not trouble her on the road. "They are shy and ashamed (*laejjayi*). If they say anything at all, it is along the lines of 'Forgive me,'" she reported. These Naeaegama drinkers retained consciousness of gender and status norms, behaving in a stereotypically drunken manner only in an allowable context.

Like rules of gender and status interactions, respect for people in uniform persists during intoxication. Ananda Thero, the head priest at a village temple, used this continued consciousness to suggest that rowdy drinkers act out a lie. He observed, "A drinker will jump in front of almost any vehicle, but not a police jeep. Drunks might yell and misbehave, but they will sober up fast if the police arrive." Therefore, he argued, "When a drunkard behaves like he doesn't have a brain, it's more act than fact." Siri replied jokingly, "Drunks will run from anyone in uniform, even the postman!" Ananda Thero's position emphasized continuity of rational agency despite liquor consumption. In contrast, Siri's joke pointed out impairments of cognition and choice.

Ananda Thero continued his discussion of a drinker's agency in the face of intoxication by noting that a sober man would not get into a dispute but a man who has had some arrack might start a fight. "People say that this is the alcohol talking. But the drunkard will tell ten years of family history, remembering to mention a vast number of shameful things about his adversary. At the same time, he will boast about his own family and status. How can the drinker remember all this history if he has no brain?" The monk concluded that calling this state *sihiya naetuwa* (being without consciousness or memory) distorted the truth. In his opinion, alcohol did not alter a drinker's consciousness, but merely served as an excuse to fight or bully. Convinced that drunken behavior was culturally learned and socially controllable, the priest prohibited drunken behavior on temple premises. Respecting the monk's authority, village drinkers behaved suitably in his presence.

Drinkers can both restrain and unleash their behavior. The absolution of responsibility acquired by drinking alcohol is a two-edged sword. Sometimes the drinker wants to be thought competent, but others think alcohol has impaired his decisions. On other occasions, people drink to be relieved of responsibility for their behavior (Fekjaer 1993). Room defines "pseudo-intoxication" as an instance "where drunkenness is feigned to take advantage of the excuse thus offered" (2001, 196). Since intoxication is understood to affect the mind, it can also affect "the capacity to form a criminal intent" (Room 2001, 195). If society allows it, drinkers can use alcohol for "deviance disavowal"; in such a case, a drinker "puts himself in a position where he will enable himself to do things he would not normally do" (Pernanen 1991, 213) and escape most or all punishment. Societies differ in how they determine culpability in such cases. In Sri Lanka, intoxication does mitigate guilt, and drinkers exhibit a degree of calculation and agency in entering this extenuating condition.

Drinkers, particularly low-status ones, can use the excuse of intoxication to accomplish things sober men cannot. Siri told a story about a coconut plantation owner, his servant, and a coconut thief.

> Once there was a very rich landowner. He had acres of coconut trees. A poor woman came and took five coconuts every day from his stock without paying money. The owner saw her from his balcony, but couldn't say anything because he was rich and she was poor. He discussed the situation with his servant man. "Sir," said the servant, "Don't come to the balcony in the morning for the next few days. I will take care of the problem." The next morning, the servant man went and had a drink. Then he stood near the coconut stock. When the woman came, he raised his sarong. Shocked, she left quickly without taking any coconuts. The next morning, he again took a drink and raised his sarong when the woman came for coconuts. The woman didn't come back a third time. The rich owner thanked his servant and said, "Shamelessness is bigger than a businessman's status (*wili laejja naeti kama maha mudali kamaTat vaDaa lokuwi*)."

By consciously breaking social rules but implicitly blaming his behavior on being drunk, the poor servant accomplished something his rich and status-conscious employer could not.

In another example, this one factual, male alcohol consumption again constrained women's behavior. In Naeaegama and most of the rest of Sri Lanka, sunset marks a de facto curfew for women: "After 8 at night it is not safe [for women to walk alone] as there are drunkards on the roads" (Baklien and Samarasinghe 2003, 136). A woman breaking this social rule sets herself outside the protective gender conventions that respectable women enjoy during the day. Villagers assume that drinking increases in the evenings and deem drunkards especially prone to insulting, aggressive, and threatening behavior. Without anyone expressly stating or enforcing this curfew, most women abide by it; the few who do not are vulnerable to drinking men's discipline. In the coconut and the curfew story, the possibility of, appearance of, and fact of male drunkenness operated to police female behavior. Because women do not drink in Naeaegama, alcohol-related behavior often takes on such gendered dynamics. Feigning intoxication, men can reinforce aspects of their social privilege.

Conclusion: Spirits and Spirits

In discussing intoxication, theory pertaining to other altered states of consciousness proves useful. In some cultures, "The special kind of altered consciousness that comes from having drunk heavily is thought to provide the ideal relationship with supernatural beings" (Heath 2000, 126). Several groups conflate drunkenness with spirit possession and trance, or liken it to witchcraft and possession by aliens (Room 2001, 194; Valverde 1998, 191). Anthropologists who study rituals have developed ways to talk about the nature of agency when a medium enters a trance (Boddy 2005). In many cases mediums and oracles claim not to remember what they said or did during their altered state (Brown 2001). Enough testimony exists that we need to take these ritual specialists seriously and assume that something besides chicanery and showmanship backs the claim. An autonomous agent animates the ritual specialist's body during possession and trance. Despite its autonomy, this personality shares many linguistic and cultural competencies with the ritual participants and behaves according to well-scripted patterns. In a number of cases, the spirits and their mediums have social, economic, and political agendas that they fulfill through ritual actions (Ong 1988). These fleetingly embodied personalities are agents in complex and intricate ways.

Like ritual specialists, drinkers change personalities and enter altered states of consciousness under the influence of spirits. But transformations spurred by alcohol are gradual and continuous, and only in the final stages of intoxication does a drinker entirely forget what has happened. Like the autonomous agents of ritual, drinkers under the influence retain a great deal of cultural knowledge and act in strategic ways. For the most part, however, alcoholic transformation does not earn respect. In Naeaegama, poems suggest that a heavily intoxicated person is no longer a man but an animal (a lion or a pig). After a night of excess, in the morning a sober drinker, "like a baby" or a partially recovered lunatic, lacks full adult status. Although moderate drinking does enhance men's standing in certain social spheres, the transformation achieved through excess alcohol use that renders him *sihiya naetuwa* does not improve the reputation of the drinker. The most shameful behaviors correlate with alcohol-dependence. In all these cases, alcohol intake undermines the ideal of "rational social man."

Intoxicated, a man undergoes a metamorphosis, transforming into someone with different attitudes, priorities, and behaviors. Societies construct careful rules for consuming such powerful substances. Although people make allowances for drinkers' behavior, those who drink to excess or drink outside culturally sanctioned times and spaces garner social stigma. But drinkers continually negotiate the rules governing their behavior. Carrying forward this discussion, in subsequent chapters I focus on issues of consumption and identity, as drinkers create and contest subjectivities based on alcohol use.

3 We Don't Say No: Drinking and Identity

Consuming things serves as a major way to display one's identity. Because people require daily nourishment, the consumption of food and drink provides a superb vehicle for symbolic action. Eating and drinking with others makes manifest not only individual but also group identity. In many societies, consuming alcohol takes on special meaning. Heath suggests, "In some circles, drinking almost serves as emblematic of membership in a social group" (2000, 174). Drinking together creates a sense of community within the drinking group and differentiates that group from others. As Dietler observes, "Drinking serves to mark social categories, boundaries, and identity" (2006, 235). Social rules govern alcohol use, shaping who can drink how much, of which substance, in whose presence, at what times, and at which locations. Within these general parameters, people indicate who they are (and who they are not) by what they ingest and how they behave thereafter. An anthropological approach to drinking patterns examines the everyday practices through which people imagine, embody, perform, and transform their identities.

Most people take cultural categories and classifications for granted. For example, English speakers accept common names for the colors of the rainbow (red, orange, yellow, and so on) and recognize common types of mammals (dog, cat, horse, elephant, etc.). Children learn the differences that mark separate categories and use those categories without questioning throughout their lives. Most categories, including classifications of colors and mammals, have few political overtones. But studying categories of people places a scholar squarely in the realm of power and politics. Categorizing requires highlighting the differences by which items are classified. It takes only a baby step to turn the recognition of difference into an assertion of hierarchy. Where differences sort items into categories, hierarchy stratifies categories into ranks. Choosing a favorite color or preferring cats to dogs are harmless types of ranking. But ranking categories of people often confers special rights and privileges. Even a short list of identity categories reveals ample ground for the study of hierarchy and inequality; consider race, class, gender, age, occupation, caste, religion, ethnicity, and nationality to name a few.

Where the stakes are high, systems of ranking and classification come under continual challenge. Studying the politics of representation around categories of persons reveals ongoing struggles over meaning. Control over cultural categories, which is tantamount to the construction of reality, forms a major dimension of political power (Bourdieu 1977, 165). Raymond Williams defines hegemony as "our shaping perceptions of ourselves and our world" (1977, 110). He suggests that this "lived system of meanings and values" is also "the lived dominance and subordination of particular classes" (1977, 110). The people in power use their power to keep that power, defending systems of classification that support their dominance. But those people whom the system exploits resist this oppression. For this reason, hegemony "has continually to be renewed, recreated, defended, and modified. It is also continually resisted, limited, altered, and challenged" (Williams 1977, 112). Examining classificatory systems dealing with human beings reveals complex histories and ongoing social negotiations (Ortner 2006; Scott 1988). Communities develop strategies to create and maintain group identity and delineate and defend boundaries between categories. In this chapter, I look at gender, age, and occupation in Naeaegama, examining how people enact their identities through the use of alcohol and how issues of hierarchy, power, and dominance play out in these consumption practices.

Gender

Gender forms one of the most basic dimensions of identity. Although "male" and "female" constitute universal human sexual categories, the cultural elaborations of these biological traits vary from place to place and time to time. I define gender as cultural knowledge about biological difference. People use this knowledge to shape their own behavior and judge the behavior of others. In most segments of Sri Lankan society including the village of Naeaegama, properly "feminine" women do not drink. Conversely, full "masculine" men can drink, do drink, and often *must* drink. Alcohol consumption provides a medium through which men form powerful social networks.

Cross-culturally, alcohol use is closely tied with gender identity, particularly masculinity. For example, Suggs (2001, 242) argues that in Botswana both older and younger men tie their masculinity to the public use of alcohol despite changes in economic conditions, drinking patterns, and concepts of manliness. Among gang members in San Francisco, drinking is a male-dominated activity. Researchers suggest that "Alcohol and group drinking work to maintain group solidarity and camaraderie, while, at the same time, operating as a distancing mechanism to exclude 'others', including both women and rival gang members" (Hunt, MacKenzie, and Joe-Laidler 2005, 229). In Chiapas, Mexico, cultural rules prohibit young women, particularly mothers, from drinking to excess (Eber 2000). Women limit their consumption to drinking at semi-annual festivals, and should not drink when their husbands are drunk. Throughout the world, men drink more, and more often, than women (Heath 2000, 72; Milgram 1993, 53). Kunitz asserts that this gendered imbalance "is widely known but has not been adequately explained" (2006, 287). Many people think of these rules as "natural" or imposed by biology (Heath 1998a), a position challenged by cross-cultural variety in drinking contexts and behaviors. Instead, I argue that societies often set formal and informal prohibitions on drinking for "those who have not been deemed worthy to use their own wills to govern their desires and their acts" (Valverde 1998, 145). In Naeaegama as elsewhere, women and children often fall into such a category.

Absolutely Not! Female Drinking in Naeaegama

Sri Lankan drinking practices illustrate an extremely gendered pattern. Although in Sri Lanka people do not see a biological barrier to female drinking, women rarely take liquor. Consider the following conversation. Michele: "Do women drink?" Dr. Sepali (an Ayurvedic physician): "Absolutely not! *(Naehaemayi!)*" Michele: "Why not?" Dr. Sepali: "Culture [in English]." Abeyasinghe suggests, "Women in Sri Lanka, like in many Asian countries, do not have a tradition of drinking....It is only a small percentage of women who drink and this is true of both middle and working classes, both urban and rural" (2002, 119).[1] Women carefully defend their own sexual reputations and those of their daughters, an undertaking antithetical to the disinhibition locally associated with alcohol consumption. When asked why women abstain from liquor, people in Naeaegama often answered by referring to Sri Lanka's Buddhist traditions. Those who used

---

1. Abeyasinghe's assertion about the drinking habits of "Asian women" requires some nuance. Compared to women in South Asia, many women in Southeast Asia have more social space to drink if they wish. Customs also vary widely within geographic regions.

this explanation seemed to conveniently forget that Buddhism forbids the ingestion of intoxicating substances for men as well as for women. Nevertheless, men drink widely. In fact, this gendered dichotomy provides essential defining characteristics of femininity and masculinity.

In Sri Lanka, the Alcohol and Drug Information Centre (ADIC) estimates that 45–60 percent of the male population drinks at least occasionally, compared to 5.0 percent of the female population that has ever tried alcohol and only 0.5–1.5 percent of the female population that drinks at least occasionally (1999, 6; 2003, 4; 2004, 11, 20). Actual figures for female drinking may rise slightly among some populations. When pressed, Naeaegama villagers suggested that Catholic women in Negombo drank beer and toddy, a habit that one scholar attributed to a lack of "religious inhibitions against drinking" (Abeyasinghe 2002, 136). Western female tourists and westernized urban women were also known to drink. Samarasinghe (2006, 627) asserts that media presentations equate beer drinking with female emancipation and sophistication. For the middle class employees of a cooperative store, "The quiet acceptance of the open sipping of alcoholic beverages by women folk, at parties…is almost a sign of 'not belonging to the village'" (Baklien and Samarasinghe 2003, 71). But female drinking also occurs among the working class. Naeaegama villagers suspected (correctly) that Hindu women who pluck tea on upcountry estates indulged in liquor (Bass 2004, 244; Vijesandiran 2004, 16). In addition, Abeyasinghe's research in a Colombo slum community revealed that some women drank at social events: "It is our estimate that 20% of the women at Thotalanga engage in social drinking, while 4%-5% are dependent on alcohol" (2002, 120). These figures and instances show that women drink in Sri Lanka more frequently than some Naeaegama informants believe.

Although Naeaegama villagers knew that many western women and some Sri Lankan women drank, these exceptions did not challenge their own gendered rule for alcohol consumption for several reasons. First, Buddhist villagers saw women from other faiths as governed by different rules; they assumed that Christianity and Hinduism did not forbid alcohol consumption in the same way. Second, alcohol consumption by women in Colombo (50 miles distant), in Negombo (70 miles distant), on tea plantations (far inland), and at hedonistic foreign-dominated beachside hotels merely served to solidify Sinhala-Buddhist village women's reputations in contrast to a list of deviant "others." Female abstinence formed a strong marker of ethnicity and religion as well as gender.

Village beliefs that women do not drink created some cognitive dissonance around beer. For example, one woman asserted that some women drank "beer" but not "alcohol." She claimed that she and her female relatives did not drink, at the same time saying that they had had a little bit of beer at a neighbor's recent wedding. This observation may indicate a cultural distinction between different types of liquor. Elsewhere as well, distilled spirits are sometimes "construed as the only real alcoholic beverage, whereas beer and wine [are] thought not to contain alcohol, or at least not enough to be worth mentioning" (Heath 2000, 94). Along the same theme, during an interview with Chandrani and her husband Perera, I asked Chandrani if she had ever tasted alcohol. Implicitly acknowledging beer as alcoholic, Chandrani said that she sometimes drank beer, as did a woman in the house next door. Perera then remarked, "People do not get drunk on beer." Perera may have referred to how much more one would have to drink to get drunk on beer than on hard liquor, or to the fact that when Naeaegama women drank beer, they did not drink to intoxication. Lee Strunin found similar patterns of reporting alcohol use among U.S. adolescents, some of whom felt that "'sips' and 'tastes' did not connote 'drinking'" and categorized certain alcoholic drinks as non-alcoholic (2001, 221). In Naeaegama, the "muscular truth" (Said 1986, 219) that "women do not drink alcohol" led people to suggest that beer was not alcoholic or would not intoxicate the female drinkers.

Several village women admitted sampling hard liquor. When I asked Padma, who was in her eighties, if she had ever drunk liquor, she said that she had once put her finger in a glass and tasted the stuff, just to see what the big deal was about. She disliked it, and never tried it again. Similarly, Chandrani tried *kasippu* once. Pointing to Perera, Chandrani said, "I once followed this one [her husband] to the *kasippu* tavern. I was angry because he had taken Rs. 50 to drink. He had paid Rs. 25 for a quarter bottle by the time I got there. I grabbed the glass from him and drank it myself because I was so angry. I drank it like it was water, in one gulp." Laughing together, the couple explained that Chandrani then had trouble walking, and Perera had to help her home. "I drank a quarter bottle with the other Rs. 25 before we left," Perera recalled. Chuckling over the memory, the couple assured me that Chandrani had never drunk any other hard liquor. I genuinely believe that Naeaegama women have not had extensive experience imbibing alcohol, though social norms now seem to be evolving toward permitting women, even those in rural villages, to drink beer at weddings.

A Drinking Woman: Joy-amma

Universally known and reviled as a daily cigarette smoker and *kasippu* drinker, Joy-amma was an exception to the rule that women do not drink. Both drinkers and non-drinkers brought up her case when asked whether any area women drank. Mentioning Joy-amma's name prompted laughter or concerned censorship. Most local *kasippu* drinkers had drunk with her, even buying her drinks and cigarettes when she was short of cash. This reciprocity mirrors the ways that men drink and smoke with each other.

Curious to meet this woman, I went with Siri to talk with Joy-amma, who lived near Naeaegama with her son and daughter-in-law in a nice cement house. During our interview, Joy-amma sat with one bandaged foot propped on a chair; she had fallen between a moving train and the railway platform and nearly lost a leg. After appropriate introductions, Siri and I asked Joy-amma about drinking. She immediately replied, "Now stopped, now stopped! [in English]." Joy-amma had spent nearly twelve years working in Lebanon as a housemaid, leaving her children with her mother. She went abroad when she was twenty-six, after her husband died. Joy-amma encountered troubles with her live-in employment, working very hard but not receiving a proper salary. She eventually paid for her own visa and moved out on her own. She started to drink at parties while she was abroad and continued to do so after she came home. She reported, "Sinhala people say that drinking is bad, but the Arabs gave me liquor with their own hand. They didn't force me to drink. They just gave me a glass while they were also enjoying. If they had coffee or cigarettes, they shared those too. That's how I got the habit. After my accident I controlled my mind and stopped drinking." Siri claimed he had met her in *kasippu* taverns. She gave him a meaningful look and said in English, "Thanks for coming." We changed the topic.

In a cultural context that forbids female drinking, many fewer women than men become addicted to liquor. Joy-amma learned to drink in Lebanon and could not shake the habit when she returned to Sri Lanka. Soon after our interview, Joy-amma started to drink again. Her son kicked her out, and she slept at the railroad station or in other relatives' houses. Joy-amma's lack of a stable home weakened her already-vulnerable social position. Siri asserted that the story she told us during the interview differed from the one he had heard at a *kasippu* tavern—that her foreign employer forced her to drink alcohol and have sex with him. Siri suggested that Joy-amma currently worked as a prostitute, servicing a man for Rs. 50 or 100 and spending what she earned on *kasippu*. Whatever the truth about the prostitution allegations, the fact that Joy-amma broke one set of rules by drinking suggested that she might break others. Heath notes that "The infamous double standard applies, so that a woman who drinks is presumed to be sexually promiscuous in many societies, and her drinking may be morally condemned" (1998a, 112; see also Valverde 1998, 85). By drinking, Joy-amma exiled herself from the category of "good woman," opening herself to other accusations and propositions (Lynch 2002, 2007).

Eight months after our interview, I ran into Joy-amma on my morning walk to the junction. Thin, red-eyed, and unwashed, Joy-amma claimed that she still suffered from pain in her foot, which had not healed completely. She asked me for Rs. 50 to go to a doctor and have the wound dressed. I had no money with me, but volunteered to go with her later that morning to Dr. Mendis's dispensary. Clearly preferring cash to company, Joy-amma proposed instead that I give her the money, and she would get some food and medicine with it. As we stood talking, a man rode by on a bike and shouted to me in Sinhala, "That woman drinks *kasippu* in the morning." Joy-amma yelled an angry retort and then assured me that the biker was crazy.

In a cultural milieu where hardly any other women drank, Joy-amma faced constant censorship from both family members and strangers. Many men drank *kasippu* in the morning, but people did not shout that information to me while passing by on their bicycles. When I asked one local gentleman, Titus, whether women drank alcohol, he brought up Joy-amma, and then said in English, "She is a mad woman, I think." In this he paradoxically agreed with Joy-amma, who called the cyclist crazy for suggesting that a woman would drink *kasippu* in the morning. A drinking woman violates firmly held cultural categories, and her drunkenness thus constitutes a form of madness.

Like a Woman: The Non-Drinking Man

Given the powerfully masculine associations with alcohol consumption, a man who does not drink receives nearly as much comment as a woman who does. Although not scorned, reviled, or called crazy, non-drinking men occupy a symbolically marginal social space. For example, Titus mentioned that a neighbor's son had earned his engineering degree and started a job. Titus described this young man as "good" and "like a woman" (*gaeaeni-wagee*). Siri agreed: "This boy comes and goes very quietly, without making any trouble in the village." In a different interview, Lalith, the retired policeman, said that people would call a man who didn't drink a "woman-man" (*gaeaenu pirimiyaa*). In each instance when I heard non-drinking men described as being "like women," the speaker asserted the positive value of this designation. Because women stereotypically do not drink, fight, shout, or waste money, being "like a woman" was often admired.

Despite this general affirmation, Siri expressed some ambivalence about non-drinking men, particularly day laborers. He suggested that a man who had a white-collar job or powerful relatives did not lose status by being "like a woman." In fact, government servants, police officers, and people from powerful families gained more respect if they did not indulge in alcohol. But working class men who did not drink or smoke held no place in the male drinking networks described below. In addition to this class-based dichotomy, Siri noted a gendered divide in the community: women appreciated a non-drinking man, but drinking men disliked him. "Drinkers will say that man is 'under the petty-coat government' [in English], controlled by his wife," Siri predicted. Participation in the male drinking community was particularly important for men who had few other claims to manly status. By not drinking, a man missed out on a source of masculine identity and marginalized himself from a powerful network of local friends and co-workers.

Professions

For its capacity to ease interpersonal interactions, scholars term alcohol a social lubricant. Dramatically reversing this fluid metaphor, Wilson calls alcohol a "social cement" (2005, 7) for its ability to bind groups together. Drinking together enhances confidence and builds trust. By drinking together, working men can cultivate professional networks that give them access to goods, services, information, and employment opportunities (Carrier and Heyman 1997, 362; Valverde 1998, 168). For example, Gerald Mars (1987) explores the role of alcohol in creating social networks among Newfoundland dock workers. Men who work together regularly drink beer together in bars on the wharf, where they talk about their jobs. Those most central to the social network receive more alcohol than they give. In exchange, these influential individuals can pressure bosses regarding whom to include in the work group. Similarly, Sharon Popp reports that "occupational drinking may be normative or constructive to the drinker within the work culture" (2001, 17). For example, men in the skilled building trades describe drinking as a way to join a work crew and reduce the chance of being laid off (Popp 2001, 20). Neither dock workers nor builders can miss work because of drinking, and it is socially forbidden (not to mention dangerous) to be drunk on the job. Drinking takes place during non-working hours, but forms a social requirement of the work role (Mars 1987, 93).

Certain professions guide men to particular drinking patterns. For example, Samarasinghe suggests that in Sri Lanka, people with distasteful occupations, such as sewer cleaners, will drink before starting work. Such a worker uses alcohol to alter his consciousness so that "he" is not actually engaged in the questionable occupation, a job he would not do in his

"normal" state (Samarasinghe 1995, 273). In contrast, for men in other occupations, drinking constitutes part of a valued identity. Baklien and Samarasinghe note that an interviewee stated, "When you are a fisherman,
you have to drink alcohol" (2003, 131). In Naeaegama, teams of cinnamon
peelers received weekly pay (*sumaana kaasi*) from the garden owners as
advances against the worth of the cinnamon they would sell when finished
peeling. Many cinnamon peelers stayed sober during the week, but binged
when they received their pay. Some salaried workers also drank heavily
on payday. In these cases, class affiliation and choice of liquor overlapped
with professional affiliations; working class cinnamon peelers often drank
cheap illicit liquor with their work gang, while middle class salaried men
drank legal arrack in bars with friends from their office or commuter train.
Men who drank with their peers chose beverages commensurate with their
class status and financial capacity, and drinking together created a sense
of camaraderie between drinkers and simultaneously separated them from
other groups.

Army arrangements exaggerate the sorts of informal norms that govern
drinking among non-military co-workers. In many countries, men in the
armed forces are reputedly heavy drinkers (Heath 2000, 85). Sri Lanka's
servicemen face considerable pressure to conform to the prevailing drinking patterns. In Naeaegama, Edward, a retired sergeant who competed in
the long jump, described his first army experience with alcohol. At a party
at the sports grounds one day, a lieutenant put beer and arrack into the
"challenge cup." When Edward refused to drink it, the lieutenant poured
the contents of the cup on Edward's head—a humiliating dousing that Edward vividly remembers forty years later. Edward also faced peer pressure in
the sergeant's mess, where "Drinking was compulsory (*anivaaryen bonDa
onaeae*)." An off-duty army officer reported a similar situation, saying, "You
have to drink in the army. They have parties with arrack. You have to drink.
Those who don't drink are out of the circle. You need to enjoy together, or
else it isn't good. You need to be comrades. If you don't drink, people say
you are a girl. Girls don't drink." Compulsory communal alcohol consumption seems to play an important role in creating a soldier's hyper-masculine
identity and maintaining a strong bond between officers.

While drinking together reinforces group identity, being unable to drink
together creates a sense of hierarchy. Men in the army drank different substances depending on their ranks. A man in army supplies elaborated on alcohol consumption patterns: "There are no alcoholic drinks at the private's
mess for the new recruits. They can have Fanta [orange soda] and other
soft drinks. At the corporal's mess, there's only beer, but they have hard

liquor at the sergeant's mess and the officer's mess. Officers either pay cash or buy on credit with the bill deducted from their pay." Edward confirmed that officers bought and drank shots of arrack before dinner. Peer pressure and the separate mess halls found in the military contributed to the sense that certain men must, without fail, eat and drink with their equals but not with men of other ranks. The off-duty officer noted that to maintain his respectability, he could not drink with "just anyone" even when he came home on vacation. Both official rules and unofficial practices reinforced the system of status and rank.

Syndicating: Male Drinking Networks

Drinking together creates bonds not only between co-workers but also between family and friends. For example, in Malta, men buy drinks in rounds that emphasize both reciprocity and the buyer's generosity (Mitchell and Armstrong 2005, 186). Among gang members in San Francisco, "drinking operates as a social 'lubricant' or social 'glue' working to maintain the social solidarity of the gang" (Hunt, MacKenzie, and Joe-Laidler 2005, 239). In Botswana, "Sorghum beer was symbolic...of the patrilineal core of [the] descent system and of the ideologies of reciprocity and redistribution" (Suggs 2001, 241). Around the world, people drink together to celebrate family rites of passage and the conclusion of collective labor (Heath 2000). In this section, I describe norms regulating drinking between peers in Nae-aegama, examining the moral imperative of generosity and its social and financial consequences.

In a classic relationship of balanced reciprocity, drinking men in Nae-aegama and elsewhere in Sri Lanka "syndicate" their money (*hawule geva-navaa*) with their peers. Someone who has money today will buy drinks for those who are broke; on another day he will receive free drinks in return. In balanced reciprocity, members do not keep exact records of exchanges, but maintain continuing exchange relationships. They anticipate that they will give and receive roughly the same amounts. Men tend to go into this sort of syndicated drinking relationship with kinsmen, neighbors, friends, or co-workers. The members' work schedules and financial liquidity determines the group's drinking schedule. Baklien and Samarasinghe report that an informant said, "I give some money from my salary to the family, but these people here have bought me food and drink when they had money—so I must treat them well when I get the chance" (2003, 60). Conspicuously paying for drinks for others confers status and power (see Baklien and Samarasinghe 2003, 130). Syndicating ties men into long-term relationships and creates a social momentum toward alcohol consumption, both allowing and forcing men to drink together.

During an interview with Sherman and Kitsiri, I asked whether people who had money gave drinks to others. Instead of translating my question, Siri turned to Sherman and said, "Can we do something?" Sherman immediately replied, "I have Rs. 50 in my pocket!"

"Drinking men don't hide their money," Siri told me with a smile. "We don't say no (*naeae kiyanne naeae*)." He then explained, "People will give a bit extra to someone who is drinking. If I only have Rs. 25, Sherman will give me more. But some people hide their money when I come by, so I won't give them money either—unless I am drunk and feeling generous!"

Perera also syndicated his drinking. He provided an example, saying, "Someone I know might be at the junction and say '*savuttuwi* (bad state, dirty). Today I have no money,' so I will call him to come drink with me. He'll return the favor another day." Perera estimated that he spent Rs. 1,000 on himself for drinks each month, and added another Rs. 200 or Rs. 300 for friends (probably receiving as much from others). Another drinker said that if he had Rs. 100, Rs. 20–25 would go for friends. Both men estimated that they spent about 15 to 25 percent of their money on other drinkers when they were flush, and received as much in exchange when broke.[2] Syndication allowed men to pool their drinking money, ensuring that they could drink even when they had no cash.

I asked Perera what he did if he saw a drunken person on the road. Like many women who answered this question (see chapter 2), Perera suggested that he would avoid the drunkard, but he applied a different line of reasoning: "If I know the drinker, that man is likely to suggest that we go drink together. If we do this, he will have had too much." Perera, his wife Chandrani, and Siri then joked how one drunken person would try to guide the second one home, then the second would want to guide the first home. On the way they would have another drink, and continue shuttling back and forth between houses all night, or until someone dropped, whichever came first. In this imagined case, the bond between drinkers led to a humorous situation where neither man was sober enough to make a wise choice.

2. Baklien and Samarasinghe (2003, 144–45) suggest that men often underestimate how much they spend on alcohol because they fail to count money others spend on them or they spend on others. They also do not count the money they spend providing alcohol for events, or the amount they drink at others' ceremonies. Men might also neglect to count money they earn unexpectedly and then spend on alcohol.

Drinking with someone implies a series of other responsibilities. Refining the scenario of meeting a drunkard described above, Siri noted that if he encountered a good friend who had helped him in the past, he would take him to a safe place. If he disliked the man, he would just let him pass by. In another context, Siri noted, "If you drink with someone, you can't leave him if there is a fight or if the police come. But some cunning people take a shot and vanish," implicitly breaking the social rules. Obligations incurred through syndication last a long time, as the following case illustrates. About a year after our interview with him, Sherman got ill enough to stop drinking for some time. Later he started drinking again, despite his doctor's orders. One day Sherman came to Siri's gate and asked for some money to drink. Siri refused because he knew Sherman was ill. Sherman scolded him and cursed him, hoping that the same treatment would happen to Siri when he got sick. Although Siri said he had Sherman's best interests at heart, Sherman interpreted Siri's act as a betrayal.

Drinking networks overlap with other forms of association. For example, Siri often drank with his neighbors Dharmadasa and Somaratne. If he needed help in his garden, he employed Dharmadasa, and if he had carpentry or plumbing to do, he called Somaratne. If either man needed a form filled out or a letter written in English, he asked Siri. Payment for labor was made in alcohol, not in cash. Siri lamented this situation, noting, "If we have a shot or two together before they finish the work, the job does not get done satisfactorily." In addition, his friends asked for drinks for several days after they completed the required labor. In these cases, drinking networks provided employment opportunities, but Siri felt it was cheaper and more efficient to hire a wage laborer for cash instead.

How Drinkers View Non-Drinkers

When drinking together reinforces social networks, refusing a drink can indicate distance and disdain. In many contexts around the world, drinkers distrust and dislike abstainers (Heath 2000, 100). For example, in Malta people have an obligation to receive an offered drink; "refusal is considered a great insult" (Mitchell and Armstrong 2005, 180). Among American Indians, drinking falls into wider cultural patterns of hospitality and reciprocity (Spicer 1997, 310). Medicine describes social pressures to join drinking groups, and suggests that among the Lakota, "To refuse a drink is tantamount to giving a slap in the face" (2007, 58), generating accusations that one thinks one is "too good to drink with us" or is no longer Lakota (2007,

82). Similarly, Spicer points out the profound ambivalence with which urban Native Americans view drinking. His informants recognized many negative consequences of drinking, but also mentioned the social costs of abstinence, especially because "to quit drinking was often perceived as an attempt to elevate oneself above others" (1997, 317). Siri faced a similar dilemma in Naeaegama: "If I stopped drinking, my family and neighbors would approve, but my drinking buddies would be sad." Refusing a drink can cause offence, break ties of kinship and friendship, and undermine ethnic identity.

In addition to enhancing comradeship, some drinkers try to incorporate others into their group in order to promote economic equality. For example, David McKnight suggests that among aborigines on Mornington Island, leveling mechanisms work to minimize inequalities. Because non-drinkers are seen as rich and self-congratulating, "Drinkers practically cheer when someone falls off the wagon or when somebody drinks for the first time" (McKnight 2002, 189). Similarly, describing a non-drinker in Naeaegama, Siri said, "Drinkers want to bring him into their group. They want to drink with his money. They are jealous, and they want to bring his status down to their level so he cannot criticize their drinking." Baklien and Samarasinghe suggest that the Sri Lankan drinkers in their sample actively tried to erode the financial status of non-drinkers: "The picture that emerges is one of nastiness and a deliberate communal complicity to keep everybody down to the level of the others" (2003, 150). The drinking men's ideal of reciprocity creates strong social groups but makes it difficult for individuals to channel money to other purposes.

Naeaegama drinkers compared themselves positively to their non-drinking peers and female relatives. They prided themselves on their generosity and open-heartedness, contrasting their own attitude favorably with what they saw as non-drinkers' stinginess and their wives' greed and demands for money. "A drinker has an open heart," Sherman said. Siri added, "There are no blades inside," suggesting frankness and a lack of duplicity.

Events during an interview with Sherman and Kitsiri affirmed the obligations that drinkers feel toward each other. Sherman asked to borrow Kitsiri's bicycle and went off to run an errand. Kitsiri told Siri and me that because he and Sherman drink together, "I can't say [he] can't [borrow it] (*baeae kiyanDa baeae*)."

In contrast to the generosity they observed between their fellows, drinkers saw non-drinking men as penny-pinching and tightfisted. Returning from his errand, Sherman said that drinkers call the non-drinking husband of a Middle East migrant "a stingy person" (*loobayek*). "People look at such a man 'from an angle' and are jealous because he is saving money. They would like him to spend, not save." Sherman claimed that non-drinking men insulted drinkers, protected their own property, and always tried to make money.[3] These traits ran counter to the drinking man's ideal of open-hearted generosity. Naeaegama drinkers maintained egalitarian and reciprocal relationships with other drinkers, and tried to draw non-drinkers into their sphere as well.

Men did not try to bring kinswomen into their drinking groups, but they did seek their cooperation in funding the purchase of alcohol. Sherman returned to the theme of greed when I asked what his wife said about his drinking. "She scolds me, saying I will die of drink. In addition, she doesn't like all the money I spend. Under all this talk, my wife is too greedy (*taan-haawa vaeDiyi*) and craves material things." With this statement Sherman made a deliberate reference to Buddhist doctrine, which suggests that attachment to worldly goods perpetuates the suffering inherent in the cycle of reincarnation. By accusing his wife of un-Buddhist behavior, he adroitly countered the doctrinal argument that taking intoxicating substances violates the fifth of the Five Precepts (see chapter 1).

After Sherman presented a religious argument against begrudging men's spending on alcohol, Siri presented a secular one, asserting that women spent money on unnecessary things for their own enjoyment: "Ladies want money for nail polish, for saris, for lipstick, and for underwear. It costs Rs. 15,000 for a bride to get dressed for her wedding! Women want to blacken their eyebrows and put their hair up like a *roTi* (round flat bread). I just put on trousers and shoes when I go to an event. But when men spend Rs. 50 to drink, they [women] give us 'a rolletting' [in English; an angry scolding]!" Siri implied that women hypocritically condemned men's drinking but wasted money on their own feminine pursuits. Although Siri focused specifically on women's luxury items and beauty interests in this instance, when women fought with men about money, they usually prioritized gender-neutral essentials such as food for the table or money for children's educational needs. By focusing on women's spending on beauty items and not on compulsory household needs, Siri equated men's spending on drinking with women's interests in frivolous luxuries. This argument supported men's right to drink for pleasure, suggested that women wasted more money on unnecessary pursuits than men did, and directed attention away from the possibility that men's drinking deprived entire families of basic necessities.

---

3. Baklien and Samarasinghe (2003, 64) report similar accusations of pride and miserliness against non-drinkers.

Siri and Sherman presented drinking with buddies and spending freely for enjoyment as the opposite of non-drinkers' stinginess and wives' craving. The drinking man's ideology promotes the common consumption of alcohol, which enhances men's social networks. Instead of viewing money spent on alcohol as a waste, this perspective suggests that people who begrudge drinkers worry too much about saving money for the future. Instead, they should live for the moment and not fret about worldly goods.

Age and Education

Societies often restrict access to alcohol by age, with consumption marking adulthood in many contexts. Although in some societies older women can drink, aging in Sri Lanka does not give a woman this right. Gradually, however, some sections of the female population have begun to drink at celebrations. Changes have also occurred for men. As noted in the introduction to this volume, village perceptions suggest that more men drink now than did four decades ago, and that boys begin drinking at younger ages. These changes indicate that cultural rules governing alcohol consumption shift over time, which raises questions about how people learn to drink (Heath 1987).

Although travelers and migrants (like Joy-amma) may discover alcohol as adults, most people receive their alcohol education as children. Scholars distinguish broadly between "wet" and "dry" societies. In wet societies, alcohol forms part of everyday life and is often consumed with meals. People learn to drink within a family context and rarely become obviously intoxicated. In dry societies, people reserve drinking for special occasions, drink only sporadically, and often drink to intoxication when they indulge (Room 2001, 193). In France, a wet society, children learn to drink gradually; but in dry societies such as the United States and Sri Lanka, alcohol is forbidden to youngsters. Heath and Rosovsky write, "To make drinking a normal adjunct to daily living has served the Mediterranean cultures well in terms of lessened risk of drinking problems, especially in comparison with other cultures in which drinking is relegated to back rooms, garages, or outdoor trips, and kept from women, children, and youths" (1998, 215). This line of argument suggests that when children learn how to use alcohol at an early age, they often become well-controlled drinkers. When they drink on the sly, they still drink at an early age, but the act becomes a risk-taking and authority-challenging behavior (Heath 2000, 80). Speaking of a coastal resort along Malta's shore, Jon Mitchell and Gary Armstrong write, "This night city of excess has become the post-independence site of the *rite de passage* for young Maltese—of growing up and throwing up due to excessive alcohol consumption" (2005, 184). Episodic heavy drinking is often associated with adolescence, particularly (but not exclusively) in dry societies where such drinking is officially prohibited.

Even in dry societies where parents keep alcohol from youth, family interactions provide children with a basic understanding of alcohol use. Kinship connections often form an axis of sociable drinking. In Sri Lanka, although brothers often drink together, fathers and sons (and, more generally, men of widely different ages and statuses) do not. Boys cringe at the thought of being drunk in front of their fathers, or, worse yet, drinking with them. Therefore socialization into drinking does not happen directly across generations. Nevertheless, some people feel that boys get used to the idea of drinking and smoking because their fathers send them to purchase alcohol and cigarettes. More than one village mother expressed anger with her husband, father, or father-in-law for sending her son to the store for such items, worrying that the child might start to sample what he delivered. Mothers also feared that the overall cultural pattern of enjoying alcohol with male friends would attract young boys to drinking groups. If they drank, young men in Naeaegama fit into preexisting gendered struggles, imitating one parent and defying the other.

In many dry societies, people try alcohol as adolescents. In the United States, boys and girls often begin experimenting with drugs and alcohol while they are in high school. Similarly, in Naeaegama some boys (but few or no girls) begin drinking around age sixteen. Several teachers held different opinions about youth alcohol. Shivanthi, a high school teacher, thought that her fourteen- to sixteen-year-old students did not drink. The boys of this age who did drink did not attend school. She contrasted these loafers and ruffians with her well dressed, "obedient" (*kiikaruwi*) students. Other teachers, however, claimed that high school students did drink. One glibly blamed this trend on the influence of tourists and media promotions. Ajith-sir, an assistant principal at a local high school, and Greta-miss, his wife and the principal of a local grammar school, placed the onset of this activity "after Ordinary Levels"—exams that students took at age fifteen. Students studying for their Advanced Levels, which they took at age seventeen, did not smoke or consume liquor during school hours. Ajith-sir noted that in the twenty years he had taught at a local high school, the administration had not expelled a single student for such a reason. But some Advanced Level students indulged outside of school, particularly at large cricket matches and other sporting events. Since liquor shops refused to sell alcohol to students in school uniforms, "old boys" (past graduates) made purchases for their juniors. School staff ignored liquor at matches provided it remained hidden and caused no disturbances. Ajith-sir and Greta-miss also thought that Advanced Level students attending private tutorial classes in nearby towns and the capital city, Colombo, had more freedom from parental supervision and more opportunity to sample forbidden substances. In Sri Lanka as in the United States, experimentation with alcohol started in the mid- to upper-teenage years.

Young men and women experience dramatically greater freedom at the undergraduate level. Writing about the United States, Heath asks, "If alcohol is forbidden but said to be empowering, sexually arousing, and disinhibiting, is it any wonder that college students, away from home schedules and supervision, often drink heavily and then behave obnoxiously?" (1998a, 115). Opinions differed about drinking in Sri Lankan universities. One professor I queried thought for several moments and then suggested that university students did not drink due to lack of money to purchase alcohol. Greta-miss, however, exclaimed, "University? My goodness, that's a cancer! University boys think they are revolutionaries, they are so big and educated. They have parties. It's not like at high school." Ajith-sir chimed in, "They have freedom. They do all sorts of stuff." Ever fair to her students, Greta-miss moderated her condemnation by saying, "Not all of them run wild. There are good boys too. Only a quarter or so go bad." She felt that few young women drank, even at the university. Radical in other ways, Sri Lankan undergraduates did not challenge the gendered norms surrounding alcohol.

Education about alcohol use takes place in both formal and informal contexts. Schools teach students about alcohol, presenting information that may or may not confirm what children learn in the wider society. Linda Wright discusses two divergent approaches to alcohol education: the medical model, which aims to reduce or prevent drinking; and the educational model, which presents information so students can make free and rational choices about their behavior (2000, 208–15). In cultures that seek to keep children from drinking, education about alcohol often sensationalizes bad outcomes (Heath and Rosovsky 1998, 213). Students see through the scare tactics and doubt the information imparted, particularly if it seems moralistic, puritanical, and distrustful of hedonism (Heath 1998a, 119). For example, in Britain, where many teens and a large majority of adults consume alcohol as part of their leisure behavior, medical models are unlikely to persuade schoolchildren to wait until they are older or to stop drinking altogether (Wright 2000, 216). Research suggests that educators would gain credibility and influence by acknowledging alcohol's real place in youth culture.

The educational model suggests that educators should discuss the use of alcohol frankly and demystify the risks so that students can make healthy, well-informed choices. For example, in Britain, alcohol-related risks for youth center on binge-drinking and related accidents rather than the chronic illnesses or addiction that plague older drinkers (Wright 2000, 225). A focus on proximate rather than distant dangers could make alcohol education more relevant to youth. Along similar lines, Heath and Rosovsky (1998) recommend that instead of assuming teenage drinking automatically correlates with car accidents and unsafe sex, educators in the United States should separate these phenomena and try to moderate teen alcohol consumption. In tandem, they should censor bad behavior and deglamorize drunkenness, preferably enlisting peers for this approach. But such educational approaches meet stiff resistance in dry cultures, "Because, after all, [youth] should not be drinking at all, should they?" (Wright 2000, 218).

Both scholars and laypeople recognize that one educational model does not fit all cultural situations (Wright 2000, 212). I asked whether either a family-based system to teach children how to drink or a school-based system advocating moderation in consumption could work in Sri Lanka. Gretamiss replied that the patterns I had said worked in France and the United States would not suit Sri Lanka's Buddhist culture. She repeated the Pali verse of the Fifth Precept aloud, emphasizing that Buddhism completely prohibits alcohol consumption. Ajith-sir noted that most students regularly attended Buddhist Sunday school classes (*daham paasael*). In a separate interview, Shivanthi also referred to Buddhism when I asked her what schools taught about alcohol. "The students recited the Five Precepts each morning. Although the words are in Pali, the children understand them," she asserted. These replies suggest that any educational approach besides prohibition would run counter to Buddhist teachings and thus has no place in local schools. Other than abstinence, norms for guiding drinking must therefore originate outside the formal education system in Sri Lanka.

In addition to relying on Buddhist teachings, organizations and schools in Sri Lanka seek to limit students' use of alcohol by educating them about its harmful qualities. Ajith-sir said that the Education Department sent around circulars with material for running programs about tobacco and alcohol use during yearly national awareness campaigns. In addition, schools have trained counselors who can offer students confidential advice on any number of topics, including substance use. Shivanthi noted that the children in her school write essays about the detrimental effects of alcohol (*mat paen*) and drugs (*mat kuDu*). In its community interventions, ADIC employs an approach denying that alcohol brings enjoyment. Instead, ADIC asserts that the pleasure people believe they get from alcohol comes from mental associations and expectations. In their approach to alcohol education, ADIC organizers urge youngsters to resist peer pressure to drink. It remains to be seen how effective this training can be against a cultural background where drinking correlates with adult masculinity and alcohol features prominently at many ceremonies and celebrations.

Conclusion

Alcohol consumption correlates closely with identity construction, particularly in the categories of gender, profession, and age. Strongly held gender norms govern who does and does not drink. Stories about compulsory drinking told by men in military service, and the hostility exhibited toward Joy-amma, a drinking woman, illustrate the pressures against violating alcohol-related gender roles. But despite the strong social norms governing drinking behaviors, community members sometimes hold contradictory views. For example, the multiple opinions on non-drinking men reveal a deep abyss between female perspectives, which praise abstinence, and male opinions, particularly those of drinkers, which condemn the greed and self-importance of teetotalers.

Youth observe drinking behavior modeled by adult men and women (Seilhamer and Jacob 1990). In Naeaegama, formal education emphasizes total abstinence from liquor. Girls receive a constant message not to drink, and with few exceptions follow these cultural dictates. In contrast, boys receive contradictory messages. While schools emphasize Buddhist ideals, informal enculturation promotes images of adult manliness closely tied with alcohol consumption. These dual perspectives set the stage for gendered consumption struggles between wives and husbands in Naeaegama households, a topic I explore in chapter 5.

The power of alcohol to create and solidify networks requires further examination. Peer groups play an influential role in social organization, and networks formed through drinking have economic as well as cultural importance. In the next chapter I explore contexts for social drinking, including public ceremonies, bars, and *kasippu* taverns.

4 Jolly Drinking: Events and Taverns

Above and beyond satisfying the body's need for nutrition, the consumption of foods and beverages conveys meaning in society. Commensality, the act of eating and drinking together, creates bonds between people. Sharing food both enhances a group's identity and distinguishes it from other groups. In addition to demarcating groups, comestibles can also indicate status and prestige. The cultural elite and hosts staging special occasions use rare and expensive items to mark their own importance and the significance of the event. The items people eat and drink, and the company in which they consume them, can reveal group boundaries and social hierarchies.

Choice of alcoholic beverage indexes different categories of people and events. For example, working class Mexican American men drink beer with barbecued meat at informal get-togethers after work (Limon 1989). In Botswana, young men with salaried jobs drink expensive bottled imported beer in bars in the evenings, while lower class laboring men drink locally produced liquor at traditional liquor stands (Suggs 2001). Similarly, Mary Thornton (1987) contrasts the consumption of locally made table wine at informal family gatherings to the consumption of commercial rum with formal visitors in an Austrian village. In each of these cases, choice of beverage serves as a key symbol for expressing status and relationship.

Given alcohol's importance in creating group solidarity and its usefulness in marking significant occasions, it should come as no surprise that alcohol is a key part of many festivals. "The predominant association with drinking for many populations is celebratory," states Heath; he continues, "drinking itself is often treated as a joyous occasion" (2000, 196). Public drinking in Malta accompanies both the annual religious feast of St. Paul and celebrations of football victories as participants enact their religious and sportive loyalties (Mitchell and Armstrong 2005). Guests at Hong Kong wedding banquets drink expensive imported cognac while creating and renewing kinship ties (J. Smart 2005). In pre-industrial Botswana, homemade sorghum beer was made by women and shared by men to celebrate the harvest; in this instance, beer consumption expressed the basic reciprocity of social life, indexing cooperative family agricultural patterns, gerontocratic control over production, and the gendered division of labor (Suggs 1996, 598). At many ceremonies, people have a responsibility to drink at least a small amount, symbolically demonstrating their group membership and joining in the celebration.

In Naeaegama, men drink in both formal and casual contexts. I begin this chapter by investigating the annual events during which men expect to consume alcohol. Alcohol also has a place in life-cycle rituals, and men drink at rites of passage such as coming-of-age ceremonies, weddings, and funerals. Drinking at these events reaffirms family relationships. In contrast, it is friendships and professional bonds that men reinforce through social drinking in taverns and bars. In both contexts, choice of beverage (highclass arrack or low-class *kasippu*) indexes status and creates group identity.

Jolly Drinkers: Drinking for Pleasure

People around the world enjoy drinking alcohol in social contexts. The pleasure arises both from the physical effects of alcohol and from the habit of associating drinking with having a good time. In small amounts, alcohol eases stress and facilitates social interactions (Plange 1998, 90–92).[1] In most cultures, most drinkers have few if any alcohol-related problems (Heath 1987). People in Naeaegama recognized this pattern. A burly shopkeeper named Wimal distinguished between two kinds of drinkers—the jolly drinkers, who drank in a moderate and acceptable way, and the people who drank because of their problems and made those problems worse by drinking. Here I examine "jolly drinking," a male activity accepted, expected, and even required in some social contexts. I will discuss problem drinking in chapter 8.

In Naeaegama and in other Sri Lankan settings, men drink for pleasure. Local men described this experience in a variety of ways. Lalith, a tall and imposing retired policeman, said that he drinks "for the jolly (*joliyaTa*)."

1. As Nii-K Plange points out, although many scholars agree in theory that drinking alcohol is okay "in moderation," they show less unanimity on what "moderation" means in practice (1998, 90).

Wimal the shopkeeper asserted that after men earned money, they wanted to have fun. The slang phrase *aatal eka* refers to a pleasurable high, and *somiya* covers enjoyment with friends. Siri explained, "To achieve *somiya*, one gathers some buddies, puts some chairs in the yard, gets a guitar, sings and plays music. *Somiya* comes from drinking legal liquor in a relaxed manner in a place where no one can question or arrest you." Making a class distinction, Siri claimed, "Rich people can enjoy this way, but poor ones can't. Instead of pleasure, a poor person gets troubles after drinking. He might be happy when he drinks, but when he goes home he will fight with his wife about the money he has spent. And both *aatal eka* and *somiya* disappear if you get caught drinking *kasippu* by the police!" Drinkers best achieve these happy states through sanctioned, legal, accepted, uncontested drinking in approved social spaces, without conflicts with wives, police, and other detractors.

Annual Cycles: New Year and Vesak

Alcohol use symbolically marks changes in activity and venue, denoting times and places for leisure and pleasure. Drinking follows daily, weekly, monthly, and yearly cycles. For example, in the United States, alcohol use correlates with the temporal organization of daily and weekly life. People mark the difference between office and home, week and weekend with "happy hour" and TGIF (Thank God It's Friday) parties. Although drinking is rarely allowed during work, play is "an area of permissible insobriety" (Gusfield 1987, 77), where more relaxed rules for social interaction prevail. Joseph Gusfield suggests that in the United States a different drink, coffee, ends a dinner party and marks the passage back to work and sobriety. In Naeaegama, as elsewhere in the world, people reserve specific times and places for alcohol consumption.

Alcohol consumption varies throughout the year in Sri Lanka. Men who drink daily will drink all year, while teetotalers will not drink even when tradition permits or promotes it. But men who drink occasionally will often indulge during particular seasons. As discussed in the Introduction, during the Sinhala-Tamil New Year in April, men often drink and gamble together, creating a carnivalesque counterpoint to the ordered traditions of auspicious times and ritual activities. In addition, men will drink during the January New Year holidays. May Day political parades and election days also enhance drinking.

The Sinhala-Tamil New Year is an especially important celebration for people of both major ethnic groups in Sri Lanka. During this period, migrant laborers try to return from overseas to visit their families, and people who work in the city often go back to their ancestral villages. New Year thus provides an occasion to reaffirm ethnic, national, and family identities. Police, politicians, and religious leaders all recognize the alcohol consumption patterns associated with New Year. For example, a newspaper article published a week before New Year in 2006 reports that "Over 1,000 policemen have been mobilized for special traffic duty in Colombo for the forthcoming festive season," including officers to handle emergency cases and "bring to book drivers driving after consuming liquor" (S. de Silva 2006a, 2). In addition, on New Year's Eve day the monk who led a small but influential political party "requested people to abstain from taking liquor during the New Year, adding his party had resolved to eradicate the alcohol menace from the country" (Bandara, Perera, and Weerakoon 2006, 1). Two major disciplinary groups, the monks and the police, strive to restrain New Year indulgence; their limited success suggests that other social forces strongly promote alcohol consumption during this period.

The legal liquor business thrives during the New Year period, as illustrated by alcohol advertisements in the local papers. For example, the English-language *Daily Mirror* contained several quarter- and half-page ads for arrack and brandy in the week before the 2006 April New Year.[2] In the month thereafter, I saw no alcohol ads, but on 19 April, five days after New Year, the *Daily Mirror* carried an ad for Hormotex™ Power Pills for Men. The text suggests that "Hormotex™ is ideal for married men over 40 years to increase libido & overcome erectile dysfunction which is caused due to poor health conditions or alcohol and smoking." The accompanying picture shows a white man with glasses kissing the forehead of a smiling blond

---

2. In the five days between 7 and 11 April 2006, I observed the following four liquor advertisements in the *Daily Mirror*. A third-of-a-page ad for IDL Old Arrack featured a picture of a glass with ice and liquor, with an image of coconut blossoms superimposed as if they were in the glass. The text reads, "Give new life to the old customs. Celebrate the festivity in renewed spirit," referring to the upcoming New Year. A half-page ad for DCSL (Distilleries Company of Sri Lanka Ltd.) Extra Special Arrack appeared in the LIFE section on 8 April. The same day a half-page ad featured Ritz Brandy in the main section of the paper. Finally, a half-page ad from the DCSL featured White Label Arrack on 11 April.

I saw no other ads in the *Daily Mirror* or its sister paper the *Sunday Times* until after the Vesak holiday, when Rockland Distilleries ran an ad in the *Sunday Times* for Limited Rockland Old (arrack). The text reads: "The old and the Beautiful. With just any old arrack, you're history. With Rockland Old, you're on," and the picture presents a gray-haired, balding, wrinkled man in dark glasses with his arm around a much younger woman. He is about to kiss her on the cheek. She is gazing directly at the camera. Two cocktail glasses with bottle labels for Rockland Old adorn the frame of the ad. The message about masculine sexuality comes across clearly. How this ad reads for women is more ambiguous and not necessarily flattering.

woman. It seems no coincidence that the company placed this advertisement soon after New Year, a period of substantial alcohol use. The ad reappeared every week or two thereafter, usually in the financial section.

While some periods see more drinking, others see less. People who drink only occasionally will avoid drinking on Poya days (full moon holidays), which are particularly significant in Buddhism. Vesak Poya (in mid-May, soon after the New Year and May Day celebrations) and Poson Poya (in June) are particularly revered. Bars and liquor shops close on these days as well as on Hindu, Muslim, and Christian religious holidays when many people abstain from liquor. Prior to the Vesak holiday on 12 May 2006, the government closed legal liquor outlets for a week, and the police instituted a crackdown on *kasippu*, steeply raising the fines for both drinkers and retailers (S. de Silva 2006b, 2; Kariyakarawana and Senewiratne 2006, 4). In this case, the state reinforced cultural habits with formal restrictions.

Rites of Passage: Drinking at Ceremonies

Sri Lankan festivals share consumption patterns common to feasting traditions all over the world. In general, feasts allow hosts to increase their social status while creating and maintaining social networks (Schmandt-Besserat 2001; Wilson and Rathje 2001). Hosts demonstrate family solidarity by working together to produce a surplus large enough to treat many guests lavishly. In some historical contexts, groups held competitive feasts, where each strove to outdo the other (Kirch 2001). By manipulating indebtedness, such feasts created the social standing that enhanced particular people's claims to leadership (Dietler 2006, 237). Felipe Fernandez-Armesto (2002) suggests that competitive feasting may have spurred the agricultural revolution from foraging to farming. Prehistoric hunters and gatherers had little incentive in a context of abundant wild food resources to switch to farming, with its attendant hard work and social inequality. Instead of seeking material advantages through cultivation, early farmers may have sought prestige and political gains. To provide abundantly for feasts, foragers may have relied on agricultural strategies to create surpluses—not just of food, but also of drink; all of the domesticated grains and roots can be used to make alcoholic beverages. When farming began to generate surpluses for prestigious chiefly feasts, alcohol may have been a vital part of the menu.

Whatever its role in prehistoric feasting and the agricultural revolution, alcohol now forms a key element around the world in celebratory occasions where people gather to reinforce social bonds (Heath 2000). The conspicuous consumption of alcohol and other goods can take on competitive aspects, with guests obligated to return the hospitality in equal or greater measure at a future date (Ngokwey 1987). Mars and Yochanan Altman suggest that in Soviet Georgia where people engaged in feasting and competitive drinking, "Prolific expense on food and drink can be understood as a rational use of scarce resources that serves to maintain and extend prestige and contacts" (1987, 271), which facilitated access to scarce resources under the socialist system. Debts and obligations incurred by guests at a feast create an unbalanced social dynamic partially resolved by reciprocal invitations and further feasts.

Alcohol use is sanctioned during most phases of Sri Lankan ceremonies, particularly rites of passage such as coming-of-age celebrations, weddings, and funerals. Hosts have served alcohol at such events for at least a hundred to a hundred and eighty years. For example, Jayawardena reports arrack consumption at local funerals in 1825 (2000, 44), and Rogers suggests that failure to serve alcohol at weddings in the early 1900s was taken as an insult (1989, 338). Perhaps borrowing from the long-standing nature of such practices, formerly alcohol-free events in Naeaegama now sometimes serve liquor. For example, liquor is currently tolerated (though not socially required) during *daanas* (Buddhist almsgivings) and *pirith* (Buddhist verses) chanting ceremonies for deceased relatives. Furthermore, in 2006 I heard of two birthday parties for small children that served liquor; one also hosted a band that played until well after midnight on a weekday. Several Naeaegama community members I interviewed disapproved of this emerging trend in children's birthdays, preferring existing practices involving ice cream and cake if they celebrated birthdays at all. These data suggest both a long-standing use of alcohol at ceremonies and continuing innovations in style.

Gift-Giving and Drinking Etiquette at Private Parties and Weddings

Hosts, even teetotalers, go to great trouble and expense to provide ample liquor for an event. Samarasinghe writes, "A wedding or other celebration is an occasion for the poorest to demonstrate that they, too, can afford to provide guests with unlimited amounts of alcohol, and the cost of just one such celebratory event often leads to decades, sometimes a life-time, of interest payments to rapacious moneylenders" (2006, 627). In exchange for hospitality, guests at ceremonies often give their hosts presents, usually cash. Baklien and Samarasinghe (2003) suggest that guests expect to eat meat and drink alcohol; if these items are not on the menu, visitors reduce the value of the present they give the hosts. Indeed, social rules in Naeaegama dictate that someone who eats but does not drink can give a smaller present than someone who both eats and drinks. Siri suggested that for a village event he would give Rs. 200 if he only consumed food, and Rs. 400 or 500 if he also drank alcohol. At a ceremony held at a tourist hotel, the price of food and entertainment is higher. At such a wedding in 2004, guests gave on average Rs. 1,000 per person. Attendees calculate their gifts to offset host expenses and repay gifts hosts have given at attendees' events in the past.

Many social rules govern eating and drinking at celebratory events. Hosts usually offer legal liquor (arrack and beer) rather than *kasippu*. As Abeyasinghe reports, at wedding ceremonies held in private homes, "it is a common enough sight to see men disappear into a little room or segregated area where all the drinking takes place" (2002, 60). Events held at hotels often have a bar with waiter service. Women will rarely drink. Men will not eat until they have finished drinking. At events with buffets, women could technically eat while men drink, but in most cases wives will show their respect for their husbands by not eating before them. At dinner parties in private homes, no one will eat until the men have finished drinking—often quite late in the evening.

Fig. 2. A village wedding. Two men are drinking behind the vehicle on the far right. Photograph by author.

Fig. 3. A hotel wedding. Photograph by author.

Drinkers consider financial statuses and degrees of relatedness when drinking at a ceremony. Siri suggested that if a middle class man drinks lavishly at a poor man's event, his reputation will suffer. But if he drinks openly at a rich man's ceremony, people will praise the generosity of the host and the quality of his liquor. The status of both host and guest affects consumption patterns. In some instances, status determines which guests drink what sorts of alcohol. Siri described his experience at a family wedding:

> My father gave me Rs. 500 as a present for the hosts. I arrived at the wedding and took a seat. No one came to talk with me, even though I am a close relation. A couple police officers arrived. The hosts welcomed them and sent them upstairs. After a half hour my cousin greeted me, asking "Did you just come?" She introduced me to her husband. They wanted me to go behind the house. I'm convinced that the upstairs drinking area had whiskey and brandy for high class people. Behind the house they had a rubber tap with *kasippu.* They sent me to the back. I sat down, and a boy gave me a buddy bottle of *kasippu,* a pack of cigarettes, and a plate of chickpeas for bites. I felt very insulted about being sent to the back instead of upstairs to drink legal liquor. I didn't know whether to drink or not. Finally I took the bottle and

the cigarettes, went out the back door, and came home without giving the present.

In this case, different liquors served in different locations demonstrated the regard in which family members held their guests.

Some drinkers feel peer pressure to drink at weddings. Siri said that he has a reputation as a heavy drinker, and he has a group of friends who seek his company:

> If I go to a wedding, everyone knows that I am a drinking man. Even if I say that I have given it up, they will force me to drink. They reminisce about how much I used to drink and dance, and they ask me if I have stopped because I am afraid of my wife, or my son, or my daughter-in-law, or Michele Gamburd. So they persuade me to join their drinking. They'll say "Don't take a lot, just one or two shots." My wife or son will tell me not to drink. My friends will promise that they will only give me two shots. But two shots become sixteen.

Siri claimed to drink less at a close relation's function because his relatives would scold him if he got intoxicated. At a friend's ceremony, he would drink more. For Siri, the amount of the present he gives, how much he drinks, of what, and where all mark degrees of relatedness, status, and obligation.

Deciding Whether to Serve Alcohol at Ceremonies

Although public consumption of alcohol is expected at major celebrations, non-drinkers often find the presence of drinkers problematic. Husbands and wives fight about how much liquor the men should drink, and drunken men fight with each other over minor disagreements. Non-drinkers often dislike and try to avoid events where alcohol will be served. One local businessman confessed that he did not like to go to weddings and other celebratory functions because people drink there. "I don't smoke or drink. Drinking and gossiping are both a waste of time, and that's what happens at weddings," he said. Another non-drinker, Virasena, felt that drinking men took the front and center spots at weddings by dancing and talking loudly, while non-drinkers were pushed to the corners. When alcohol is central to social functions, non-drinkers feel marginalized.

Guests expected hosts to serve alcohol at weddings, coming-of-age ceremonies, and housewarmings (collectively known as *magul gewal,* literally auspicious houses). Sunil, a heavy-drinking cinnamon peeler, said that if wedding hosts failed to serve alcohol, male guests would have a bad heart (*papuwa honda naeae*) and would go elsewhere and pay for their own drinks if the host did not provide them. "Hosts have to have at least a bit of alcohol at a wedding," he assured me. Despite these common expectations, several non-drinkers questioned the importance of alcohol. Bandula said that "foolish people" might call the hosts "stingy" if there were no alcohol at a ceremony, but refuted this idea, saying, "People can enjoy [themselves] without drinking. They can sing and clap their hands. The drinkers might sing and dance—and fight too!" Manori, whose husband drinks heavily, thought that many wedding guests were more interested in the drink than in the food: "Some men go in a coat and tie and come home on hands and knees!" She felt that guests should attend a wedding to show respect to the hosts; drinking too much could cause embarrassment instead.

Men expect to drink liquor not only at weddings but also at funerals (*mala gewal*, literally death houses, or *avamagul gewal*, literally inauspicious houses). Village funerals go on for an average of three days, with the corpse on display at the family home. Friends, neighbors, and family members visit and accept hospitality of tea and soda pop during the day. The people who help with the funeral preparations receive food and drink from the hosts. Someone from the family must attend the corpse at all times. During the long nights, male friends and relatives often drink alcohol while playing *Karom* (a billiard-like game played by hand with wooden disks). Manori called alcohol "the main (*praDhana*) refreshment" at such times. Although it is expected and accepted for men to drink alcohol at night, villagers frown on obvious intoxication during the daytime public functions. A large crowd gathers in the afternoon before the burial to attend religious ceremonies and listen to public speeches by politicians. The hosts should be sober to greet their guests. In addition, custom disallows intoxication in the presence of corpses and Buddhist priests. Although villagers expect and accept drinking at funerals, local gossip about such events often includes reports about who had too much.

At regular intervals after a funeral, family members hold *pirith* chanting ceremonies and *daana* ceremonies in memory of their deceased relative. On the night before an almsgiving, families put on all-night *pirith* ceremonies for relatives, friends, and neighbors. Manori thought that serving alcohol at ceremonies where monks were present was not proper, but because men stayed up all night, they drank secretly. The following day, the hosts cook a lunch for a designated number of Buddhist monks, whom they invite to their house or serve at the temple. After the monks eat, receive gifts, chant more *pirith*, and return with the sacred relics to the temple, the rest of the invited guests eat. Drinking usually takes place away from the center of ceremonial activity, and often increases after the monks and the relics leave the premises. On all these important social occasions, hosts use alcohol to solidify relationships with male relatives, friends, and neighbors.

Spending on Alcohol at Village Ceremonies

Hosts often spend large percentages of their entertainment budgets on providing alcohol. To quantify this tendency, I collected data on alcohol purchases for a number of local celebrations. Here I present information on two girls' coming-of-age ceremonies and a wedding to illustrate how much was spent and how hosts evaluated the success of their events.

Like families from all Sri Lankan ethnic groups (Winslow 1980), Nae-aegama families often celebrate a girl's first menstrual cycle in great style. Coming-of-age ceremonies announce to the whole community that a girl has reached puberty and will soon be eligible for marriage. Some families hold only a small ceremony, while others have a large one. Parents pragmatically note that if their daughter elopes instead of entering an arranged marriage, they might not have an opportunity to put on a lavish wedding. After secluding the girl for about a month while the family makes preparations for the ceremony, at an auspicious time the family will hold private rituals for the girl (including an early-morning ritual bathing and presentation of new clothes and jewelry). Later that day they will host a large feast for friends and family. Guests bring presents. Parents who have given presents at other people's ceremonies expect to collect what is owed them from the people they invite.

Hosts serve food and often alcohol at these celebrations. For example, Perera talked about his daughter's coming-of-age ceremony. The family sent out 150 invitations and 125 people came, including relatives, neighbors, and friends from the police station where Perera did manual labor. Perera said his family spent Rs. 32,000 on the ceremony. They did their own cooking, which saved some money. They had twenty bottles of *kasippu* and ten bottles of arrack. This much alcohol would cost Rs. 5,920, which would put cost of liquor at 18.75 percent of the event's total budget.[3] Estimating half of the guests to be men, sixty-three men consumed twenty-nine bottles of hard liquor, or about half a bottle apiece. Siri remembered this celebration

---

3. Here are the calculations for the cost of the liquor at Perera's daughter's coming-of-age ceremony: 10 bottles of arrack at Rs. 400 apiece cost Rs. 4,000. Perera reported having 12 liters of *kasippu*, or 19.2 625 ml bottles, worth Rs. 100 apiece, costing Rs. 1,920. The total is Rs. 5,920 or US$59.20. Siri speculates that some of Perera's friends may have provided the *kasippu*. If Perera received the *kasippu* for free, the cost of the liquor would come to 12.5 percent of the event budget.

fondly and joked that his cousin drank too much and came home "on his ass" (*puken,* unable even to crawl, let alone walk).

In a second case, a grandmother talked about the celebration her family held at her house for her granddaughter's coming-of-age. They invited a large array of villagers and served high-status items at the party. The girl's aunt said it was compulsory (*anivaaryen*) to serve alcohol, despite its cost; they bought a great deal to make sure that they did not run out. They also purchased 75 kilograms of chicken, a more expensive and prestigious menu item than the usual protein—fish. "But the chickens were all bones," the grandmother laughingly lamented. Nevertheless, she stated with evident satisfaction that they had liquor and food left over. This family saw meat and alcohol as essential elements for a celebration where status is demonstrated through conspicuous consumption.

Like coming-of-age ceremonies, weddings are often celebrated in grand style. Arranging suitable marriages for their children is an important duty for Sri Lankan parents. Marriage not only unites a couple; it also creates a complex set of social, economic, and political rights and obligations between their families (Stone 1997). Forming strategic alliances through marriage constitutes a significant aspect of a family's social status (de Munck 1996; Nanda 1992; Yalman 1967). Marriage celebrations in Naeaegama require two large parties, which might or might not occur near the time that the union is officially registered. The wedding celebration takes place at the bride's residence and is arranged by her parents. After the honeymoon, the couple returns to the groom's house or to a festival hall for a homecoming ceremony arranged by his parents.

Although Siri's son does not drink, there was quite a bit of alcohol at his homecoming ceremony, a 250-person event hosted at a tourist hotel. Beverages included forty-eight bottles of old arrack, three cases of beer, and two cases of Coca-Cola. The liquor cost approximately US$250. Siri and Telsie spent Rs. 350,000 (US$3,500) on the homecoming; therefore, alcohol made up about 7 percent of the budget. There were about 125 male invitees and 120 bottles of beer and arrack.[4] Several bottles remained unopened at the end of the ceremony, indicating that everyone drank his fill. The groom initially did not wish to serve alcohol at the homecoming. But because the bride's side had provided alcohol at the wedding and many of the bride's relatives drank, the groom felt obligated to offer liquor in abundance. In

---

4. Here are the calculations for the cost of the liquor served at Siri's son's wedding: 48 bottles of arrack at Rs. 400 each (Rs. 19,200 or US$192); and 72 bottles of beer at Rs. 80 each (Rs. 5,760 or US$57.60) for a total of Rs. 24,960 or US$249.60.

this case, as in many other feasting instances around the world, the hosts strove to equal or outdo their social partners in hospitality while creating and reinforcing kinship networks.

Social Drinking Venues: Bars and *Kasippu* Taverns

Drinking solidifies social relationships between drinkers. At ceremonies, relatives reaffirm family connections. Even men who seldom drink elsewhere will indulge themselves in solidarity with their kinsmen. Drinking in bars and taverns, in contrast, draws together groups of friends and co-workers. In Naeaegama, men can buy alcohol in several nearby locations. Although the area has a licensed bar, few of the village men drink there. Instead, most men patronize *kasippu* taverns—ordinary-looking houses that sell illicit liquor. *Kasippu* costs about one-quarter the price of legal liquor, and the difference paves the way for many social distinctions based on consumption choices. As I discuss below, intricate rules govern social drinking behavior in both bars and taverns.

Bars

Many bars and restaurants dot the southwestern coast along the main north-south coastal highway. Although the local liquor shop at the highway junction has an attached restaurant licensed to sell liquor, few men from the Naeaegama area drink there. I did not do research in this or other bars. Instead, I rely on descriptions from other scholars and Naeaegama drinkers to provide a feel for the setting.

A bar holds many advantages over a *kasippu* tavern. In a bar, the drinker does not need to worry about encounters with the police over illicit liquor. Siri said, "You can drink freely to your heart's content (*ata paya diga aerila bonDa puluwan,* literally you can spread out your arms and legs and drink). You can sit leisurely at a table, enjoy good service, and stay as long as you like." Despite the comforts offered at the local bar, village men rarely if ever drink there because of the amount of money required. In addition to local and foreign liquor, the bar provides "bites" such as prawns, chicken, and deviled fish. Siri claimed that one should have Rs. 500 or 750 in hand to drink there. He said, "For Rs. 210 you can get a half bottle of arrack, for Rs. 85 or 90 a plate of fish, and for another Rs. 45 five cigarettes. The bill at the restaurant comes to Rs. 400, just for a half a bottle and a few pieces of fish to eat with a toothpick. You can get the same high on local liquor for Rs. 60 or 75." Because most villagers recognize the expense involved, visiting the bar is a form of conspicuous public consumption. Naeaegama men might occasionally buy arrack from a liquor store but would drink at a bar only on special occasions. For example, cinnamon peelers who have received their pay after finishing work in a garden might drink in a bar. Siri also thought that men who worked for companies sometimes drank in bars, as did lawyers and other professionals on the weekends. Such men could syndicate their money, with one providing a vehicle and the others paying for drinks. This class of drinkers might also visit a tourist hotel in the off-season to drink. In all these instances, visiting a bar provided a claim to high social status.

Baklien and Samarasinghe (2003) describe drinking patterns in bars. They claim that richer customers drink quietly. In contrast, poorer drinkers who visit a bar for a special occasion make a display of their drinking. They state, "Unlike the regular, better-off customers[,] these groups are very loud and conspicuous. They want attention, and want to demonstrate that they are having fun" (2003, 84). A man might speak loudly, walk around holding his glass conspicuously, exaggerate his unsteadiness, and talk about his intoxication (2003, 84). "The themes [of such drinkers' discussions] are nearly always sex, enjoying drinking occasions or getting into fights and assaults. The fighting is reported to be after alcohol, and they describe their own tendency to assault others when drunk. Remarkably none of them becomes aggressive in this setting" (Baklien and Samarasinghe 2003, 86). The researchers report that women rarely visit bars, even with their husbands. Men will share the bill and might spend Rs. 400–500 (20 to 50 percent of their monthly discretionary money) on this sort of occasion. "The money is spent in a setting where more wealthy people 'enjoy,' so the evening has some value beyond the alcohol and the food consumed" (2003, 86), the researchers suggest. Men boast about their bar experiences, particularly the expensive food and drink they purchased, using their experience to take on a mantle of middle-class sophistication.

Taverns

Choice of drinking location segregates men by social status, with those who can afford to drink in bars indulging in conspicuous consumption of expensive, legal liquor. Based on his research in a Colombo slum, Abeyasinghe reports that young men drink beer, old men drink toddy, rich men drink beer or arrack, and poor people, particularly alcohol dependent men, drink *kasippu* (2002, 67). Although Naeaegama villagers drink a slightly different array of alcohol beverages, they use them similarly to delineate class and status. In Naeaegama, relatively few people patronize bars or drink arrack with any frequency. Poor laborers and daily drinkers (many of them alcohol dependent) visit the *kasippu* tavern instead.

Although I call the houses where families sell *kasippu* "taverns," the buildings are indistinguishable from ordinary houses. In the Naeaegama area, several *kasippu* taverns are located at the junction of the local road and the railroad tracks. Several others are in a large cinnamon garden recently divided and sold as housing plots.[5] With Siri, I visited two houses that sold *kasippu*. While I was there, men purchased and drank liquor out of my sight. In this section I discuss general information about drinking in *kasippu* taverns and then provide some detail about one of the taverns I visited in person.

Kasippu taverns are popular mainly because the illicit liquor sold there is cheap compared to the price of legally manufactured arrack, which is heavily taxed (see chapter 1). The trade-off comes in terms of risk: drinkers can feel at ease in a bar, but visiting a *kasippu* tavern puts men at odds with their wives and the police. Local women know the locations of the taverns and disapprove when their fathers, brothers, husbands, and sons visit them. Men therefore drink *kasippu* surreptitiously. For example, Siri and Edward explained that one day they wanted to go drinking but could not walk either of the two available routes together. Siri could not go down the road because it would take him past the school where his wife taught, and Edward could not go down the railroad tracks because that would take him past his daughter's house. "What a fix!" they laughed.

Although drinking is a male activity, all the *kasippu* retailers in the Naeaegama area are female.[6] Women's gender roles facilitate their work. First, serving guests is a standard female domestic duty. Second, women are culturally constrained not to drink what they sell, whereas men might succumb to temptation and consume the stocks themselves. Third, male *kasippu* retailers would find it difficult not to sell liquor on loan. Women, in contrast, easily refuse such requests, even from their own husbands. For example, Monika, one of the local tavern operators, did not let her husband, Ariyaratne, touch the liquor she sold. Ariyaratne drank at a different tavern. While women sell the liquor, men take care of manufacture and transportation and keep a close eye out for the police (see chapter 6).

5. Cinnamon would grow into a tree if allowed to, but cinnamon garden owners trim the plant back regularly. A mature cinnamon garden consists of closely planted six- to eight-foot tall bushes.

6. The gendered pattern observed in Naeaegama correlates with data gathered by Abeyasinghe (2002, 122), who reports that in his study area, the largest *kasippu* wholesalers were women, as were two-thirds of the retailers. Women also worked as bartenders and waitresses at *kasippu* taverns. In contrast, no women were involved in the trade of legal arrack and toddy.

Taverns do not provide the sorts of facilities available at bars. Only in rare cases, such as around the New Year holidays, do they provide clients with "bites" (snack food). Treatment depends on the customer. A daily customer gets a clean glass. An occasional customer shares a common glass. The respected regulars come in through the front door and take a chair in the living room. The occasional customer takes a shot served from the window, and is not invited to come in and sit down.

Retailers employ various strategies to regulate their clientele. They drive away people without money and cater to those who have it. A beggar outside the door might put off paying clients, so sellers discourage men from lingering to syndicate enough money for a drink. The term for such beggars, *kamba kaarayoo,* translates literally as "rope guys," or people who catch a reluctant acquaintance the way a cowboy might lasso a wary steer. Retailers encourage people with extra money to drink more. The retailer might tell someone who does not have money that someone else has money in his pocket. "Why don't you ask him for a drink?" The seller might also assure the person with money that the other guy is respectable; "Why don't you buy him a drink?" In this way, sellers cater to drinkers' image of themselves as generous and open-hearted (see chapter 3). Retailers strategize to get the maximum profit from the male networks each day.

Women who sell *kasippu* use their feminine wiles to attract customers. Although associating with strange men could blacken the character of the *kasippu* retailer and her female children, only some of the local tavern managers are thought to have loose sexual morals. Their husbands' presence in the tavern helps protect their reputations. However several of the women, according to one informant's description, walk around "with their bra straps falling down their shoulders and their skirts hitched up." This attracts the interest and the business of the local men. In addition, even retailers with "good" characters flirt with their clients. One informant told me, "When I go to Monika's, she is so kind—better than my wife. She takes me by the elbow, she invites me to sit down, she puts a piece of fish into my mouth from her own hand, and she glances in my pocket to see how much money is there. Then she flatters me and says something nice about my family, and says 'Even if you don't have money we will give you something to drink,' because she can see I have Rs. 500 in my pocket. When she serves my glass, she touches my hand. She knows that from my Rs. 500 I will spend Rs. 150 there." My informant thought of this behavior as a form of prostitution, with the woman doing "everything short of offering sexual favors" to please her clients.

Retailers and clients have a double-edged relationship. Like bartenders around the world, sellers often know personal details about their clients.

Retailers can use the information they gather as confidants and friends to flatter their customers and get them to buy more alcohol. Siri said,

> If I have money, the seller will come tell "fairy stories" and praise me, saying my wife is the vice principal at the school, my son is an executive at a tourist hotel, my father is a JP [justice of the peace], and I'm very generous with my money. After a couple of drinks I will become "King Rajasinghe" [full of pride]. Then someone will come and ask for Rs. 15 to drink. I will say, "What Rs. 15? Take a quarter bottle [worth Rs. 25], and here's some money for a cigarette." Then I will come home and find that out of Rs. 500 I only have a balance of Rs. 150. I will have spent Rs. 75 for my own purpose, and the rest is gone.

A skillful retailer can use her personal knowledge about her clients to get them to spend lavishly.

Many *kasippu* drinking patterns reflect tactics that minimize risks. In restaurants and bars, customers can sip their drinks. In contrast, *kasippu* is consumed in a gulp. Discussing a similar situation, Beatrice Medicine suggests that "imbibing until all the evidence is gone seems a logical act to those drinking illegally" (2007, 38). In restaurants and bars, customers can linger. In contrast, in a tavern the retailer tries to limit the clients' stay to a half an hour maximum, saying she wants to make sure nobody is caught by the police. The danger presented by raids probably heightens the excitement of drinking in a *kasippu* tavern. But it also limits the sociability possible, as people do not linger long after they spend their money.

Manufacturers distribute cans of spirit to the *kasippu* dealers, who dilute it with water. Several *kasippu* drinkers agreed that the retailers give a proper dilution for the first one or two shots served, but further water down subsequent drinks.[7] Perera said, "They are making money. They're selling us water and putting up buildings!" I asked why someone would buy a second or third glass that he knew would be mostly water. Perera replied, "Because we are greedy (*pereeta-kamaTa,* literally like [hungry] ghosts) and want to drink without a limit." Siri agreed, saying, "The first and second shots are good stuff, and after you start swaying and repeating one thing three or four times, they will give worse stuff. They think that if they give you more, you will pass out or talk with the police! So they give you water." (Interestingly enough, this business strategy acts to protect drinkers from excess

---

7. Shorting measures and watering down drinks has a long history in Sri Lanka; see Peebles (1986) for a discussion of such practices in the nineteenth century.

consumption.) Clients can either drink their *kasippu* at the tavern or take it away in pre-packed polythene bags. Much less conspicuous than a bottle, these soft packages are easy to hide in the fold of a man's sarong. The packaged liquor is sold at the proper dilution level.

Some drinkers can buy *kasippu* on credit. Like local grocery shops, *kasippu* taverns give loans to salaried or pensioned men with predictable, regular incomes. For example, other drinkers suggested that Edward drank on credit and often owed Rs. 5,000 or 6,000 of his pension to Monika's *kasippu* tavern by the end of the month. Monika reportedly waited for Edward at the post office on pension day to collect her money. No merchant wanted a client to buy on credit and fail to pay the money back, or to build up a large debt and then start patronizing a different outlet. Drinkers suggested that men who bought on credit had to stay faithful to their source. Sherman asserted that other *kasippu* taverns would refuse to sell loan holders liquor, even for cash. As day laborers, Sherman and Kitsiri could not get loans from *kasippu* taverns. Kitsiri complained, "I drink more by the end of the month than the people who drink on loan do, but the sellers won't give me even half a bottle without seeing the cash." Sherman saw a positive aspect in this situation, claiming, "If you buy on credit, you're bound to one person. If you pay cash, you're free." People with pensions or regular salaries have more bargaining power in getting alcohol and other goods on credit, but concurrently acquire duties and obligations to their source.

Tavern money transactions are fraught with risk. Retailers sometimes take advantage of clients, both those who pay cash and those who pay credit. For example, a drinker might pay with a Rs. 100 note and ask for Rs. 25 of alcohol. The retailer will place the change in the client's shirt pocket. Siri said, "I don't have the attitude to count it. I just assume the balance will be correct. But I'm Rs. 20 short when I get home." Drinking on credit is equally uncertain: "The sellers put extra money on the account book after you get drunk. You can't remember what you drank, so you have to take their word for it. Or they give you watered down stuff but charge the standard fee." Because all of these transactions are illegal, drinkers cannot complain to the police.

Monika's House

Monika, a slender woman of about forty, sells *kasippu* out of her house, which was at the time of my visit a half-completed cement structure in the middle of a large cinnamon garden that had recently been divided and sold as housing plots. At the time, Monika's house was one of the most popular *kasippu* taverns in the Naeaegama area. Siri and I visited at about 10:30 on a March morning in 2004. Present were Monika, her husband Ariyaratne, some neighbors (both male and female), and quite a number of regular customers. During the interview, six to twelve people occupied the room at any one point. Although *kasippu* retailers usually try to minimize the number of people in their houses in case of a police raid, on this particular occasion no one seemed worried about the crowd.

I found the atmosphere open and welcoming. Although I realize my presence changed the dynamics in the tavern, drinkers seemed to find companionship as well as cheap liquor at Monika's house. In contrast, Baklien and Samarasinghe suggest that while people who drink legal alcohol report having fun while doing so, few people say they have fun with illicit liquor. Baklien and Samarasinghe write, "The easiest possible explanation is that the illegality of the brew does not permit people to openly sit around consuming it, so there is no possibility of building up rituals around consumption. Nor is there much symbolic 'status' built up around *kasippu*. It is cheap and the poorest folk drink it" (2003, 147). My informants agree that *kasippu* is a low-status drink, but when all present are drinking it, *kasippu* becomes a basis for solidarity instead of exclusion (see Limon 1989). My observation suggests that the regulars find Monika's tavern a center of convivial camaraderie where they can share lively conversation and warm, joking relationships.

Siri and I visited Monika's house under pretext of talking about labor migration to the Middle East, so the conversation turned in that direction. Most of the people present had been abroad themselves or had an immediate family member who had worked in the Gulf. Subash (one of Monika's neighbors and a regular customer) had a wife working as a domestic servant on a two-year contract in the Middle East. Also present in the room were Subash's fourteen-year-old daughter, who was looking after her two-and-a-half-year-old brother although she should have been at school that day. The group explained that Subash's wife had been abroad for eight months without sending so much as a letter, let alone any money. Subash's older sister commented on how much Subash drank, and people debated whether he had started to drink more or less since his wife left. Senerath, another regular customer, said Subash earned money for a week and then stayed home for a month, drinking at Monika's. People joked that Monika did not let her husband drink at home. Siri said that his own wife "took him by the ear" and forbade him to drink. People then commented that Siri's wife had taught all the girls in the area at the local school. Someone joked that she taught Siri at night, a comment ripe with both sexual nuance and the suggestion that Siri's wife tried to control his evening drinking.

I asked the handsome, wiry Subash how much he drank. He replied, "I drink what I get." Charith, another regular customer, held up four fingers, meaning Subash drank four quarters or one bottle (625 ml) a day. I asked how he managed to drink if he had no money. Someone in the crowd asserted, "He catches someone" (*kamba gahanawaa*, related to the phrase used above to discuss catching a cow with a rope). "He gets Rs. 10 from here and Rs. 10 from there, and manages to collect Rs. 100 whereas the guys with money only have Rs. 50 to spend. But then he has to buy them drinks when he has money later." This description suggested that Subash syndicated with other drinkers, but often had too little money to reciprocate fully.

A tall, thin, gray-haired man came in with a ripped sarong, a bare chest, and three English letters painted in white on his right shoulder. The gathered crowd explained that he peeled cinnamon for a living, his wife worked in the Middle East, and none of his three children would let him stay at their houses because he argued with them when he was drunk. Someone asked what was on his shoulder. He said that he had passed out after drinking, and some boys had painted "PIA" on him. The regulars joked with him, speculating on what "PIA" could mean. He sat down on the floor next to Charith, who rubbed his shoulder briefly but none of the dried paint came off. The gathered crowd discussed what this man had done with the money his wife sent from the Middle East. Consensus suggested that she sent money to her daughter-in-law, who was building a house with it. One of the women said that men fought with them after drinking. Another person said that Senerath's older daughter went abroad because Senerath was sitting on the porch one day, naked and drunk. "Men swear when they are drunk." Some joking about swearing followed.

I asked whether people had a daily pattern for drinking, and mentioned the U.S. tradition of five o'clock cocktails. Senerath said that in the village, people can be drunk as early as 4 a.m. Charith grabbed a cigarette from Subash. I learned later that Subash had taken it from Siri. The gray-haired man said that Charith had two wives. Charith (divorced and remarried) replied that if he could, he would take another wife. The guys joked that he should marry seven or eight women, like a Muslim. The cigarette made its way around the room.

As Siri and I left, some political canvassers from the United National Party (UNP) came down Monika's cul-de-sac. A loud confrontation followed between Subash and the visitors. The tavern regulars tried with no success to head Subash off. Various canvassers engaged him briefly, then backed away, complaining he was drunk. After Siri and I left, Subash reportedly lifted his sarong and told the election workers that he was going to vote for the penis this year, not the UNP elephant logo or the opposition party's betel leaf.

The men gathered at Monika's tavern seemed more demonstrative than they would have been in other interview settings. Research suggests that drinking liquor increases displays of laughter and affection (Pernanen 1991, 196). In addition to the physical effects of alcohol, drinking settings create cues for relaxed social behavior (Heath 2000, 169). At Monika's tavern, men touched each other casually, shared cigarettes, and spoke frankly about topics that might not be discussed in a more formal setting. They teased each other and joked freely in a scatological, sexual, and sometimes risqué manner. I attribute the laid-back atmosphere at the tavern to the alcohol some of the participants had consumed and their learned expectation that they could enjoy themselves in this context. Subash's confrontation with the election canvassers suggests that drinkers at the tavern may be a bit more likely to fight, though here again the element of humor lifted its sarong. As Pernanen suggests, drinkers may display aggression, but in many cases it remains playful (Pernanen 1991, 201).

The tavern hosts a community of friends who know each other well and talk about their problems openly. Siri said, "People start telling old secrets from the bottom of their heart in the drinking place. A man might talk about having sex with his wife, or about how many pots he has broken in the house." Baklien and Samarasinghe (2003) take a disapproving tone when they report that drinkers openly admit unacceptable behavior and laugh about it in their drinking group. The researchers suggest that these practices normalize socially disapproved behaviors and warn that "A society that allows its rules to be broken in the alcohol setting risks losing those rules altogether" (2003, 146). One might argue that this dynamic came to the fore in the conversation at Monika's when the gathered people seemed to condone Charith's divorce and support Subash's choice of political symbol. But although the people at Monika's did laugh about some behaviors discussed, they did not condone all the actions described. For example, people tried to defuse the confrontation between Subash and the election workers, and they disapproved of male behaviors that prompted female labor migration, including excess drinking, nakedness, and swearing. I read the group's laughter as acknowledgement of and gentle chastisement for breaking the accepted rules for behavior, within the safe context of a supportive network. Knowing and naming a member's faults but keeping him within the circle of friends reaffirms the solidarity of the drinking group.

Conclusion

Alcohol forms a major element of sociability in Naeaegama. Use of alcohol punctuates the yearly cycle, with annual peaks and lulls in consumption guided by secular and religious holidays respectively. Drinking at the New Year is an established tradition that even the police and monks cannot successfully check. Alcohol use also characterizes commemorations of life cycle rituals and rites of passage such as coming-of-age ceremonies, weddings, and funerals. Men who drink only occasionally will often indulge at such events. Even non-drinkers recognize that providing alcohol is an important element of hospitality. At these rituals, family members make and reaffirm kinship connections. Drinking together creates social solidarity not only at family functions but also at informal gatherings held in bars and *kasippu* taverns. Bars offer opportunities for conspicuous consumption, and both bars and taverns provide a social sphere where men share their feelings, laugh, and joke together. This arena may be particularly important for or attractive to men marginalized from their families; for example, those whose wives are working in the Middle East. But while male alcohol consumption reaffirms social networks, it can also put husbands at odds with their wives, a topic addressed in the next chapter.

5 Home Wars: Gendered Consumption Struggles

Under conditions of poverty, husbands and wives negotiate the use of scarce financial resources. Household economic decisions set the stage for many gendered struggles over consumption, including confrontations about male alcohol use. Given the low salaries and the relatively high cost of liquor in the village, almost any alcohol expenditure harms family well being (see World Health Organization 2004a, 62). Non-drinkers (predominantly women) feel that by drinking, men violate their obligations and neglect their responsibilities. In contrast, drinking men recognize many relevant and persuasive reasons to drink. In chapter 4, I describe how male drinking buddies form reciprocal networks to "syndicate" drinking money, and I present drinking patterns in taverns and at ceremonies. In these social contexts, the people involved generally agree that buying and drinking alcohol is good or necessary. In contrast, in this chapter I explore instances where household members come into conflict over consumption choices.

Scholars interested in identity explore how people express themselves through their purchases. James Carrier and Josiah Heyman (1997) caution that a focus on individual desires provides only a partial understanding of consumption choices. In this chapter, I situate men's drinking activities within the larger contexts of family financial dynamics (particularly ongoing struggles with their wives over household budgets) and global economic trends (particularly the migration of women to work as housemaids in the Middle East).[1] Relying on the holistic perspective embodied in political

---

1. I use "the Middle East," "West Asia," and "the Gulf" interchangeably to refer to a varied and diverse region with many cultural traditions. This rich complexity gets lost in many Sri Lankan

economic theory, I argue that poverty, financial insecurity, lack of economic opportunities, and international inequality all influence men's alcohol consumption. In Sri Lanka as elsewhere around the world, colonial legacies, continuing neo-imperial political domination, and neo-liberal economic realities impose structural violence and social suffering that many individuals combat with alcohol use (Chatterjee 2003, 203; McKnight 2002, 202; Singer 2001, 204; Singer et al. 1998, 295). A full understanding of village drinking requires analysis of both the symbolic intent of individual choices and the concentric social and economic contexts in which these men and their choices are embedded.

Fights between husbands and wives in Naeaegama often revolve around domestic duties performed at home for free and overseas for money. Many women now work abroad as domestic servants in West Asia; thus elements of household labor, including cooking, cleaning, and caring for children and the elderly, have become waged employment. Foreign labor migration has fragmented the bundle of responsibilities formerly allocated to wives and mothers (Gamburd 2000, 2002; Nicholson 2006). As women become the primary breadwinners, men take over some of the household chores previously done by their wives. Many men find that this shift threatens their masculinity. Concurrently, due to national and global economic trends, for local men "traditional pathways to dignified employment have collapsed" (Singer 2001, 205). These circumstances are altering the relationship between the sexes in Naeaegama, giving women more control over money and making wives more skeptical about their husbands' prerogative to drink. But because alcohol use is a powerful symbol of male identity, and because drinking provides short-term physical and emotional gratification in the face of social suffering, circumstances may prompt men to drink. These twin trends put men and women on a collision course for disputes over alcohol consumption.

In the sections that follow, I first consider household economic strategy and division of labor. I explore how men and women negotiate different consumption priorities, particularly those around alcohol use. I then examine how female labor migration affects relationships between husbands and wives. Although many local politicians claim that migration causes the disintegration of the family, I suggest that the relationship between family fights and foreign employment is more complex and nuanced. I focus in particular on the links between alcohol consumption, masculinity, and male self-esteem. Finally, I investigate instances of domestic violence and

---

accounts of migration, where migrants are said to work in "Arabia," "the Middle East," or merely "abroad."

divorce from male and female perspectives. In all these cases, issues of rights, respect, and household responsibilities come to the fore.

Gendered Struggles over Consumption Choices

Family members often hold disparate household economic agendas. In cases of poverty, kin make compromises and trade-offs when allocating resources for various needs and desires. Summarizing local expectations, Perera said, "There is an informal rule in the village. If a man earns Rs. 500, he has a right to keep Rs. 50 for his own needs, like for bus fare and beedies and blades for his razor. He has to give Rs. 450 to his wife. And he can't drink. He has to eat whatever is cooked at home, sambol, jack fruit curry [a cheap food], and so forth, and then sleep."

Although he himself had told me something similar in the past, Siri jokingly asked, "What husband works by this law!?" Perera smiled in acknowledgement, but continued with his theme, setting up a contrast.

"A drinking man will earn only Rs. 250 and bring Rs. 100 to the house. His wife has to cook dinner that day and breakfast and lunch the next day with that money. The guy comes home in the evening drunk and asks, 'Where's the fish [an expensive food]? Where's the sambol?' His wife can't afford good food with the money he has given her, so she has prepared something humble. He'll shout, 'I can't eat this stuff,' and then there's a fight. The guy tips over the plates and hits his wife."

Siri added, "If he does this for three or four days, he'll go to jail, and then he'll worship at his wife's feet asking her to bail him out."

Wage laborers, who may not have employment every day, rely on their wives to earn what they can and to budget and save the money.

In Naeaegama households, the housewife has the responsibility to collect her husband's pay, pool it with whatever she makes, and assure that the household runs smoothly. I asked Perera's wife Chandrani how women learned to control family finances. Chandrani said, "Women must save." She seemed surprised by the question, as if she found saving money so automatic that she had never thought of it as a learned skill. But many village men lack budgeting abilities; they rely on their wives and mothers to do it for them. For their part of the household duties, men earn money, run errands outside the house, do the shopping, and bring home goods for women to cook. Most families in Naeaegama operate on this widely accepted gendered division of domestic labor.

National estimates vary on how much people spend on alcohol. A small survey revealed that among families where men drank, nearly 30 percent of them spent over 30 percent of their total outlay on alcohol (ADIC 1994, 8). In another survey, Abeyasinghe found that on average non–alcohol-dependent men were willing to spend 20 percent of their earnings for liquor, whether they got paid daily, weekly, or monthly; alcohol-dependent men were willing to spend even more (2002, 127). In contrast, Abeyasinghe found that women prioritized food and other necessities for their family, particularly for their children (2002, 128). Abeyasinghe's research confirms that men and women often have different agendas for spending household income. In Naeaegama in 2004, Rs. 500 (a day laborer's average pay) would cover a day's consumption needs for a family of four. Reducing this by Rs. 100 (20 percent) or Rs. 150 (30 percent) would leave a housewife with insufficient money to feed the family, let alone save for the future. Both sets of statistics suggest that even moderate expenditure on alcohol endangers household economics in situations where day laborers drink.

Masculinity and Unemployment

In a setting where the male gender role includes earning money for the household, having a job affirms masculinity. Men who cannot achieve a sense of manliness and power through their employment can use another avenue: drink (McClelland et al. 1972; World Health Organization 2004a, 47). Lack of employment opportunities can lead men to over-consumption, habituation, and addiction to alcohol (Baer, Singer, and Susser 2003). Researchers suggest that among the Navajo "Poverty and deaths from alcohol-related causes are related," and that employment decreases substance abuse (Kunitz and Levy 2000, 6). Similarly, incidents of alcohol abuse and addiction increase among Puerto Rican men under uncertain financial situations, prompting researchers to suggest that high rates of male unemployment can lead to increased drinking, particularly among the marginalized working class (Singer et al. 1998). In a study of injection drug users in Hartford, Connecticut, Singer suggests that entrenched structural inequalities, the collapse of traditional sources of respectable employment, discrimination, and boredom can lead to substance use and abuse as people seek relief and instant gratification (2001, 205). Critical medical anthropologists urge researchers to look beyond individual situations and choices to understand epidemiological patterns.

In Sri Lanka, Baklien and Samarasinghe see a connection between employment and fulfillment of the masculine role model: "He has to be the 'man' who provides the needs of the family, and when he is not able to deliver, there may be no way to show his masculinity through that criterion" (2003, 60). Baklien and Samarasinghe describe a conversation that one of their researchers had with two intoxicated men waiting for a bus at the long-distance bus station in Colombo. The men asserted that they could not earn enough money to solve their economic problems. They said, "We might as well spend what we get for today's fun and see what happens tomorrow. To-morrow is going to be terrible anyway" (2003, 62). The researcher reported that the men seemed disgruntled about their obligation to support their families, and conspired together to keep their drinking money secret from their wives. "There is an undertone of not 'obeying' your wife.... He keeps out of her reach and keeps company with men and enjoys men's fun" (2003, 64). Baklien and Samarasinghe suggest that these drinkers "appear to be men who cannot win in the struggle to show their masculinity by providing conspicuously—or even by providing adequately" (2003, 64). The associa-tion of threatened masculinity, unemployment, and alcohol consumption aptly characterize many cases in Naeaegama.

Sri Lanka is not the only culture where male alcohol consumption leads to domestic disharmony. In Botswana, men think of drinking beer as part of an adult male's social identity. Just as women should have a yard and a house with furniture, men should have alcohol. A man sees drinking as part of "provisioning the household," and "needs alcohol to be the man society expects him to be" (Suggs 1996, 607). Women have different goals and agendas, and often see drink as wasteful and irresponsible, particu-larly in the modern context where a man might ask his wife for money to get drunk if he cannot afford to do so on his own. This dynamic has led some women to ask, "Why would I want to get married? A man will just drink my earnings" (Suggs 1996, 607). Suggs suggests that women in Bo-tswana have enough independence to wait and marry men with different attitudes. Sri Lankan women also complain when their earnings finance a man's drinking, but they often lack the power to change the situation. This state of affairs is changing, however, with increased female labor migration to the Gulf. Having discussed issues of masculine identity and household dynamics above, I now examine how global economic trends, particularly the global "care crisis" (Ehrenreich and Hochschild 2002) and the feminization of the global working class, affect men's drinking habits in Sri Lanka.

Female Migration to the Middle East

Many Sri Lankans, including newspaper reporters and scholars, assert that women's migration to the Middle East can lead their husbands to overin-dulge in alcohol (see Baklien and Samarasinghe 2003, 137). For example, speaking of migrant families, a high-ranking Sri Lankan politician report-edly stated, "The husbands and boys go astray. Most of them become ad-dicted to alcohol and drugs" ("GL: Women's Status" 2003, 4). A feminist scholar asserts, "Many families disintegrate when the wife leaves the hus-band and young children during a crucial period of life. The husband frit-ters away the wife's hard-earned income on dissolute living and fails in his parenting role. Thus, the children get neglected. In many families, sons take to drugs and young daughters, who have become substitutes for the mother, are subjected to sexual abuse, rape and incest" (W. de Silva 2002, 230). I chal-lenge the direct causal arrow that some writers and politicians draw from migration to family disintegration and substance abuse. I agree that the phe-nomena are connected, but see poverty as the root cause.

International labor migration currently forms a key element of the Sri Lankan economy. Since the early 1980s, women have gone abroad to work as housemaids in the Gulf Cooperation Council countries, particularly Ku-wait, Saudi Arabia, and the United Arab Emirates. In 2005, the Sri Lanka Bureau of Foreign Employment reported that over 1.2 million registered Sri Lankans were working abroad, 89 percent of them in the Gulf (SLBFE 2006, 57). Overseas guest workers make up 16.25 percent of Sri Lanka's labor force (SLBFE 2006, 88). Of these migrants, two-thirds are women. Most migrant women are married; they leave their husbands and children behind when they go abroad on two-year contracts. Several studies sug-gest that each migrant woman supports an average of five members of her family (Jayaweera, Dias, and Wanasundera 2002, 1; Weerakoon 1998, 109). It follows that the approximately 800,000 women working abroad support roughly 4 million people (over 20 percent of Sri Lanka's estimated popula-tion of 19.5 million) (Institute of Policy Studies 2005, viii; SLBFE 2006, 57). Thus labor migration, particularly of women, clearly affects domestic arrangements in a large number of Sri Lankan households.

Families choose to send a woman overseas for a number of reasons. First among these is lack of money for vital needs. Consider, for example, the laborer whom Perera described, whose daily salary of Rs. 500 is spent immediately for family consumption. While many families manage to make ends meet with such wages, they cannot save enough money to buy land and build a house (an expenditure of at least Rs. 500,000). Most migrant women go abroad with the primary goal of funding large pur-chases. Other reasons include gathering money for children's education, a daughter's dowry, major household appliances, or a business venture (M. Gamburd 2003). In addition, some women go abroad to escape abu-sive marriages.

Although women have always worked, particularly in the domestic sphere, they have not always received a wage for their efforts. In the past, they have worked at home, for their families, providing economically vital but unpaid domestic services. The current demand for household labor in West Asia brings domestic work out of the home and into the labor market. Migrant women now control a paycheck of US$100 which, while a mere pittance on the global economic scale, represents in local perspective a significant monthly salary in Sri Lanka (Rs. 10,000). But despite the economic necessity for this arrangement, both men and women get blamed for breaking traditional gender roles.

Migration throws the older gendered division of labor into question, turning women into breadwinners and men into homemakers. Stay-at-home husbands find themselves denigrated for taking on childcare and other domestic duties (M. Gamburd 1998, 2008). Once his wife has left, a husband is stereotyped as a drinker. But village research reveals that in cases where a husband drinks heavily, in most instances he drank before his wife went abroad, and continues to do so after her return. In several such cases in the village, the man's drinking provided a primary motive for the woman's migration. The stereotype suggests that "most" or "all" migrants' husbands take to liquor, but in reality many do not, or drink only occasionally (for example, to celebrate receiving a check from abroad). Nevertheless, some men do drink, perhaps to assert their masculinity in the face of their wives' migration but doubtless for other reasons as well.

Female gender roles are slowly shifting to accommodate the new situation, but older ideals still abound. Caricaturized as greedy and money-loving, migrant women are accused of abandoning their children and husbands and going abroad for personal advancement. Reality often differs dramatically from stereotype. Women rarely use their wages for their individual pleasures, instead spending money on family projects, particularly housing and education. Women who have gone abroad to work uniformly reject the accusations that they have gone for selfish purposes. They claim instead to have migrated to improve their children's lives. What they cannot give in care, they hope to give in material goods. Women fight fiercely and strategize to make sure that the money they earn is spent the right way, for example on land and a cement house with a tile roof (M. Gamburd 1995). The presence of these properties proves that a woman has indeed provided well for her family. If money is spent on other, less substantial matters, a woman has nothing to show for many years' absence. Spending money on alcohol is the antithesis of these women's dreams and desires. This context clarifies the stakes when migrant women struggle over consumption choices with their husbands.

Narrating Masculinity: Sherman

While social drinking can enhance positive experiences, some people drink to cope with negative experiences. In the latter case, Bateson (1972) argues that drinking provides an alternative to an unpleasant sober state. This explanation for drinking could fit the situation of migrant women's husbands whose sense of masculine identity suffers when their wives take over the breadwinner role. Danny Wilcox suggests that people use alcohol to enhance their sense of self-worth. Peer pressure and unrealistic expectations of affluence and self-gratification can motivate drinking (Wilcox 1998, 39). As a man consumes alcohol, Bateson asserts, "His anxieties and resentments and panic vanish as if by magic. His self-control is lessened, but his need to compare himself with others is reduced even further. He feels the physiological warmth of alcohol in his veins and, in many cases, a corresponding psychological warmth toward others. He may be either maudlin or angry, but he has at least become again a part of the human scene" (1972, 329). People drink in search of sociability, togetherness, and equality. But, Wilcox argues, eventually alcohol loses its effect for the heavy drinker, instead bringing problems, a sense of failure, and a loss of self-esteem (1998, 40). Although written about dynamics seen in American alcoholics, Wilcox's and Bateson's observations also ring true for the situation of heavy drinking men in Naeaegama, who distance themselves from prestige struggles and feminine family improvement projects by engaging in reciprocal drinking with male friends.

Siri and I interviewed one of the village's heaviest daily drinkers, Sherman, about female labor migration and male alcohol consumption. The conversation started on the topic of Sherman's wife, who spent several years overseas, and then went on to cover Sherman's own experiences in Saudi Arabia. Sherman said, "Before I went abroad, I was home while my wife worked in the Middle East as a housemaid. I was drinking then." I asked why migrants' husbands drank. Sherman answered, "Maybe because they have no job. They can't help their kids. While their wives are abroad, the husband is doing the housework. Then this goes to work in his head and he gets confused and upset (*awul venawaa*)." Sherman tapped his head at the temple. "Then men will drink and forget." With this statement, Sherman neatly illustrated the challenge raised for male self-esteem by unemployment, female migration, and disrupted gender roles.

One solution for reasserting threatened masculinity is to drink heavily. While Sherman's wife worked abroad, his son joined the army. "I had no responsibilities at home, and spent time at this junction and that junction [presumably drinking with friends]. I came home at 10 at night [well after dark, when most people are already asleep.] My mother prepared my food." In this section of his narrative, Sherman emphasized that unlike other migrant women's husbands, he himself did not stay at home and do women's work. Instead, he seems to have preserved his masculinity by enacting the stereotype of the migrant woman's drinking husband.

In 1992, Sherman went to Saudi Arabia, where he worked for several months as a maintenance man at the air hostesses' hostel. He borrowed money to pay the job agency Rs. 55,000 [Rs. 130,350 in 2004 figures] and had to repay Rs. 80,000 [Rs. 189,600] to the moneylender. Overseas, Sherman earned Rs. 10,000 [Rs. 23,700] a month. He also earned another Rs. 6,000 [Rs. 14,220] a day in tips for carrying the air hostesses' bags into the hostel area. Also, during the Ramadan period, the Muslim air hostesses gave money away according to their religion (probably following the custom of Zakat). Relating this information, Sherman clearly conveyed that he had held a desirable and lucrative job. He then brought out his wallet and proudly showed the receipt for sending his first pay home to his wife (a symbol of affluence) and his green plastic insurance card (a symbol of employment). Then he laughed a bit sheepishly and admitted that he only stayed abroad for three months.

Sherman did not stop drinking when he went overseas. "Although alcohol is forbidden in Saudi Arabia, there were ways to get it secretly. It cost Rs. 2,000 [Rs. 4,740] for a bottle of hard liquor. Pepsi was a lot cheaper, just Rs. 60 [Rs. 142]. While I was there, I bought seven packs of cigarettes a day and shared them with my friends. I used my tip money." In telling us about this sharing, Sherman made it clear that he networked with other men and created relationships of obligation with other drinkers and smokers as he would have done in Naeaegama.

The other activity Sherman described would not have been condoned under village fishbowl scrutiny. "One evening a call came for me to go replace a bulb. I went." Sherman then broke his narrative to ask me and Siri not to get mad at what followed, because he was telling the truth. "I went and knocked on the door. An air hostess opened it. Usually there were four girls to a room. But there was only one there, an Indonesian. I was there for 45 minutes. She would not let me go." The prestige of marital fidelity paled in comparison to the temptation offered. Having an attractive woman find him irresistible, and telling others about the event, affirmed Sherman's masculinity and self-esteem.

Sherman's story, told in response to a question about being a migrant woman's husband, integrated three demonstrations of masculinity. First, he drank large quantities of alcohol before he went abroad and continued to drink in Saudi Arabia despite the risk. The mention of shared cigarettes suggests that Sherman smoked (and perhaps drank) in syndication with other men, establishing his place in male networks. Second, he earned money and sent it home to his wife, fulfilling a husband's duty to provide for the family. Third, he was found irresistible by an Indonesian woman. In all three ways, Sherman distanced himself from the stereotypical image of the docile, obedient, stay-at-home dad.

Self-esteem is necessary for any person's mental health. As social animals, humans also need respect from their peers. Poverty and women's migration threaten the self-image of many men in Naeaegama. While alcohol consumption diminishes men's status in other ways, it acts to shore up their masculinity. Unfortunately, in a situation of poverty, men's spending and drinking habits could put them in conflict with their wives. This conflict sometimes led to domestic violence.

Domestic Violence

Violence simultaneously shapes and is shaped by identity (Afflitto 2000). Certain people are prone to particular types of violence, and experiencing violence enhances associated aspects of identity. Gender often channels interpersonal violence, particularly between spouses. Telsie once remarked, "Drinking men eat their wives as 'bites.'" Worldwide, researchers observe a correlation between alcohol use and gender-based aggression (World Health Organization 2004a, 64). Kenneth Leonard and Marilyn Senchak write of a western sample, "Excessive alcohol consumption and alcohol abuse are significant risk factors for marital aggression" (1993, 96). On tea plantations in northeastern India, women are often wage earners and oppose their husbands' drinking (Chatterjee 2003, 200). Piya Chatterjee suggests that "control of finance is a source of considerable tension and men's consumption of alcohol manifests this tension into physical abuse and violence against women" (Chatterjee 2003, 200). Historical data suggest that similar conditions have existed for over 150 years. Writing of peasant villagers in 1850, a colonial official suggested that drinking men "squander their earnings on strong drinks and instead of ministering to the wants of their families, they return like madmen to torment them" (Jayawardena 2000, 97).

Although alcohol use might heighten aggression, interactions still follow culturally shaped trajectories. Pernanen sees violence as "a form of gendered behavior, with rules and expectations that are applied and generally followed despite at times very intense arousal states" (1991, 194). His

research in Canada revealed no radical abandonment of normative stric-
tures on what violent acts are "permissible" against women and men, but did
show that people experienced more violence when drinking was involved
(1991, 154–55). In addition to alcohol use, Leonard and Senchak (1993)
identified other factors that influence violence, including attitudes toward
aggression, degree of marital satisfaction, and hostility between spouses.
Individual relations and personalities may spark conflicts, but fights play
out within wider cultural contexts.

Domestic violence against women is both common and expected in
Sri Lanka, especially if the husband is drunk (Baklien and Samarasinghe
2003, 138). A study performed at the Colombo North General Hospital in
1994 found that "most instances of assault, including wife battering, were
alcohol-related" (World Health Organization 2004b, 5). Discussing findings from her research on gender-based violence, Ameena Hussein writes,
"Many of the women perceived alcohol as being a causative element in
violence" (2000, 37). Women also mentioned adultery, financial problems,
dowry, and disputes over domestic responsibilities as causes. Domestic violence occurs within economic and social relationships with pre-established
power dynamics, and usually "takes place in the privacy of the home with
only the victim and perhaps other family members as witnesses" (Gomez
and Gomez 2004, 216). Despite the privacy of specific fights, domestic violence is widely acknowledged.

In Sri Lanka, wife beating is a sign of masculinity that men might boast
of, justifying their act by asserting a man's right to discipline his wife when
she misbehaves (Baklien and Samarasinghe 2003, 138). Siri confirmed that
local drinkers shared these attitudes about male prerogatives to discipline
and punish their wives. An example Siri provided suggests that drinkers
apply "discipline" to change women's spending priorities. During a conversation at a *kasippu* tavern, one man said, "After I give my wife money, it's as
if she has put it under Sigiriya Rock [a huge stone monolith with a ruined
palace on top—think "Fort Knox"]. I gave her Rs. 500 but can I get Rs. 50
back to drink? No!" A fellow drinker told this man to keep some money at
a shop instead of bringing it all home in order to avoid such struggles with
his wife. Someone else advised him to toss some chairs and plates around,
and predicted that his wife would give him whatever he wanted. This conversation illustrates the relationship between household economics and
domestic violence, and highlights how consumption struggles affect relationships between spouses.

Another example further demonstrates the interrelationship between domestic violence, gender expectations, alcohol, and household consumption

struggles. Lalith discussed domestic violence in terms of the common themes of food, alcohol, sex, and family obligations: "The man comes home drunk. He sees shortages (*aDu paaDu*). Maybe there's no food. Or maybe there are only a few vegetables, or things that he doesn't like to eat. There's no fish. Then he will fight with his wife. The plates will fly like flying saucers. After a man quarrels with his wife like this, when he sobers up a bit, he will want sex. The man has urinated in his sarong, he hasn't washed, and he has bad breath. His wife won't want to go near him. So then the second war will start." This example suggests that husbands and wives come into conflict in kitchens and bedrooms about the fulfillment of domestic responsibilities.

I asked Lalith whether the dispute he described would contain physical violence. Lalith answered, "In my experience, drunkards will scold in filth (*kunuharpen baninawaa*) but they don't come to blows because they have no strength. If someone hits a drunk, he will fall down. His wife will hit him with a broom." In Naeaegama, hitting someone with a broom or a slipper, while not physically very dangerous, expresses utmost contempt. Lalith emphasized the significance of such a blow, saying, "It is a shameful thing for someone to get beaten up (*guTi kanawaa,* literally 'eat fist') by his wife." Evidence in local narratives suggests that men and women select violent acts for their symbolic effects on victims and witnesses (see Pernanen 1991, 145). In Naeaegama, a blow from the fluffy end of a coconut-fiber broom damages pride more than body. Similarly, throwing something is less serious than laying hands on someone; the aggressor has a large chance of missing, and the target can dodge. But in addition to the communicative value of throwing pots, plans, and plates, the threat to damage china carries economic importance. In the village context, such breakage can set a household back financially. A man might hold a Rs. 100 plate hostage in exchange for Rs. 50 to drink. Although the scenarios discussed above contain elements of physical violence, the aggressive acts most commonly described seem to relate more to symbolic communication than actual intent to harm.

In the cases below, I present two discussions of domestic violence, one related by men, the other by women. Different perspectives on domestic rights and responsibilities emerge in these conversations. One theme focuses on household finances, especially gendered consumption struggles over alcohol and assigning blame for shortages. Another theme focuses on interactions between drinkers and their family members, particularly the sort of respect the drinker expects and whether he receives it. Failure to fulfill role obligations forms the core of these disputes.

Fights with Wives: Siri and Sherman

During an interview with Sherman and Kitsiri, the topic of fights came up. Siri said, "If I am drunk and someone interferes, I get mad. I have told my family, 'If the dog has eaten a disgusting thing (*jaraavak*), let him sleep. Don't poke at him.' If my wife asks, 'Where did you get the money to drink? Did you take a loan?' then I will get mad."[2]

Carrying on Siri's themes, Sherman declared, "If I drink and go home and I'm only half drunk [as in half-a-bottle drunk], if my wife is in a bad mood, then I'll get as mad as if I have had a full bottle."

Kitsiri chimed in with, "And if your wife's mood is good, it's as if you have had only a quarter bottle." (They have obviously had this conversation before.)

Sherman continued, "If my wife feeds me, that's good. If she just says, 'There's food in the kitchen, go feed yourself,' then I get mad. If I get in a bad mood, I go out for more liquor."

Siri finished the story, saying "And then you come home and fight with your wife. There will be flying saucers and plates." Sherman laughed and agreed. Siri reflected, "Some evenings I fight with Telsie and then I forget what has happened. In the morning her face is like this [he mimes a mad face] and I can't remember what happened but I know it was bad." He continued in English, "It's a very bad thing, drinking. My God."

The drinking men related these instances with a fair bit of humor and only a touch of concern for the seriousness of their actions. In both Siri's and Sherman's accounts, their temper after drinking depended on the actions of the women in their households. These men blamed their wives for not providing the right food with the right attitude, and they resented

---

2. During a different conversation, Siri related a fuller version of the same hypothetical argument with his family: "I tell my family that when I am drunk, I am a dog who has eaten a dirty thing. I warn my family, 'Don't interfere with the dog. Let him sleep.' They should not confront me, asking 'Are you drunk? Where did you go? Why aren't you eating?' Those questions are a reason to start a fight. 'Did you drink with Wasantha? Did you drink with that other one?' That is also a reason to fight. 'Don't interfere,' I tell them. But they'll ask 'Where did you get the money? You had Rs. 500 in the morning and now you only have Rs. 20!' I tell them, 'That money is gone for good. You can't get it back. Don't interfere and ask questions. Only a policeman can ask questions.' If a policeman asks, 'Where did you drink?' I will answer humbly, 'Sir, I went to Monika's place.' A drinking man is afraid of getting put in the cell." In this hypothetical case, Siri has broken cultural rules about family responsibility but refuses to acknowledge his family's right to question and condemn his behavior. He wants them to let him drink in peace, which few family members of heavy drinkers can successfully do, especially if the drinking behavior threatens the family's economic situation and social status. Although in this narrative Siri challenges his family's right to try to limit his drinking, he bows before the authority of the police.

inquiries about how they financed their drinking. Men assumed that they had a right to drink and their wives had a duty to provide them politely with food and conversation. These men focused almost exclusively on their wives' faults when explaining household disputes.

Bateson notes that alcoholics have unrealistic views of the people on whom they depend, whom they may actually love (1972, 328). The stories above suggest that these heavy drinking men in Naeaegama may have distorted images of domestic relations. In particular, they fail to recognize their own shortcomings and refuse to let their wives raise issues about alcohol use. Drinkers dislike household members' negative reactions to their intoxication, but not enough to stop drinking. Instead, as Sherman suggests, angry interactions may lead them to drink more.

Home Wars: Ruwani and Chandrani

Siri and I went to Ruwani's house in May 2000, where we talked with Ruwani and her sister-in-law Chandrani (Perera's wife). We were having an awkward interview about the civil war, which had heated up to fever pitch at the time (M. Gamburd 2004b). The women answered many of my questions about the war with long silences or "We don't know." Finally Ruwani said to me, "We know about home wars!" An animated discussion of domestic violence followed.

"There's a war if there's money; there's a war if there's no money," said Ruwani.

Chandrani asserted, "Things are worse if there is no money."

Ruwani disagreed, saying, "Things are worse if there *is* money, because then my husband drinks more." Some joking followed about "breaking heads" (physical fights).

Siri opined, "At least army soldiers get compensated for their injuries."

Someone mentioned that Ruwani used to run into the cinnamon gardens if she fought with her husband. "I have more experience now. I fight when I think I can win, and I run when I know I can't win," Ruwani said. She told me to come by one day when she and her husband, Sunil, were fighting.

I said, "I am not married. I don't have any training in this sort of war." She assured me her husband would stop fighting if I came by.

I asked what the children thought of this sort of clash. "They are scared if their father is drunk. They are scared of him anyway." Some joking followed about how Ruwani's sons might start drinking themselves someday soon.

The conversation took several more alcohol-related turns before settling on health problems. Chandrani said about her husband Perera, "I think he will drink until he dies. But at least he eats before and after he drinks."

Ruwani compared Perera to her husband Sunil, claiming, "Sunil doesn't eat before he drinks, and he can't eat for a few days after, either."

Chandrani replied, "Perera drinks every day."

"Sunil only drinks every once in awhile, but then he goes over the top," replied Ruwani. Ruwani later continued this theme, saying, "Sometimes I go to the tavern and tell Sunil not to drink. Then he's ashamed. It's okay if someone drinks, as long as he doesn't cause trouble, and as long as it isn't every day." Ruwani then went on to talk about alcohol-related violence. "When Sunil goes drinking with his friends, he doesn't fight with them. He knows that they'll beat him up if he does. He is afraid of his friends. He just comes home and fights with me."

Chandrani confirmed this, saying, "If they are drunk, then they will fight over any small fault."

"If you talk, that's a fault. If you don't talk, that's a fault. If you smile, that's a fault. If you don't smile, that's a fault," claimed Ruwani.[3]

"Can't you go to the police?" I asked. The women said that they would call on the authorities if an outsider threatened them but they did not do so when they fought with their husbands.

"My husband is good when he's sober. Then he forgets that we ever fought. I'm the one who starts fights in the morning," Ruwani said.

The women saw money as a major factor in domestic disputes. Having more is not always better, however, because more money may lead to more drinking. Cash, a vital necessity, could become a source of conflict and violence. The women felt helpless to control or stop men's drinking, and feared their violence. They worried about their husbands' health, especially when they drank without eating. The women also noted that men did not totally lose control of their aggressive impulses when intoxicated: men did not fight with their friends, and would stop if the village ethnographer came to visit, but felt free to clash with their wives. The women felt that no matter how carefully they acted, the men would seize on insignificant faults as reasons to fight. By noting this, the women implicitly countered the men's assertion that women's behavior triggered their temper when drunk.

The men and women shared a number of assumptions about domestic relations and concurred on many points about domestic violence. They agreed that confrontations occurred over food and money. They did not see eye to eye on how much respect a woman should give a drunken husband, and they differed on men's right to consume alcohol. The men put a

3. In his Canadian research, Pernanen suggests that "trifling" circumstances bring about drunken wrath (1991, 133) and suggests that alcohol may create hypersensitivity to social cues.

high priority on drinking with friends; for the women, household finances and men's health took precedence over men's need to drink with their network of associates. Women and men shared the opinion that a fight in the morning differed from a fight at night, when the man was drunk. In these confrontations, each side felt that the other had neglected gendered obligations and responsibilities. And both men and women seemed to assume that women would not fight back or go to the police.

No specific legislation deals with domestic violence in Sri Lanka. Women are often unwilling to report such violence, and weaknesses in law enforcement in this realm further undermine women's positions (Goonesekere 2002, 59). A plurality of traditions, including Roman-Dutch law, British Law, and various religious and ethnic systems of personal laws govern family relations. Many of the values enshrined in law "reinforce discriminatory and stereotyped views on women's role in the family" (Goonesekere 2004, 50). Legal scholar Savitri Goonesekere suggests the need for "wholesale reform" of Sri Lanka's legal system, to harmonize laws with international and constitutional human rights standards (2004, 52). But even with legal backing, the common social acceptance of domestic violence will make it difficult to eradicate.

In situations of systemic destructive drinking, community members— often women—sometimes take corrective action. For example, in Chiapas, Mexico, "Women are making significant contributions to the dialogues… about problem drinking based on their roles as household managers of meager resources and as newly empowered political actors in their communities" (Eber 2001, 252). Women leaders in the Zapatista movement seek to abolish hierarchical and male-dominated power structures, and see drinking as a practice to reject (Eber 2001, 257). They take this stance as both primary breadwinners and as guardians of cultural traditions. Sri Lankan women, even those who bring in significant portions of the family income, face similar household hardships, but as yet lack the political mobilization to confront destructive drinking and domestic violence in an organized fashion. Instead, relatives step in when violence escalates to dangerous levels.

What Outsiders Do and Say

Fights between spouses occurred regularly in the village. Although outsiders stepped in to solve other sorts of disputes, they hesitated to interfere between husband and wife. Virasena noted that if a domestic dispute got serious (he offered "breaking plates" as a benchmark), then the neighbors would step in and calm things down. But in most cases, as Manori suggested, "If there is a fight between a husband and wife, it only lasts for a short period. The neighbors know this so they don't interfere. In the night the couple fights, but in the morning they are okay together." Villagers distinguished between fights where husbands were sober and drunk. In a conversation with Edward and Bandula, Edward asserted, "A drunken man fights with his wife because he's drunk. A sober man fights for a reason. A drunken man just comes and hits his wife." Bandula agreed, saying, "A drunk doesn't need a fault to start a fight." I asked them if people stepped in to stop domestic violence when a man was drunk. Edward and Bandula laughed and said that in most cases, no one would step in. "That man is drunk, and tomorrow he'll come fighting with you!" Even though a drunken fight might have little objective cause, sober neighbors hesitated to confront intoxicated men about domestic violence.

Close relatives took the responsibility for settling domestic disputes, and they often paid a high price for interfering. Edward told us that he used to step in when his older brother was drunk, protecting his brother's wife and children by drawing his brother's wrath on himself. Despite Edward's help and his elder brother's death, relations between the households remained strained. Siri declared, "Drunks dare to scold close relatives. They know that their relations won't beat them up. But outsiders would." Certain family obligations to the drinker persisted, even though the drinker had violated a number of social rules. Paradoxically, the people most likely to step into a dispute are those most constrained in their methods of intervention.

In another case, Misilin spoke about stepping into situations of domestic violence in her sons' families. The scenarios she described went well beyond symbolic communication into physical violence.

> If my sons are drunk, they will hit their wives. Otherwise they won't do that. They are very good in the morning. They will eat their lunches happily. And then for dinner there's a world war. I live just across from Janith's house. I can tell if he starts yelling and hitting his wife. I go across the path and stop the fight. The other neighbors don't like to get involved in a domestic dispute, but I can go as the mother. If I didn't step in during fights, my daughters-in-law would be dead by now. My sons would have killed their wives. They drink and they don't know what they are doing. I hide the knives and machete (*kaetta*) because when Charith comes home drunk, he will use those.

Misilin then related a Buddhist story of a man who got drunk, killed his son, and ate him. When he sobered up, he asked where his son was. When he found out what he had done, he left the kingdom and went to live in the forest. Misilin's tale of filicide and cannibalism indexed the extreme shift in judgment she witnessed when her sons got drunk, and the violent extremes that they might go to while intoxicated.

Baklien and Samarasinghe suggest that if a couple fights, the community often blames the wife (2003, 141). While some people shared these views in Naeaegama, many villagers, especially women, understood the impossibility of living with a heavy drinker. Misilin said that she told her son Charith's first wife to separate from Charith. "After she returned from the Middle East, he hit her when he was drunk. Chasing Charith off was the best answer." Generalizing, Misilin continued, "No woman likes to be hit. Once or twice is okay, but not habitually." Although not officially divorced, Charith and his first wife had been separated for over ten years, and Charith lived with another woman. Misilin felt that her other son's wife remained with him because she did not want to lose ownership of their plot of land. "If not for that land, she would have left and gone a long time ago." That daughter-in-law managed a temporary escape, working for a number of years in the Gulf.

Aggressors follow social rules about violence even when they drink, and the cultural expectations of both perpetrators and victims shape the violent acts. Pernanen asserts that in his research in Canada, he found "Very strict, graded, and rather finely calibrated rules...for intergender aggression and violence" (1991, 172). If an aggressor exceeds limits, then people do not see the fight as a good or just one. In Sri Lanka, when domestic fights move from symbolic gestures to physical attacks, near relatives step in. Pernanen suggests that when aggressors break social rules in this way, they will often express their actions as involuntary (1991, 172–73). In such cases, drinking can serve as an excuse: because the man claims he was drunk, there is no need for his wife to take revenge or initiate reciprocal action. After numerous reiterations, however, domestic violence can lead to divorce.

Divorce

In much of Asia, married women are unlikely to leave their husbands. In middle-class households in Japan, for example, men earn money and women manage the home and take care of children and elderly relatives (Borovoy 2005, 75–76). Patience is a traditional female virtue, and women are expected to endure a great deal on the home front. Furthermore, people assume that domestic disputes are the wife's fault. Amy Borovoy writes, "A husband's abuse is often perceived as a source of shame for the wife—a failure on her part to meet his needs or to diffuse his anger" (2005, 103). Women thus feel obliged to keep family disagreements quiet. Similarly,

Naeaegama villagers felt strongly that women should not leave their husbands. I asked Edward's niece Shivanthi whether a woman would seek a divorce in a case of extended domestic violence. She said forcefully, "No! People don't get divorced! The lady just lives with the man. They have to keep living together even with big problems. Those couples get back together again. They forget in the morning what happened last night." During another interview, Siri related a common Sinhala saying: "Spouses fight just for the length of time the rice is cooking (*bath haTTiya ivenakan vitarayi ranDuwa*)." In both contexts, social norms dictated that couples should not separate or divorce.

Unable or unwilling to leave stressful family settings, women often do what they can to make their marriages work, including facilitating life for abusive drinkers. In the discourse of Alcoholics Anonymous (AA), smoothing the way for a heavy drinker to continue drinking is "enabling" the destructive behavior. Euro-American counselors suggest that enablers nurture irresponsibility and immaturity in the drinker and unwittingly abet and promote his addiction (Perez 1992, 39). I question, however, whether Euro-American categories can adequately account for the wider social context within which Asian women make their decisions. In urban Japanese culture, alcohol forms a main part of men's lives and ties in closely with masculinity (Borovoy 2005, 46–47). Women are responsible for managing their husbands' drinking and ensuring that it does not disrupt the rest of the family or society. Borovoy argues that the normal role of the Japanese housewife and stay-at-home mother has much in common with what U.S. therapists would call "codependence" (2005, 15). What AA would see as pathological enabling behavior is the embodiment of domestic virtue in Japan. In Sri Lanka, a woman similarly bears responsibility for her family's health. Tasked with restraining her husband's alcohol consumption, she takes the blame if he drinks. If a woman leaves her husband, it is expected that he will drink more (see Hussein 2000, 57). Women's work on the home front doubtless prevents some drinkers from, in Euro-American parlance, "hitting bottom," a state from which they might initiate change for the better.

Resolving the question about whether Japanese and Sri Lankan women "enable" their spouses' drinking requires examining the issue of divorce. In Naeaegama, only a serious marital breakdown combined with unusually supportive relatives will make it possible for a woman to leave her husband permanently. If a woman has children or if she married for love rather than by arrangement, she will often find it problematic to move back in with her parents. It is socially unacceptable, not to mention very difficult, for a woman to live alone. In Japan, divorce creates economic hardship for middle-class women. While married, they are financially dependent on their husbands but relatively secure in their socially valued role as a wife (Borovoy 2005, 168). In both Japan and Sri Lanka, divorced women lose their social status and often encounter financial problems. Because women often expect different things from marriage in Asia than they do in the West, and because divorce causes many difficulties, fewer women divorce problem drinkers in Japan and Sri Lanka than in the United States and Europe.

In Naeaegama, reluctance to divorce reflects social disapproval and legal hurdles. Siri and I consulted a lawyer who claimed that getting divorced was more difficult in Sri Lanka than in western countries. She told us that according to the Marriage Registration Ordinance 19(1) of 1995, the petitioner had to prove a fault and show at least one of the following faults to divorce: a) malicious desertion or the connected reason constructive malicious desertion, b) incurable impotency, or c) adultery (see also W. de Silva 2002, 217). Divorce was most commonly initiated after two years of legal separation or seven years of de facto separation. Even if the husband and wife had not separated, a lawyer could argue that a husband was guilty of "constructive malicious desertion" if the man drank regularly; beat, assaulted, or treated his wife badly; and failed to maintain his family. But if the couple continued to live under one roof and never reported problems to the police, outsiders might not be able to testify about the case. Despite these difficulties, the lawyer said some people did get divorces. But even if both sides consented to the divorce, the judge would only grant it if the petitioner could prove one of the three reasons listed above. In Naeaegama, separations were much more common than divorces, and neither was socially acceptable.

Despite hurdles, some women did leave their husbands, particularly if they had strong family support or had earned significant sums of money while working abroad. Misilin's first daughter-in-law's permanent separation from her husband followed this pattern, and was accomplished with the full approval of both her parents and her in-laws. Perera, whose daughter was in an abusive relationship, stated, "Women who have troubles with their husbands are very sad. Many of them feel like committing suicide. They are fed up. They will go crazy or jump in front of a train or drink poison. The mother is distressed because the children are hungry." Although Perera did not suggest that a woman in this situation should divorce her husband, he and his wife Chandrani took care of their daughter's child while she worked as a live-in domestic servant in a nearby town—an arrangement that removed her from her husband's purview.

In the West, the incidence of divorce has risen as women have become
more able to support themselves. Women leave marriages if they can get
by financially, even if it means living in greatly reduced circumstances (Stacey 1990). In Naeaegama, women who do not leave abusive drinkers are
not deliberately enabling their spouses. Rather, they are making the best
choice available to them given the internal and external constraints they
face (Bourdieu 1977). But the stigma surrounding divorce in Sri Lanka is
slowly changing. Women's ability to support themselves and their children
through migration and other jobs has earned them some independence. At
the same time, men's sense of inadequacy might exacerbate confrontations
and contribute to a rising rate of separation and divorce. This lends some
indirect support to the assertion that migration contributes to the disintegration of the family, though the causal relationship is much more complex
than a straightforward statement of connection would suggest.

Conclusion

Speaking of an American context, Bateson (1972) suggests that the error
or pathology that leads to abusive drinking must be found in the state of
sobriety. Some people suggest that an alcoholic is saner than others, and
thus he finds the situation around him intolerable while others can bear it.
Intoxication provides a subjective but transient correction for the problem,
for example offering an escape from the false ideals of materialistic society
(1972, 310–11). Elements of Bateson's scenario parallel the drinking situation in Naeaegama. Some men in rural Sri Lanka face what they feel to be
an intolerable situation: they are culturally required to be breadwinners but
cannot successfully fulfill the role. Simultaneously, the opportunity to work
as domestic servants in the Gulf provides many wives with an income that
greatly surpasses what their husbands could make locally. In search of self-
esteem that they cannot achieve through their traditional economic role,
some men turn to alcohol as a source of egalitarian social connection and
an affirmation of their masculinity.

Carrier and Heyman propose that individuals, families, and households
try to maintain or improve their position in a world with unequal social
groupings (1997, 362). Within families, however, men and women have
different and sometimes conflicting agendas for improving status. To understand male alcohol use and female migration, one must look at the poverty underlying both phenomena. Lack of money for food and housing is a
source of men's humiliation and a primary reason that women go abroad.
Responding to the same cause, men and women sometimes take actions

that set them at odds. While some men seek to achieve individual status in male drinking networks, many women seek to increase family standing by educating their children and providing superior housing. Different goals and agendas set men and women on a collision course for gendered struggles over household expenditures and domestic duties.

Studying male drinking in the context of household disputes and international migration of labor helps to put alcohol consumption in broader perspective. In the next chapter, I continue the focus on political economics by examining the place of the illicit liquor industry in the local economy.

6 *Kasippu:* The Political Economics of Illicit Liquor

"*Kasippu* affects everyone. For the people who drink it, it's bad, and it's also bad for their families. For the manufacturers, it's good. They can get very rich—much richer than the sawmill owner or a housemaid working in the Middle East. In this area, *kasippu* is an industry, like garment factories and tourist hotels. There are a few families living quite nicely on this income." This is how an informant[1] portrayed the size and scale of the local *kasippu* industry when I first started my fieldwork in Naeaegama in 1992. In previous chapters, I have shown the major role that alcohol consumption plays in public ceremonies, identity construction, and household economics. In this chapter I examine the manufacture and sale of *kasippu* as an industry in its own right, albeit an illegal one.

A political economy theoretical approach considers how economic and political dynamics overlap and interact. The study of economics covers the production, distribution, and consumption of goods and services. The conversion of grains, tubers, and fruits into alcohol "turns large-volume low-value material into a good that has small volume but high value and that is easily transportable, almost infinitely divisible, does not spoil, but is often readily consumed" (Heath 1998a, 107). Alcohol has facilitated commerce for many centuries. For example, colonial traders exchanged rum, sugar, and slaves across the Atlantic (Dietler 2006, 240). Issues of power and control lead researchers from economics to the study of politics, which considers the creation of legitimate authority and the dynamics of domination and

---

1. Because the activities discussed in this chapter are illegal, I do not acknowledge many of my informants even by pseudonyms in order to protect their identities.

resistance. Here again, stakeholders can use alcohol for their purposes. For example, Hillel Levine documents the economics of alcohol production in Poland in the eighteenth century, noting how landlords used alcohol both to offset declines in farming and to control an unstable labor force (1987, 255). In Chiapas, Mexico, alcohol formed part of a debt bondage system to keep workers on coffee plantations (Crump 1987). In Sri Lanka, alcohol plays an important role in generating both economic and social capital and solidifying social status. Here I look at the economics of the *kasippu* industry and examine the political maneuvers by which *kasippu* businesspeople negotiate their ambiguous status in the Naeaegama community.

Economics of *Kasippu*

Administrations all over the world tread a fine line when regulating alcohol production. Many governments earn significant revenues by taxing and licensing the alcohol industry. At the same time, exorbitant taxes strike many populations as unfair, and can be used to justify illegal production with associated black market activities (Saunders and de Burgh 1998, 147). In Sri Lanka, 50 to 90 percent of the alcohol consumed may be illicit. The state tries to suppress the illicit liquor industry, but high taxes on arrack— *kasippu*'s legal equivalent—raise demand for the cheaper alternative.

The manufacture of illicit liquor is hidden from the state's supervising organs: the police, the Excise Department, and the Police Narcotics Bureau (Excise Ordinance 1956; Police Narcotics Bureau 2006). *Kasippu* businesspeople try to get around the authority figures using a combination of subterfuge, trickery, and bribery. In Naeaegama, manufacturers and retailers play cat and mouse games with the police. Police constables hunt down *kasippu* makers, arrest them or their proxies, and confiscate their equipment. Manufacturers allegedly bribe authorities to ignore their activities. Many aspects of the *kasippu* industry reflect the extra costs associated with illegal production.

Understanding the political economy of *kasippu* depends on examining not only economic but also the social and political aspects of the industry. Local villagers openly object to *kasippu* but sometimes protect its makers and retailers from the police. Distributors hide stocks in gardens; landowners either welcome them or chase them out. Retailers send tips to the police about their rivals' deliveries; tips allegedly flow back from the station to the *kasippu* sellers before a raid. Drinkers and retailers develop jokes, idioms, and short-hand secret languages to speak about *kasippu* and police scrutiny without openly stating their topic of conversation. These cloak and dagger interactions form part of the political fabric of everyday village life.

Sajith's Distillery

An informant related the following story about a visit he had made many years before to a *kasippu* manufacturing site.

Sajith was the *kasippu* king of this area for about fifteen years starting in the early 1970s. He had thirty-one people working for him in a remote area in what was then called the Cemetery Demon's Forest. His manufacturing site was like a small distillery for the Southern Province. He used to distribute big containers of *kasippu* openly, during the day, riding on his motorbike. He made about a hundred gallons a night. People were afraid to give tips or evidence to the police, because they were afraid he would kill them.

I went to the distillery once. At that time, a village friend drove a Land-master [small tractor with a trailer]. He came by one evening with a big load of firewood and told me to hop in the back. He wouldn't tell me where we were going. We drove quite a distance, and went deeper and deeper into the Cemetery Demon's Forest. In the middle of the forest, we started to unload. Six people with guns were guarding the place, using flashlights as large as car headlights, and the bearers had to take the firewood another half a mile into the forest from where we left the tractor. We went along with them. This was Sajith's *kasippu* manufacturing site. Even though Sajith transported the *kasippu* during the day, he brought the raw materials (sugar, fruits, firewood, and so forth) and did the distilling only after dark.

In the forest, near the distillery setup, there was plenty to eat and drink. They had a huge fish and all sorts of curries. Sajith was a very large man, and he used to eat a whole fish in a single sitting. There was also a lot to drink. They gave me a couple of glasses of strong, undiluted *kasippu,* and I can't re-member much more. My friend timed his drinking better, and got to eat and drink all night. We left home about 9:30 in the evening, and got back about 10:00 the next morning. Sajith didn't worry about us telling anyone anything about the distillery, because he knew we were drinking men.

Sajith was a thug, but he also helped the poor people. For instance, if a local person had a wedding, they'd invite Sajith, and he'd contribute a big bag of rice or fifteen kilograms of fish. Because of this, people wouldn't tell the police about the distillery. He was also good to me. One day when I was unemployed, I was standing by my gate watching the road. I saw Sajith trans-porting a barrel of *kasippu.* Sajith asked what I was doing; I said "*ohee inneva* (just waiting [implying that the speaker is without opportunities, has prob-lems, or needs something])," and Sajith said, "Wait just a little bit." He drove off on his motorbike and came back in about fifteen minutes with a bottle of arrack and a pack of cigarettes for me.

Later Sajith was killed by the police.

This story about Sajith's distillery incorporates many elements of the political economics of the *kasippu* industry. In addition to logistics of manufacture and transportation, the story reveals the manufacturer's ambiguous status in the village community. Despite Sajith's wealth and power, he depended on the good will of local villagers who could have told the police about his operation. Sajith enforced his standing with armed guards and the threat of force. But he also earned the loyalty of his workers by paying them well and giving them plenty to eat and drink, and he obtained the cooperation of local villagers by contributing generously to their ceremonies. *Kasippu* manufacturers and dealers were, and are now, integrated in contradictory ways into the local community.

Manufacturing

Sri Lanka's legal hard liquor, arrack, is distilled from toddy, the fermented sap of the coconut palm. I knew of no one who illegally distilled toddy in the Naeaegama area. *Kasippu,* the most popular illicit hard liquor in the area, is made from fermented fruit. In 1993, the manufacturing process began with a large barrel, in which producers combined water, yeast, cheap sugar, and ripe fruit into a thick, sticky mixture called *gooDa.*[2] The manufacturers covered the barrel and let the contents ferment for five or six days. One local group fermented *gooDa* in ten or twelve barrels at a time, and distilled the contents in one night. Diluting the gummy contents of one barrel of *gooDa* with ten barrels of water, they could distill about 340 liters of pure spirit and earn Rs. 8,500—9,000 [Rs. 17,765—18,810 in 2004 figures].

By 2005 some changes had occurred in the manufacturing process. Since 1999 or 2000, local tourist hotels had started buying most of the ripe fruit in the market, driving the prices up, so *gooDa* rarely contained fruit. *Kasippu* manufacturers relied instead on yeast and white or (preferably) brown sugar. In addition, police pressure made the lengthy maturation of *gooDa* risky. Manufacturers experimented with speeding up the fermenting process by adding a couple of spoonfuls of cement powder or urea fertilizer to make the barrels "mature" faster—at a maximum within a day and a half (compared to the five or six days previously required). Instead of having a sweet, fruity flavor, the current product sometimes tasted like cement or kerosene (a by-product of transportation in a canister fresh from the filling station). Some producers put coriander seeds into the mix to improve the flavor. In addition to facing shortages of fruit, a regulation briefly required yeast dealers to sell only to bakers with permits. Until repealed, this regulation created a black market for yeast—an essential ingredient for *kasippu* production. Producers

---

2. *GooDa* rhymes with "soda."

regularly paid more than market rate for sugar, yeast, and firewood. Despite these business expenses, they still made a good profit on their product, receiving an estimated Rs. 20,000 from a barrel of *gooDa*.

Kasippu is made by fractional distillation. The most expensive part of the operation, a coil made locally from copper pipe, in 1993 cost about Rs. 2,700 [Rs. 5,643] and required replacement every three or four months. The manufacturers stashed the rest of the equipment in the forest, but the kingpin kept the coil. In the past, *kasippu* producers such as Sajith had permanent setups in remote, forested areas. But recently, they began to shift their production sites frequently to avoid police detection. Because they could not move the heavy *gooDa* barrels around openly, the manufacturers set up several different sites.[3]

To distill, manufacturers set up two large metal drums. They light a fire under the drum that holds *gooDa* diluted with water. They cover it and seal the coil over a hole in the top. As the fermented mixture boils, steam rises, entering the coiled copper pipe. Because alcohol boils at a lower temperature than water, this steam is nearly pure alcohol vapor. The pipe angles down through the next drum, which workers constantly fill with cold water. The cool temperature causes the alcohol vapor to condense, and the liquor flows out the bottom of the pipe. The best alcohol (first *kooD*) comes out first, with two lesser quality *kooDs* (containing more distilled water) coming out later.

Distilling *kasippu* requires considerable manpower. One local operation running in 1993 employed six people for each two-drum setup, and usually had three setups going at any one time. Two people kept the fire hot (cool fire smoked more, drew attention to the process, and decreased the quality of the alcohol).[4] Two people constantly poured cold water into the second drum. Two people collected the final product; one of them filled bottles and cans, and the other transported them away quickly, in case the police raided the operation. The manufacturer operated twice a week, with eighteen people working all night. In 1993, each worker received Rs. 150 [Rs. 314] plus food and alcohol. For comparative purposes, consider another manufacturing operation. An Excise Department raid on an illicit distillery in the marshes north of Colombo in mid-July 2006 revealed a sophisticated setup with twenty large barrels resting in a fire-pit of burning

3. Both iron and plastic barrels were inexpensive and easy to replace. An iron barrel costs about Rs. 450 wholesale. But the courts held regular auctions of materials confiscated during *kasippu* cases, at which such a barrel cost about Rs. 75.

4. Distilling at too low a temperature can create methanol (which is toxic) instead of ethanol (Heath 2000, 149).

peanut shells (Kariyakarawana 2006, A10). Alcohol vapor from the boiling *gooDa* passed through rubber hoses to coils submerged in the marsh water, then condensed and flowed into collection containers. Three people ran the distillery, which went into production twice a week. Each worker earned Rs. 1,000 [Rs. 827] a day, or about Rs. 8,000 [Rs. 6,616] a month.

The raw final product, *kasippu*, is a brownish-white liquid. The first alcohol that comes out of the distilling process, called the first *kooD*, is extremely potent. This liquid will burn if placed on a fingertip and lit with a match—a safe test due to alcohol's low kindling point. The second and third *kooD*s are less potent and do not burn in this way. Both the manufacturer and the retailer add water to the pure spirits. By the time drinkers consume *kasippu*, the first *kooD* has usually been mixed 1:2 with water. Both drinkers and non-drinkers worry about the quality of the water used in the dilution. Contrary to its reputation, however, Abeyasinghe (2002, 92) suggests that *kasippu* is actually quite pure according to content analysis done during his research project. Its alcohol content, however, can vary significantly from time to time and tavern to tavern. Drinkers expect *kasippu* to have the same "kick" as arrack (33.5 percent alcohol by volume), but neither drinkers nor dealers have a scientific way of measuring alcohol content. One drinker told me, "Sometimes, if I'm in a hurry, I will take a shot from a tavern and drink it quickly. I only realize on my way home that I have paid Rs. 25 for a glass of water." In general, the strength of *kasippu* has decreased in the past fifteen years, as the ingredients have decreased in quality and manufacturers and retailers have begun adding more water to the final product.

Distillery Sites and Property Owners

Because the unlicensed production of alcohol is illegal, *kasippu* manufacturers have to keep their distillery sites secret. They seek out locations with ample water far from well-trafficked areas. Manufacturers usually get the landowner's consent before using a site. In 1993, landowners received Rs. 50 [Rs. 105] per barrel each time a manufacturer filled it with *gooDa*, and from each manufacturing session three bottles of undiluted first *kooD* alcohol (equaling twelve bottles of regular strength *kasippu*, which sold for Rs. 45 each in 1993 [Rs. 94]). If a manufacturer stored twelve barrels on a property and produced six batches of *kasippu* a month, he would give the landowner Rs. 6,840 [Rs. 14,296] in cash and liquor for the period.[5] This figure is at the top end of what a civil servant would earn in a month.

5. I calculate the landowner's share of income from storing a dozen barrels of *gooDa* on his property and distilling six batches of *kasippu* a month as follows, using 1993 figures: 12 barrels ×

While one member of the family might approve of hosting a manufacturing site, other family members might not, particularly because the police could and did arrest landowners if they discovered barrels of *gooDa* on their property. But in the early 1990s, rousting a *kasippu* manufacturer was neither easy nor safe if he had established a location. At the end of December 1992, I visited a distilling site. My guide showed me an empty, sweet-smelling tub buried in the ground, where the manufacturer stored *gooDa*. At the nearby distilling site, a patch of ground was still warm from the fire used to boil the *gooDa,* and another was still muddy from the water used for cooling the coil.

Soon after my visit to this location, the landowner's teenage son, who resented his father's drinking habit, got a tip from a friend at the police station that the police suspected that his family land hosted a distillery. Out of respect for the family, they asked the boy to destroy the setup before the police came to raid it. The police had already asked the boy's father to clear the overgrown area. Without clearing the area, the landowner had passed the information on to the manufacturer, who had dug the *gooDa* barrels into the ground in an unsuccessful effort to hide them. On a Sunday morning, the landowner's son and several of his friends cleared the undergrowth in the back corner of the land. They found and broke three full *gooDa* barrels and filled another one with dirt. Their actions cost the *kasippu* manufacturer Rs. 35,000 [Rs. 73,150].

Furious, the manufacturer investigated who had destroyed his gear. At first he suspected a rival producer, but several days later he found out the truth and threatened all the young men involved. The boys' families, scared and upset, confronted the landowner and his father, blaming them for hosting a *kasippu* manufacturer in the first place and letting their sons get involved in the dangerous activity of clearing the site. The landowner's family members, none of whom had known of the production site prior to this, criticized his disgraceful association with the illegal industry. The landowner in turn condemned his son for acting so rashly, claiming that he could have asked the *kasippu* manufacturer to remove his barrels after the next production session, getting rid of the problem without danger. The landowner feared that despite his intervention, his son and the other boys might be punished for their actions. This case illustrates that people within a

---

6 distillations a month × Rs. 50 per barrel = Rs. 3,600 [Rs. 7,524] in cash for the barrels and 12 bottles × 6 distillations × Rs. 45 a bottle = Rs. 3,240 [Rs. 6,772] in *kasippu,* for a total of Rs. 6,840 [Rs. 14,296].

family may have varying opinions about alcohol and different relations with the liquor producers in the area.

Landowners felt ambivalent about having *kasippu* manufactured or stored on their land. Although the landowner in the former story agreed to host a distillery, the landowner in the following one did not. In 2004, a heavy drinker had an altercation with a *kasippu* seller. Soon after, he received a tip that his adversary was hiding manufactured *kasippu* in the drinker's family's cinnamon garden (several acres of closely planted six- to eight-foot tall bushes). The drinker called the police. He and two police constables searched the garden but found nothing. My research associate Siri speculated that a message went from an insider at the police station to the retailer, who removed the offending liquor before the police could seize it. Siri asserted, "If I were in that position, I would send a message to all of the retailers asking the owner to remove the liquor. I would not bring in the police." By calling the police, the heavy drinker in this story earned the disfavor of the local *kasippu* retailers and drinkers. Because there was a less confrontational but equally effective way to get the *kasippu* off the land, the drinker's decision to call the police was probably prompted in part by his dispute with the *kasippu* retailer as well as the fact that he had not been offered any compensation for hosting the stock. In interactions between *kasippu* businesspeople and Naeaegama villagers, interpersonal politics often impinge on economic interests.

Transportation

Manufacturers must transport *kasippu* to retailers—an activity that leaves them vulnerable to police scrutiny. Transportation strategies have developed over the years. In 1993, manufacturers stored stocks of *kasippu* in various secret places, and the retailers came to buy from them. By 2000, some manufacturers brought *kasippu* to their retailers using teams of three motorcycles. By 2004, many manufacturers employed workers to distribute their product to the retailers directly from the distilling site, without keeping stock on hand. These transporters used trishaws (covered, three-wheeled motorcycles) rather than motorcycles. They transported the liquor at about 4:30 A.M., distributing their stock in six or seven different vehicles. The deliveries coincided with early morning bakery deliveries. The police stopped trishaws along suspected delivery routes. Because local officers grew familiar with the trishaws used to move liquor, the transporters changed vehicles frequently. When they hired a vehicle, they paid ten times the normal rate for a trip. Transporters and retailers also moved small quantities of *kasippu* over short distances by foot and bicycle.

Manufacturers and transporters chose their associates carefully and treated them well, because they needed a closed-mouthed, reliable staff. *Kasippu* businesspeople fed their workers and looked after their families when needed. This relationship reflected older systems of patronage between patrons and clients, who were bound in more intimate ways than those embodied in the wage labor contract agreements that are more common today. But the relationships also reflected the political exigencies of running an illegal business.

Retail Distribution

Manufacturers sell or consign their products to local *kasippu* retailers. Drinkers, retailers, and manufacturers measure *kasippu* in units of .625-liter bottles. In 2004, a .625-liter bottle of *kasippu* sold for Rs. 100. People in the business called a five-liter can an "eight" because it contains eight 625 ml bottles. A retailer could buy an "eight" for either Rs. 450 or Rs. 550. The Rs. 450 "eight" contained *kasippu* that the manufacturers had already watered down. The retailer could sell the eight bottles for Rs. 800, reaping a

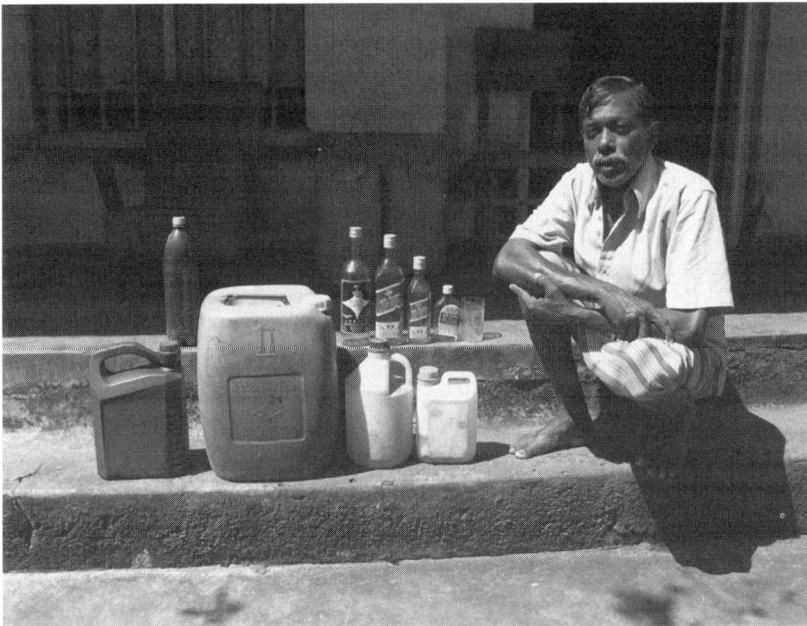

Fig. 4. These sorts of containers are used for transporting *kasippu*. The biggest container is a "forty-five," the second biggest is an "eight," and the glass is a "quarter." Photograph by author.

profit of Rs. 350. The Rs. 550 "eight" contained more highly concentrated spirits. The seller could add another two or three bottles of water without damaging the taste. Retailers got a better profit margin on the Rs. 550 containers, the contents of which yielded ten or eleven bottles of *kasippu*, which could be sold for Rs. 1,000 or Rs. 1,100, leaving a profit of Rs. 450 or Rs. 550. If a dealer could sell six "eights" a day, the distributor brought a bigger "tap": a 28-liter container (called "a forty-five" because it contained 45 bottles of *kasippu*) or a 37.5 liter container (called "a sixty").[6]

The local retailers stored their stock in "eights," which they hid in forested places (for example, cinnamon gardens). A retailer might dig a hole in the ground, cover it with a wood plank and some leaves, and mark the spot so she could locate it again. Despite these precautions, the police could often find hidden stocks of *kasippu,* especially after they received tips. Retailers diluted the spirit with water and poured it into smaller containers before bringing it to the tavern. They preferred to use 2.5-liter containers, but if they feared a police raid they might store the liquor in smaller bottles. (The smaller the container seized, the lower the fine.) A retailer often waited for several customers to arrive before bringing a bottle from her hiding place. If she had six clients, she could give each drinker "a quarter" (one-fourth of a 625 ml bottle), empty a one-liter bottle, and not have to hide the remaining liquor.[7] One drinker I knew liked to be the last person served from such a bottle. He said, "The last shot is a little bit over the usual 'quarter,' but the dealer still only charges Rs. 25."

Business as Usual with the Police

According to local informants,[8] intricate relationships linked the representatives of the state and those who operated outside its purview. Some policemen

---

6. For a little while in 2005, distributors and dealers shifted from using plastic containers to plastic bags. They later returned to using plastic containers, which are easier to hide and less likely to be punctured.

7. A "quarter" (156 milliliters) is the equivalent of three and a half 44-milliliter "shots" in the United States.

8. I want to emphasize that I have never observed a Sri Lankan police officer do anything illegal. All the information below is based on hearsay and reports from village informants who may have misinterpreted events, imagined police corruption, or exaggerated the number of officers involved in such activities. But because a number of people independently offered similar information, and two of my informants were or had been policemen themselves, I feel confident that the information below represents the Naeaegama view of police complicity in the *kasippu* industry. In addition, Abeyasinghe (2002, 152–57) reports similar complicity between police and *kasippu* businesspeople. I present this information as a village "view," not hard evidence of

genuinely wanted to stamp out illicit liquor production. Others were willing to ignore it in exchange for a bribe. Both police crackdowns (with their resulting court fines and loss of *kasippu* stocks) and protection (in exchange for bribes) increased the price of illicit liquor. Nevertheless, the high tax on arrack kept *kasippu* in demand. The *kasippu* trade proved profitable for all involved: producers, retailers, and, in some cases, the police. In the following section, I describe the events that preceded, took place during, and followed a police raid. Issues that informants raised during discussions included police investigations, raids, stand-ins, bribes, court cases and fines, and selling confiscated materials back to the manufacturers. (For further discussion of the state apparatus for controlling trade in illegal substances see Gamburd n.d.)

Police Investigations

Because *kasippu* producers and distributors worked secretly, the police employed investigative strategies to obtain information about when a manufacturer delivered new supplies, where the retailer hid her stocks, and at what times taverns hosted the most customers. Drinkers commented that during police raids the police seemed to know all the escape routes from the tavern; they also knew where the liquor was hidden. In such cases, drinkers inferred that someone had passed information to the police.

Drinkers also suggested that *kasippu* retailers sent tips to the police against each other. One drinker told me,

> If one seller feels that her competition has higher sales, she will ask one of her regular drinkers to find out some vital information about the rival, like where she hides her big tap. The seller will give that information to the police. The police might jump [raid] and fine the rival Rs. 35,000 and put her out of business for a few days. During that time, the rival's regular customers have to drink from a different outlet. But if the rival finds out where the police information came from, she will retaliate in the same fashion!

Thus *kasippu* retailers can use the police to increase their own sales and regulate their relationships with other dealers.

Raids and Bribes

Police officers allegedly took bribes for all stages of the *kasippu* trade. One informant told me that in 1993, a large-scale manufacturer made

---

corruption. What I write here should not reflect on the many honest and hardworking policemen in the local area and the rest of Sri Lanka.

a monthly payment of Rs. 10,000 [Rs. 20,900] to the police. The manufacturer also lent his car to the bribed police officer, who used it when he met his lover at a rest house. In addition, the *kasippu* manufacturer gave several parties each month for a small group of high-status police officers. The manufacturer provided whiskey, good quality arrack, and "bites" for his guests. In exchange for these favors, when the police planned to raid the production site, they sent a message ahead of them, so that the producer would have only a small amount of liquor on hand when the police arrived, thus reducing the court fine. The *kasippu* manufacturers and the policemen were bound to each other by common economic interests and shared secrets.

Certain policemen also reportedly made semi-permanent arrangements with *kasippu* transporters. The police recognized the vehicles involved and stopped them regularly. In 2006, an informant told me that if a policeman was receptive, the driver would give him a bribe of Rs. 500 [Rs. 414] each time he was caught. Some drivers arranged their travel with the police officers ahead of time, telling them the route and schedule, so the policeman on duty would know which vehicles to ignore. In exchange, a policeman involved would regularly ask "favors" from the transporter, claiming for example that he needed Rs. 5,000 [Rs. 4,135] for his grandmother's funeral. Higher-ups would send a messenger of lower rank with similar requests. My informant said that Rs. 5,000 was half a day's profit for a manufacturer, and on bribe days, "Drinkers find a bit more water in their *kasippu!*"

Kasippu taverns developed strategies to circumvent raids. Retailers posted people at strategic places along roads to warn the tavern if they spotted the police. One informant told me that the lookouts had "eyes like owls"—round and wide open. Usually the retailer was a woman, and her husband formed part of the warning team. Originally the police did not suspect women of being involved in the *kasippu* business. Although the police quickly grew to know the local sellers, female retailers retained some advantages. A police officer told me that some retailers packaged *kasippu* in plastic bags. He said,

> Women put the parcels in their bras, under their shirts. A male police constable cannot reach into a woman's blouse, or there will be a big fuss. In a raid, the police will catch all the people in the building, search the place for *kasippu,* and seize what they find. If they find illicit liquor, they will take someone with them to the police station. If the police arrest a woman, the "matron" at the police station supervises her. The police don't put women in cells; women have a separate place to sit down without being locked up.

While this policeman emphasized the care taken to avoid inappropriate gender contact, another informant suggested that some female *kasippu* dealers accused others of trading sexual favors for reduced or dismissed fines, particularly if they returned quickly from the police station after an arrest.

In 1993, an informant suggested that police inspectors took about Rs. 2,500 [Rs. 5,225] a month from a tavern as protection money. In 2004, various informants suggested that if the police caught a retailer with *kasippu,* in some instances the retailer would bribe the police. For Rs. 2,000 or Rs. 3,000, the police would agree to seize only a quarter of a bottle instead of a bigger container of *kasippu.* If a raid took place in a relatively crowded area during the day, the police seized everything they found. Negotiations took place later, at the police station. A police officer I spoke with confirmed that if the police seized a large tap of *kasippu,* after receiving a bribe they would send only one bottle to the courts. This reduced the fine and did not leave a large black mark on the person's "character," the official record of criminal charges. If the police received a bribe from someone whom they had caught multiple times, they would file a report as if they have never caught the person before, reducing the fine. These data suggest that police could use the court system to their advantage. Despite the high price of bribes, the possible court fine was greater than the sum of the protection money, bribe, and reduced fine. The police acted with the cooperation of the *kasippu* businesspeople to cheat the state of its due income.[9]

While police could claim to have found less *kasippu* than they had actually seen or seized, they might also assert that they had found more. For outlets that did not pay protection money, or retailers who failed to cooperate, the police allegedly increased the court fine by claiming they had found additional *kasippu.* A police officer told me that police stations had a stock of confiscated *kasippu* that they could use for this purpose. In such cases

---

9. Abeyasinghe (2002, 146) reports from his research in a Colombo slum that *kasippu* salesmen and tavern owners gave monthly payments of Rs. 100 [Rs. 121] to police constables, Rs. 150 or 200 [Rs. 181 or 241] to police sergeants, Rs. 300 [Rs. 362] to sub inspectors, and Rs. 2,000 or 5,000 [Rs. 2,415 to 6,037] to the officers in charge (OIC). Abeyasinghe asserts, "All those involved in the Kasippu trade vouched for the need to pay off the police" (2002, 146). In addition to money, the OIC received gifts of food and legal liquor (2002, 146). Standardized for inflation assuming that Abeyasinghe's research was performed in 2001, his figures corroborate amounts and activities reported in Naeaegama. Abeyasinghe also reports that police raids avoided *kasippu* wholesalers, netting only small quantities of liquor from small-scale suppliers and outlets (2002, 151). The police undertook many raids but never caught the big fish; the small fry got off lightly too.

the police used *kasippu* against the manufacturers to discipline them and encourage them to accept the protection system.[10]

Police raids generally disrupted tavern supplies for forty-five minutes or an hour. Regular customers waited for the new supply to arrive, but men who wanted a drink badly often visited another outlet. Rival taverns experienced good sales during the hour it took the raided retailer to restock.

Retrieving Confiscated Supplies

If police raided a production site, they took the barrels and other items to the station. For a certain sum, they allegedly reported having found fewer items. For example, the police might find ten *gooDa* barrels and ten large taps of *kasippu* but, if bribed, take only one or two barrels and one distilling drum to the courts. In some cases the police sold the equipment back to the producer.

An informant told me the following story about police raids and an honest police sub inspector (SI):

> The police arrive and make a lot of noise kicking things over and crashing around. Then they take the barrels and the other equipment. The village people think it has been a big raid. But the equipment comes back to the producer the same night!
>
> The IP [inspector of police] here was doing this for awhile. Then a new SI came to the local police station. The SI didn't take bribes. He raided a *kasippu* manufacturing site in [a nearby village], and discretely put little blue marks on the seized equipment. On their next raid, in [another nearby village], he found the same barrels in use.
>
> Bypassing the IP, the SI told the ASP [assistant superintendent of police] about the situation. Soon thereafter, the SI was transferred to another station! In other words, some of the IP's bribe went up to the ASP, and they weren't pleased to have someone interfering with the system.
>
> Another local IP has the same trouble. He has been an IP for about twelve years. He would have been promoted a thousand times over, but he doesn't take bribes.

This story implies that money from bribes made its way up through the system of command, with a wide array of police officers complicit in the protection racket. Junior officers risked transfers and other disciplinary actions if they disrupted the system. In 2006, however, one informant suggested

10. Abeyasinghe reports that in the Colombo slum he studied, police conducted raids if their monthly payments were late (2002, 147).

that younger police officers were often unwilling to take bribes, as were people in the Excise Department and Police Narcotics Bureau. These officers, relative strangers to the village area, reportedly upheld the letter of the law instead of entering into complex interdependent financial relationships with those in the illicit liquor industry.

Stand-Ins, Court Cases, and Fines

Minor players on the front line of the illicit liquor industry frequently risked police arrest. In the Excise Department raid of the large-scale *kasippu* distillery north of Colombo, a suspect who spoke with the newspaper reporter anticipated a fine of Rs. 100,000—200,000 [Rs. 82,700—165,400] and hoped that the *kasippu* kingpin would pay the fine and bail him out, otherwise he faced long-term imprisonment (Kariyakarawana 2006, A10). Those in the trade usually came to the aid of their loyal workers.

Fines increased with repeated encounters with the law. In Naeaegama, wealthy, large-scale *kasippu* retailers made arrangements with some of their clients, usually alcohol-dependent men, to stand in lieu of the seller in the event of a police raid. These men agreed to claim to own the illicit liquor, be remanded at the police station, and have a court case filed against them. The *kasippu* retailers tried to send a different stand-in each time; if the magistrate recognized the individual, the fine went up. The *kasippu* seller paid the court fine, which in 2005 could be as high as 12,000 [Rs. 10,176]. Cases from my research area were heard on a particular day of the week at the local court. (*Kasippu* retailers and drinkers knew the court day and relished the thought that the local police would spend the morning at the courts, not raiding the tavern.) Once the court assigned a fine, the retailer paid the money at a nearby bank and brought the receipt to the court. The police then released the remanded person. In exchange for his services, the stand-in received a sum of money (about Rs. 500 [Rs. 414] in 2006) and a few days worth of free liquor.

In 2004, I heard that Monika, a local *kasippu* retailer, had to pay between Rs. 2,500 and Rs. 5,000 every few months to the courts for fines. During raids, she had to give Rs. 500 to various policemen, in addition to giving them free liquor. Court fines, bribes, and fees for stand-ins greatly increased tavern expenses.

Interview with a Stand-In

In 2004 I interviewed Mangala, a heavy drinker who had gone to the courts several times when the police raided a local *kasippu* retailer, Sri Lal. Mangala claimed that he stood in for Sri Lal because they were friends; he also received Rs. 500 and free drinks for his service. Sri Lal paid the fine and bailed him out. The last time Mangala did this, the Officer in Charge cited three prior offenses and set a higher fine. Mangala stated that the fine for the first offence was Rs. 1,000, the second Rs. 1,500, the third Rs. 2,000, and the fourth Rs. 4,000. Mangala did not want to go to court again. To keep his brush with the law secret, when he went to court, Mangala left the house in a sarong, fearing that if he were to wear more formal attire, his family might ask him why he was dressed up.

When we asked if the *kasippu* retailers had a connection with the police, Mangala claimed that the two sides cooperated. He said, "If the police need to forward a court case, they raid a tavern. But even if they find a 'forty-five,' they only take one or two bottles for the case. The sellers can get the rest of the tap back from the constables for a small fee."

When we asked if *kasippu* retailers had a connection with politicians, Mangala agreed that some sellers called politicians if they were caught. The politician then called the police and got the retailer released. Money flowed from the *kasippu* businesspeople to the politicians and back again; retailers contributed to political campaigns, and if a seller was raided or arrested, she could get money from the politician to restart her business. In addition, if a politician needed thugs for a fight, he could come to a tavern and buy a drinker a couple of drinks. "Then he will tell the drinker whom to stab." Mangala waved his hand in a warding-off gesture and stated categorically that he would never do such a thing. But another person present asserted that a local *kasippu* manufacturer took such contracts from politicians.

Two years later, in 2006, Mangala was caught drinking at Amarapala's tavern and had to pay a fine of Rs. 5,000 [Rs. 4,135]. Since he had no money and none of his relatives would bail him out, he spent nine days in jail. Presumably his prior arrests increased his fine, but this time he did not serve as a stand-in and the *kasippu* retailer did not come to his rescue. Personal obligations and alliances shift frequently in the illicit liquor trade.

Who's Who in the *Kasippu* Business

Local people agreed that while manufacturing and transporting *kasippu* were difficult, selling *kasippu* was an easy and profitable job. Siri said, "They just bring the stuff, mix it with water, and sell it! They don't need to go to school and study a lot. They don't need to get tired. They just stay at home twenty-four hours a day. Those people eat chicken every day. If they buy fish, they purchase huge quantities. They have large families, but they eat well. They are wealthy." In the Naeaegama area, the job of selling illicit alcohol ran in families. Although richer than other villagers, these families carried a stigma from their profession. Family members who acquired educational qualifications got out of the business, and others started legitimate businesses with their gains from illicit liquor.[11]

History of Kasippu *Manufacturing in the Naeaegama Area*

Over the past fifty years, many different individuals from a half dozen village families have been involved with *kasippu* production and distribution. The business landscape changes frequently. Here I sketch out the broad picture with some of the larger players.

The first person to produce liquor in the area was an Ayurvedic physician (*veda-mahattayaa*) who started making *kasippu* around the time of Sri Lanka's independence in 1948. He carefully and cleanly made an alcoholic mixture according to Ayurvedic principles, using healing leaves and roots. Whenever the police questioned him, he insisted that his medicine should be taken by the spoonful. He denied responsibility if people insisted on drinking whole bottles in a single sitting. The police never convicted him for making illicit liquor; the Excise Ordinance "does not apply to bona fide medicated articles" (Excise Ordinance 1956, 297). He stopped manufacturing because the constant stream of male clients damaged his daughters' reputations. For many years thereafter, people in the Naeaegama area had to travel four or five miles to nearby coastal villages for toddy if they wanted to drink.

In the early 1970s, Sajith, whose distilling site is described at the beginning of this chapter, started making and distributing *kasippu*. In those days the demand for *kasippu* was lower. Sajith supplied a number of taverns along a fifteen-mile stretch of the main coastal highway. At that time in the Naeaegama area about twenty people drank each day, many fewer than in the early twenty-first century when several hundred clients might visit one of many taverns in a single afternoon. Sajith manufactured *kasippu* for about fifteen years before he was killed by the police.

Four or five years after Sajith started his business, Gunasinghe, a friend of Sajith's, started producing *kasippu*. His brother sold the product in Naeaegama. As of 2006, Gunasinghe was still making *kasippu*. He had built a large house and bought several acres of cinnamon land with his profits.

---

11. Jayawardena (2000, 130–31) reports a similar trajectory during the colonial period, with arrack renters investing their profits in graphite mines and plantation lands.

His brother no longer sold *kasippu* because his daughters pressured him to stop, saying their reputations suffered from his activities. Around 1980, Ranjan, a friend of Gunasinghe and Sajith, started manufacturing *kasippu*. His entire family engaged in the business. His sisters and many of his nieces and nephews sold Ranjan's *kasippu* in conjunction with four other families who also had a long history of retailing. Ranjan and several other local producers supplied the area market. Ranjan stopped manufacturing in the mid 1990s, when he moved his profits from alcohol into more respectable and legal industries. By 2006, when he was in his mid-forties, he owned four trucks and a tractor, which he hired out for construction projects. Ranjan turned his *kasippu* manufacturing business over to his niece's husband, Gihan.

Between 1995 and 2005, more people began producing *kasippu* because of a greater demand in the area. Gihan manufactured until about 1999. Then, when his sister-in-law Rani and her daughter were jailed for selling drugs, Gihan and his wife stopped making *kasippu* and took over the easier and more profitable drug trade. Toward the end of Gihan's manufacturing career, two other local men started producing but went bankrupt after getting caught and fined several times by the police. Rani's brother then manufactured for a short while, until he was jailed for using drugs. Manufacturing shifted to a nearby town, where several different producers worked to supply the local taverns. The increased demand opened up a space for competition in the local industry, leading to a local power struggle. In most of the surrounding areas, the *kasippu* manufacturers had settled the distribution boundaries, with Gunasinghe and two other large producers supplying the neighboring areas. In the area around Naeaegama in 2004, however, several different producers and their supporting factions vied for supremacy. By early 2006, no one made *kasippu* in the local area, and all four of the main retailers received their supplies from elsewhere. As this brief sketch illustrates, the manufacturing landscape shifts fluidly and frequently.

Relationships and Rivalry between the Retailers

The *kasippu* trade, sometimes supplemented with drug dealing, was run by five main families linked by a bewildering number of intermarriages and sibling connections. These families ran their main businesses near the junction between the road and the railroad tracks, and relatives had in the past five years set up outlets in a newly developed cinnamon garden area. Rivalries and alliances shifted regularly, but generally played out in two main factions, each of which had outlets near the junction and in the cinnamon gardens. Among the retailers, Rani, her brothers Sri Lal and Tushara, and

Sri Lal's wife's brother Amarapala formed one faction. Monika and Fernando formed another faction.

In 2004, an informant suggested that Rani, Sri Lal, Monika, and Fernando all sold about five or six "eights" (25–30 liters) of liquor a day, giving each tavern a daily profit of Rs. 2,500 or Rs. 3,000 (not including fines or bribes). Amarapala, Monika's rival in the cinnamon gardens, had just started selling and had a smaller clientele. The retailers competed fiercely for business. Siri said, "If the police raid Amarapala's house, his wife will say, 'Why don't you go trouble Monika? We only have ten or fifteen people drinking here; Monika has two hundred. We only have these two small bottles, which we sell each day to make a living. But Monika sells ten gallons, and people line up over there like in the theater hall queue!'" Each side tried to hide its activities from the police while simultaneously using the police to harass the others. In addition, the distributors vied for customers, sometimes beating up those who drank regularly from the competitors.

The *kasippu* industry in the area changed quickly depending on internal dynamics and police activities. In late 2005, a large number of places began selling liquor on a small scale. The retailers were always related to the families who specialized in this trade. Soon afterward, the Police Narcotics Bureau cracked down on sales, raiding establishments twice a week. Only the larger establishments that could afford to pay bribes and court fines survived. Both Amarapala and Monika stopped selling for about five months, but the businesses on the railroad track thrived. Rani and one of her daughters, imprisoned on a drug charge, turned their business over to female relatives, causing several outlets to consolidate along the railroad tracks.

After the crackdown ended, Amarapala and Monika resumed selling in the cinnamon garden area. Amarapala's business soared from three to twenty-five "eights" (15 to 125 liters) a day due to a police crackdown in a neighboring area that sent clients south in search of liquor. Still living in a small wooden house, Amarapala and his wife began work on a larger cement structure with the profits from selling *kasippu*. While Amarapala's business prospered, Monika's declined. By 2006 she claimed to have stopped selling altogether, perhaps because her brother, who had been supplying her with *kasippu*, stopped manufacturing. (In addition to the damage done by police raids, a rival tossed a hand grenade into Monika's brother's house. The grenade exploded in a fish tank, slightly injuring Monika's brother but sparing his wife and four children.) Monika started a broom-making business, which initially offered a convenient excuse for customers during a police raid: "I'm here to make brooms, officer!" Later the broom business generated enough money to support Monika's family.

This brief sketch illustrates the volatile nature of the local *kasippu* industry. With a few shot glasses and Rs. 500 in cash for an "eight," families with connections and experience could open a tavern. But raids, bribes, and court fines could bankrupt a retailer just as quickly. Outside pressures and forces within families changed the landscape swiftly. For example, retailers both benefited and suffered from police actions; although a local crackdown temporarily drove many producers and sellers out of business, a crackdown in a neighboring village benefited Amarapala. Despite disputes between retailers, the business remained within a small range of families in the local area. Various family members took up or abandoned selling, depending on the climate and the competition.

Ambivalent Relations with Villagers

As the narrative about Sajith's distillery told at the beginning of the chapter reveals, *kasippu* businesspeople occupied an ambiguous position in the social landscape. Manufacturers were feared as fierce and violent thugs. Many housewives cursed retailers for selling liquor to their husbands. Yet those same husbands often had quite close relationships with tavern owners, and even villagers who disliked *kasippu* manufacturers and retailers often admired them for contributing generously to community events and family celebrations. Bourdieu's discussion of symbolic capital helps make sense of this dynamic (1977). Bourdieu argues that people can interchange cash (economic assets) and status (political clout). For example, *kasippu* businesspeople spent money for the public good or engaged in conspicuous consumption in ways that enhanced their status, which was often considered marginal due to the illegal nature of their work. In turn, people could use social status, or symbolic capital, to benefit their businesses. For example, *kasippu* manufacturers requested business favors from politicians whose campaigns they helped fund. As the following cases illustrate, *kasippu* retailers used their money and their networks to try to enhance their social status. But factors other than wealth affect how much an individual or family can rise in status (Ong 1999). The Naeaegama *kasippu* retailers' efforts met with limited success.[12]

12. Manufacturers of illicit liquor have faced similar stigma in other places and times. For example, Navajo bootleggers acquire wealth and accumulate possessions, but not in a socially acceptable way (Quintero 2002, 11). Historically speaking, a similar dynamic occurred in nineteenth-century Ceylon, where ordinary people made their fortunes in the arrack industry (see chapter 1). Colonial authorities "rented" to local middlemen the right to distill, distribute, and trade liquor in Ceylon. Elites from the highest caste did not want to get involved with the

Hendry's Funeral

While I was in the village in 2004, Fernando's father Hendry, an elder in a *kasippu*-business family, fell ill with throat cancer, and news spread quickly through the village that he was close to death. Villagers' opinions about this man varied. An older laborer I met on my way to the post office told me that Hendry was sick because he drank too much *kasippu*. The laborer insisted that he himself "didn't touch that stuff." Siri also condemned Hendry and his family, calling them "pointless people" (in English); nevertheless he took powdered milk to him when Hendy became unable to eat solid food.

Manori came over to our house soon after Hendry's death. She said, "That man deserved all his suffering, because he sold *kasippu* and destroyed a lot of families. Men drank at Hendry's and then came home to kick over all the pots." Manori went on to call Hendry's daughters "prostitutes." Implicitly supporting Hendry's family, Siri commented, "Lots of people will eat and drink at that house in the days before the funeral." Manori retorted that the place was "dirty"; she did not like the idea of eating there. Siri said, "Villagers will come in droves to Hendry's funeral. He was good with the people, and he knew some important politicians." This conversation revealed the range of opinions villagers held about Hendry's place in the community.

During the three days before his funeral, Hendry's family distributed free liquor to regular customers and to people who came to help with the funeral work. Having a crowd at a funeral is a sign of the family's importance in the village, but Siri felt that many of the people at Hendry's were "third class drinkers." Three influential politicians also attended. Hendry had been an avid supporter of the United National Party (UNP) that was in power at that time, and had organized political meetings for these politicians, who came to the funeral to express their solidarity with Hendry's family and to give a speech to the gathered mourners.

Many villagers disapproved of Hendry's profession, especially wives of drinking men. But quite a few people helped Hendry during his illness and paid respects to his family after his death. Despite the dubious nature of his occupation, Hendry had amassed significant social capital, especially in the

---

business because of the attached stigma, leaving the field open for Karaava-caste Christians. After making their fortunes, these businessmen diversified their holdings and provided their children the cultural capital to advance. "Entrepreneurial wealth did not bring elite status to the arrack renters; the inherited wealth of their sons enabled them to achieve elite status through education, favorable marriages, professional careers, life style, and government" (Peebles 1995, 162). It took at least a generation for the "red blood" of entrepreneurship to fade into the "blue blood" of aristocracy (Carby 1985).

drinking community. His political contacts reaffirmed his status as an important organizer in the UNP, and their presence boosted his standing. The politicians benefited from speaking to the crowd who gathered to honor Hendry. At the same time, many people in Naeaegama condemned Hendry as a drinker and cynically commented on the connection between *kasippu* businesspeople and politicians, both of whose reputations suffered in the process.

Monika's Daana

Contradictory dynamics surrounded the death anniversary almsgiving (*daana*) that the retailer Monika gave for her father. Monika set up six small pavilions in her yard, and had a big table covered with biscuits and cakes brought by her regular clients. During an interview soon after the *daana*, Lalith speculated that Monika might have provided free drinks for her guests, and called the function a *kasippu daana* for drinkers, comparing it disparagingly to an authentic *daana* of free food given to the temple monks. Siri, somewhat enviously, said that he had not received that many presents when he gave a *daana* for his mother. Lalith speculated that all Monika's regular customers probably had to bring a gift.

Monika had a large number of people in her network, many of whom felt socially obligated to her. For example, Edward, a heavy drinker with an account at Monika's tavern, attended the *pirith* chanting ceremony at Monika's the night before the *daana* and the religious function the morning of the event. Aside from Edward's *kasippu* connection, no member of Edward's much higher-status family would have had anything to do with Monika's family. By their presence at her family ceremony, influential drinking villagers lent respectability to Monika and her kin. The large size of the *daana* also indexed the family's financial standing, a point that counted in their favor in the community.

Buddha Statues

Respectable and affluent villagers often made contributions to Buddhist temples. In a bid to raise their ambiguous status, *kasippu* makers attempted to create social capital and legitimacy by building visible religious structures. Although two chief monks told me that they would refuse donations from *kasippu* businesspeople, others did not know or care about the source of contributions (see also Abeyasinghe 2002, 38; Jayawardena 2000, 266). In 2006, three small, covered Buddha statues were constructed in the village area. One, completed by a man whose mother had died in the Indian Ocean Tsunami of 26 December 2004, stood on the school grounds. Another, sponsored by Fernando (Hendry's *kasippu*-selling son), stood on temple land near the railroad tracks. Fernando's mother had also died in the tsunami, and Fernando used his compensation money as well as *kasippu* profits to make the statue. The third structure graced the gate area of another local temple and was funded by Fernando's wife's sister and her husband Tushara (Rani and Sri Lal's brother, who sold *kasippu* at the junction). Siri suggested that Tushara and his wife were jealous of Fernando and his wife, and decided to make a statue of their own. They chose the most visible position, along the road outside the temple compound, so that many people would be able to see the donor's inscription.

An informal survey of villagers revealed the following opinions about Tushara's statue. School principal Greta-miss said that Tushara and his wife were making the statue to offset bad karma. "They want to try to get rid of the sins (*pawu*) they have committed. It is against the Fifth Buddhist Precept to consume alcohol and against the Eightfold Noble Path to produce it. *Kasippu* destroys families. But this statue won't erase the sin. If someone builds a statue with money earned though honest hard work, then he or she can gain merit (*pin*) from the building. But selling *kasippu* is neither honest nor difficult work." In Greta-miss's opinion, the nature of the family business and the source of the money nullified the merit of the donation.

During a conversation with Siri and myself, Siri's neighbor Dharmadasa said that the statue's sponsors offered him some milk rice (*kiribath*) on the day they laid the foundation stone, but he refused to eat it. (Refusing food is a strong negative gesture in Sinhala society.) Dharmadasa said, "That statue was made with *kasippu* money. Neither the milk rice nor the statue is worth anything. Many village people have lost their money and their health by drinking *kasippu*. Tushara and his wife are making the statue to try to escape from the bad effects of their business."

Siri disagreed: "A woman going down the road to bathe at the communal well might pluck a few flowers and offer them to the statue. That gesture will benefit the sponsors. People will think that even though the people who made the structure sold *kasippu,* they did a good deed in providing the statue. This well-wishing offsets the cursing that *kasippu* sellers receive from a man's wife when her husband comes home drunk and makes troubles."

"We go and drink and curse, saying they've put dirty canal water in the *kasippu*. But the women who go by will say that whoever made this statue did a good thing, and bless as they go," Dharmadasa concurred.

Some money buys symbolic capital more easily than others. While drinkers implicitly and explicitly supported the *kasippu* businesspeople, others (particularly drinkers' wives) condemned them. And yet the community appreciated the benefits that the *kasippu* industry could offer. These final comments suggest the ambivalence villagers feel toward *kasippu* business-people and reveal the complex calculations considered by community members when people who engaged in an illegal industry try to convert their wealth into higher social standing.

Conclusion

Political economy includes the study of production, distribution, and consumption of goods and services, as well as the social relations that surround the economic exchanges, including issues of social status. In Naeaegama, subtle and flexible norms govern both the economic and the political relationships between *kasippu* businesspeople, police, and members of the community.

Villagers both feared and respected *kasippu* manufacturers. Employees received special treatment in exchange for their loyalty and silence about illegal activities. Manufacturers also spent their money to maintain good relationships with the local people, who could make their lives difficult if they reported distilling activities to the police. Landowners who hosted *kasippu* manufacturing and storage sites might willingly conspire with the *kasippu* businesspeople, especially if paid for their services. Various villagers and rival retailers gave tips to the police, but at the same time, whether due to fear or a sense of solidarity, people protected *kasippu* manufacturers from the law. Although some landowners reported illicit distilleries to the police, others preferred to handle such situations without making enemies of these powerful village businessmen, who were both dangerous and valued community members.

In addition to the official negative sanctions brought against *kasippu* manufacturing by the law, the community administered informal negative sanctions against the disrespectable business. Because *kasippu* businesspeople could and did make quite a bit of money, they used their money and influence to try to increase their social standing, transforming cash into symbolic capital. But the local discourse on merit and sin allowed villagers to talk about and condemn the moral aspects of these families' activities and to hamper their conversion of financial capital into social status. The three cases above show *kasippu* retailers simultaneously as valued and marginalized members of the community. Retailers used their financial capital to try to obtain social capital, but the harmful and illegal nature of their work made the conversion of cash to status difficult.

Kasippu manufacturing, like other businesses, obeyed laws of supply and demand. But its illegality added another layer of complexity, as police officers simultaneously harassed and allegedly protected the business. The overall governmental regulatory structure, especially the high tax on legal liquor, promoted the profitability of the *kasippu* industry, providing a prime example of the links between the economic and political spheres. Patterns of police complicity with the illegal industry suggested that people created de facto rules for breaking the official laws. Both *kasippu* business-people and complicit police officers profited, but lost respectability from their association.

7 Over the Red Line: Social Rules for Drunken Comportment

A consummate storyteller, Siri had a bottomless stock of jokes and yarns. On the breezy veranda after dinner, he related the following tale: "A man owns a coconut tree. He has cut a blossom and set up a toddy pot to collect the sap, but for three days he has found it mysteriously empty. The next day he hides to see what is happening to his tree. A man who cuts grass for cows comes with a sickle and bag, climbs the tree, drinks what's in the pot, and comes down. The owner confronts the thief, saying "You drank my pot of toddy!" The thief replies, "No, I climbed up the tree to cut the grass." "There's no grass up there!" exclaims the owner. "You're right," says the thief. "That's why I came down!" As this quirky story suggests, an intoxicated drinker lives in a context not quite like the one sober people inhabit, governed by a different set of rules.

In the late 1960s, MacAndrew and Edgerton argued that when people use alcohol as a form of entertainment and recreation, in many cultures they enter a "time out" state where, within limits, "various of the normally operative prescriptions and proscriptions can be set aside" (2003 [1969], 99). Using historical and ethnographic examples, MacAndrew and Edgerton refuted the common assumption that drunkenness leads inevitably to disinhibition and uncontrolled behavior. Instead, they showed that specific cultural rules govern how people drink and how they behave when drunk.

Following MacAndrew and Edgerton's lead, anthropologists who study alcohol use have supported the theory that much of drunken comportment is learned behavior. Psychological experiments show that people are often affected more by what they think they have drunk than by what they actually did drink (Fekjaer 1993, 95; Room 2001, 190). Heath asserts that

"People who expect drinking to result in violence become aggressive; those who expect it to make them feel sexy become amorous; those who view it as disinhibiting are demonstrative" (1998a, 115). He concludes suggestively, "If behavior reflects expectations, then a society gets the kinds of drunks it deserves" (Heath 1998a, 115).

Research in Naeaegama reveals the complexity of "time out" drinking behavior and within-limits conduct. Although within limits, drunken actions sometimes violate expectations for sober behavior. In addition, excess consumption sometimes leads people to violate the limits for drunken comportment. As an intoxicated person violates rules for sober and drunken comportment, his actions can run the gamut from funny to aggravating, dangerous, and even deadly. Those around the drinker may tolerate, ridicule, or curb his behavior. I argue that both humor and hurt spring from breaking the social rules for sober behavior. Laughter and ridicule act as informal correctives to drunken conduct. When these gentle sanctions on intoxicated behavior fail, stronger and more formal ones come into play.

What things do drinkers do in Naeaegama, and how do interlocutors deal with these men? In this chapter, I look at what happens when people exceed tolerated levels of intoxication or, to use a local phrase, go "over the red line" (*ratu ira paenalaa*). I examine funny stories told by both drinkers and non-drinkers about intoxicated people. In addition, I consider some serious ill consequences of drinking and how various members of the village community conceptualize such events. These data reveal what sorts of drunken comportment village norms allow and what sorts they condemn.

Narrating Expectations for "Time Out" Behavior

When men get drunk, they sometimes do things they would not do when sober. Villagers share a fairly standard set of expectations for intoxicated behavior. They claim that intoxicated people often behave without modesty, shame, or fear—the principles governing respectable behavior.[1] If no injuries or lasting damage occur, people may find drunken violations of village norms funny. Laughter simultaneously reaffirms the existence of the broken rule and enforces the belief that drunkards can and do set aside many of the normal demands for accountability.

---

1. Several interchangeable phrases cover the condition of being without modesty, shame, or fear: *vilibaya naetuwa* (without modesty and fear), *vililaejja naetuwa* (without modesty and shame), and *laejja baya naetuwa* (without shame and fear).

Villagers in Naeaegama enjoy telling and laughing at funny stories about inebriated people. In this section I examine two sorts of stories told about drunken behaviors. The first set of stories, told by drinkers themselves, emphasizes the theme of the drinker as a trickster who outwits the plodding policeman by cleverly manipulating social expectations. The second set, related by both drinkers and non-drinkers, vividly illustrates repelling things drinkers do when drunk. Both groups of stories carry a moral and teach a lesson. Taken together, the narratives reveal a gradient of tolerance for a spectrum of drunken behaviors.

Drinkers as Tricksters: Clever Escapes

Along with a man's female relatives, the policeman sets out to constrain alcohol consumption. Police raids at *kasippu* taverns provide a great deal of local excitement. Non-drinkers feel a certain satisfaction when troublesome drunks are hauled to the station, and drinkers rejoice if one of their own can outwit the police. Instances when a drinker avoids arrest or bests a policeman provide excellent material for stories. These stories feature the drinker as a witty trickster and policeman as a plodding straight man.

My research associate Siri had some close calls with the police. He periodically related a favorite story of how his quick thinking got him out of trouble:

> On one occasion, I inadvertently blundered into a police raid at Monika's tavern. I walked in the door with Rs. 100 in my hand. As soon as I entered, I saw the policemen. One officer confronted me and asked me rudely how much *kasippu* I wanted. I thought very quickly, and I replied politely that I didn't know anything about *kasippu;* I had come to contribute Rs. 100 for the *siitu* [communal savings venture] that Monika was organizing. Monika came over. I gave her the 100 rupee bill in my hand and said, "Next Monday's *siitu* is mine; I need the money badly so please don't be late." Then I walked out of the gate and came home. The police caught all the other drinkers. Now the regulars at Monika's place call me "Mr. Siitu." They were amazed at my brain.

After relating this story, Siri emphasized the mental dexterity of drinkers not yet incapacitated by alcohol.

A drinker of my acquaintance narrated another police encounter as follows:

> I went to an out-of-the-way *kasippu* tavern. It was in a cul-de-sac, and suddenly the police appeared at the only exit. What to do? There was a small red calf tied to a coconut tree. I spoke loudly as if I was talking to someone in

the house, and said "I'll go tie the calf somewhere else." I untied the animal. "Come, come, Little Red, we'll go," I said, and I walked past the police toward the gate with the cow. I went out the gate, tied the calf to another tree, got on my bike, and came home.

The expectation that the police will easily round up their suspects makes it especially funny when the crafty drinker outwits the law.

These same dynamics and expectations reappear in a favorite drinking joke: On Vesak Poya day, a policeman catches a drunkard. "Why are you drinking on Vesak Day?" he asks. The drunkard replies, "Oh, Sir, on this day Lord Buddha was born, and I am happy. And on this day he attained Enlightenment, and I am happy. But today is also the day the Lord Buddha died, and I am very sad about that, so I have had a half bottle of arrack." This joke makes use of a number of common cultural patterns, working up to a justification of drinking on Vesak Poya (arguably the most important Buddhist holiday of the year, the one day above all on which not to drink). In the local cultural logic, death causes sadness and justifies drinking. Village men regularly drink at funerals and *daanas* (almsgivings commemorating dead relatives). But drinking violates many Buddhist tenets. If they follow the Fifth Precept, Buddhists should never take intoxicating substances. Villagers are particularly observant of the precepts on Poya (full moon) holidays, particularly on Vesak Poya. The joke above derives its humor from the drunkard's audacious assertion of chummy familiarity with the Lord Buddha, mourning his death as he would that of an ordinary villager and in the process behaving in a distinctly unreligious fashion.

In this type of joke and story, the drinker character draws on common cultural expectations—the duty of a grass-cutter to search out cow fodder, the right of a *siitu* member to hand over his weekly contribution, the right of an owner to move his cow to fresh pasture, and the assumption that a villager will drink to mourn a death. The protagonists manipulate these expectations to trick a critic (the policeman or toddy tree owner) and slip out of trouble. The drinking men who relate these stories set their protagonists (and by proxy themselves) in contrast to ordinary people who obey all the cultural rules or are caught and get into trouble for their offenses. The clever trickster transgresses without punishment.

In the trickster genre, the protagonist's mental dexterity proves that drinking has not incapacitated him. These stories about outwitting the police emphasize a state short of visible intoxication. In contrast, stories about the unappealing things drinkers do usually focus on extreme stages of inebriation.

Vomit Stories

Although the jokes and adventures related in the trickster genre suggest that drinkers can break cultural rules without suffering consequences, stories about extreme intoxication emphasize the unacceptable category crises that drinking can bring about (Douglas 1966). This genre focuses on the unappealing things that drinkers do when they have had too much alcohol.

At the village temple, the monk and a visitor related several stories about distasteful events. During this conversation I heard two versions of a story about vomit, quite similar to a third related to me in another context. The most elaborate version of the story came from Mahanama Thero, who narrated some verses written by a famous monk named Miripaeni Dharmaratne. "A drinker drinks, then falls in a ditch. He vomits. A dog comes and licks the vomit off his face. The guy feels the dog's rough tongue and thinks that a barber is shaving him. He enjoys it. When the dog has finished one side, the guy turns the other cheek. The dog lifts his leg, pees on him, and goes away. That's the result of being a drunkard."

When our laughter subsided, the visitor told a story about the aftermath of a wedding. "One drunk was sleeping on a bed, another on the floor. The one on the bed vomited, and the one on the floor licked it up." The audience made appropriate noises of disgust.

In a different context, Siri recounted a similar story. "A drunk passes out on the side of the road, and a dog licks the vomit off his lips. The man says, 'Okay, *machan* [buddy, male cousin, brother-in-law], give me another kiss.'"

These three vomit stories condemn extreme intoxication by highlighting the many social conventions broken by drunkards. In two of the stories, the drunken man thinks a dog is a human being (first a barber, then a cousin), and in the last story the drinker happily accepts a homosexual kiss. In one story a man gets peed on by a dog; in two stories dogs pollute men's mouths by licking up vomit; and in one version the vomit-lapping dog has been exchanged for a vomit-lapping drunkard. The stories suggest that drunkards forget a series of basic rules: what to eat, where to sleep, whom to kiss, how to stay clean, and how to relate to dogs. No one gets hurt, but the drinkers in the stories lose dignity and breach hygienic standards in the starkest possible ways. The stories derive their humor from the violation of cultural rules and categories. Each story enforces a message: "Don't drink to excess, or you too might do things like this." Both drinkers and non-drinkers related stories of this nature, suggesting that they shared a common concept of unacceptable drunken comportment.

Stories About Hooting, Pissing, and Failing to Zip

Clever-trickster stories tacitly condone moderate drinking, and vomit stories condemn excess. Another set of real and fictitious stories, these concerning attire and urination, reveal limits for drunken comportment of casual drinkers and wedding guests. In the following examples, the narrators paired stories about drunks with comments about informal social sanctions, particularly those imposed by teenage boys.

Two tales about improper dress included remarks allegedly made by hotel staff at family weddings about the effect of liquor on sartorial elegance. A witty observer of human foibles, a chef manning the buffet line reportedly dubbed one drinker "the guest who ate the meat curry with his tie." A doorman referred to an intoxicated individual who lost the sarong to his outfit and wandered around clad only in his tunic as "the gentleman in the dress." Placing these simultaneously respectful and dismissive words in the mouths of strangers heightens their humorous effect. These examples suggest that although men can and sometimes *must* drink at weddings, they should regulate their high to safeguard their dignity.

Stories about inappropriate urination also drew disapproving laughter. Siri and Manori had the following conversation one afternoon. Siri reported that a drunk at the junction had peed behind a shop into an alley that led to someone's house. Manori called this man "out of his right mind" (*sihiya naeae*). Siri added that this man forgot to zip up afterward. Siri then related a famous incident where an important political figure attended a fancy wedding held at the four-star Bentota Beach Hotel. This man drank too much and urinated in the swimming pool. Siri said that "everyone" knew this story, and the carpenter working at Siri's house confirmed the fact.

Manori replied that when a heavy-drinking neighbor went by on the road without zipping, the boys would hoot. Siri and Manori then discussed the case of another neighbor, who swore in a rhythmic and poetic way when drunk. The previous day some boys had hooted at him. That neighbor had scolded Manori because her son participated. Manori said that she retorted, "If you were sober, no one would hoot. If a person is naked, boys can hoot at him! You go swearing on the road. Today you just got a hooting. Next time you'll get hit! If you want the hooting to stop, stop swearing as you go on the road. Stop swearing while you're drunk. The kids are just kids. Next time they'll throw stones." She asserted that boys had a right to hoot at a drunkard who came down the road like a madman (*pissek*) "without his sarong." Siri then related a favorite story about Sumanapala, a man from a neighboring village, who passed out in a ditch from drinking too much.

The local boys got some "chicken dye" (a cheap water-soluble coloring used for making brooms) and painted it all over Sumanapala's body, even under his sarong.

In this conversation, Siri and Manori touched on various category violations and the steps taken to admonish the offender. When intoxicated, drunkards may forget where to urinate, where to sleep, and how to wear their clothing (ties unstained, trousers zipped, and sarongs securely fastened). Hotel staff reportedly noted excesses, and the local teenage boys chastised drinkers by hooting at them and painting them bright colors—attention-grabbing and humiliating but harmless and humorous sanctions. Manori's assertions that the boys would beat and stone a drunkard were couched in a fictive "next time"; informal sanctions rarely involved physical violence. A drinker and an adamant anti-drinker, Siri and Manori saw eye to eye on the limits of acceptable drunken comportment and the informal steps taken to enforce them.

The examples above portray a continuum of comportment. Judging from reactions to the vomit stories, both drinkers and non-drinkers concur that drinking until one is nearly comatose clearly exceeds the limits of acceptable conduct. Lesser levels of drunkenness, especially at wedding celebrations, are tolerated, unless or until individuals violate norms for respectable dress, speech, and bodily functions. Breaches of these cultural expectations result in humiliating but otherwise harmless consequences. At the other end of the continuum, trickster stories laud the state where the drinker is still clever enough to outwit his opponent. By telling trickster stories, drinkers lay claim to an acceptable high, and by laughing at these stories, non-drinkers tacitly agree.

Mishaps and Accidents

Respectable demeanor is not the only casualty of inebriation. When men go "over the red line," unexpected and unfortunate consequences can result. Both drinkers and non-drinkers find drunken outcomes funny unless or until someone gets hurt. Often the line between tragedy and harmless foolishness is drawn only in retrospect. Focusing on the less frequent but most regrettable outcomes, the World Health Organization sees intoxication as integrally involved with "acute adverse health consequences" such as "accidental injury and poisoning, suicide, interpersonal violence and assaults" (World Health Organization 2004a, 46). In the rest of this chapter, I address Naeaegama norms governing humorous alcohol-related mishaps as well as more serious accidents, fights, and suicide attempts.

Mishaps

Drinkers sometimes told stories about funny (but not dangerous) things that happened when they were drunk. For example, Siri talked about a time that he and his friend Wijepala had two baby pigs in a large box.

> We were both drunk after riding home on the office train from Colombo. We were each carrying one side of the pig box. Near the school, the rope around the box broke and the pigs ran into the forest. It was dark out, so we couldn't search for the pigs. We both went home without telling anyone about the problem. After a few months, local people began to complain that bark from cinnamon plants had mysteriously been eaten. Wijepala and I took a gun and went to see if we could find the pigs, but we couldn't. Three years later, a fellow came running saying, "There is a strange muddy creature in that forest. Come quickly and bring your gun!" Wijepala and I thought it could be one of the pigs. We took the gun to the garden. That pig was three feet tall and six feet long! He was stuck in the mud. We shot him, butchered him, and gave the meat to various people. A few months later there was a complaint in a nearby village of eaten cinnamon bark, but we never found the other pig.

Siri also liked to tell a story about what happened at his wedding.

> Botin was dead drunk. Three other wedding guests, also fairly drunk, decided to take him home. He was heavy. Liilawathie had left her rope bed outside. The guys took the bed and loaded Botin on it. One took the front and two took the back. Near the paddy field, there was a hole in the road. They had forgotten about it, and the guy in front stepped into it. The guys in back fell down too. Botin and the bed fell into the paddy field, and the bed broke. Botin was all muddy. They somehow got him the rest of the way home and left him near his house. Botin's wife couldn't recognize him because he was covered with mud and looked like a devil. The others took the broken bed back to Liilawathie's and came home. In the early morning Liilawathie came shouting, complaining to my father that the bed was broken. My father replied, "The married couple's bed is fine, so how come yours is broken?" But he gave Liilawathie some money for the bed.

The consequences of these two cases involved minimal damage: a broken bed and some nibbled cinnamon bushes. In other cases, drunken accidents have more serious fallout, and the stories are no longer laughing matters.

Over the Red Line: Serious Accidents

Villagers used the phrase "going over the red line" to describe a stage of serious intoxication, particularly one that results in adverse consequences.

The term refers to the red mark on a car's speedometer that indicates the official speed limit. People gauged whether someone had exceeded the acceptable level of inebriation based on behavior, not on the quantity of liquor consumed. When "over the red line," a drinker can cause harm to himself and others.

Experts and laypeople alike agree that drinking alcohol impairs physical coordination. In Euro-American contexts, many examples of alcohol-related accidents involve driving under the influence (Single 2000, 125). In Naeaegama, few people own cars, but accidents occur with other forms of transportation. For example, one drinker told me, "One night I went to a friend's ceremony and got very drunk. I 'lost the red line' and had trouble cycling. About a quarter mile from home, I met an oncoming van, which didn't dim its lights. I couldn't see. I lost control of my bike, and I fell into a drainage ditch by the side of the road. I broke my left wrist in the fall. In the future I will make different arrangements for transportation home from celebrations!" Much like revelers who arrange for a designated driver when traveling by car, this drinker vowed to take steps to diminish the dangers he faced while intoxicated.

Clouded judgment caused the demise of a drunken village peddler. Karunasoma, fifty-three years old at the time of his death, drank daily, especially in the afternoons after selling his bicycle load of brooms. His wife often tried to intercept him at the junction to collect some of his money for home consumption. Siri related this story to me:

> At about 9:00 one evening, Karunasoma and his wife went to the junction. They bought some goods for home, and Karunasoma, who was already drunk, wanted another quarter. His wife refused to give him any money for this purpose, and they had a loud fight. When they reached the railroad tracks, the rail gate was closed for the 9:15 night train. [In such a situation, many bikers go around the barriers instead of waiting the three or four minutes for the train to come.] Angry, Karunasoma said, "I'm going home," and tried to cross the tracks even though the train was very close. The rail gatekeeper and several other men tried to pull him back. But Karunasoma was "over the red line" and they couldn't stop him. He was on the tracks when the train came through. The engine hit Karunasoma directly and dragged his body about forty feet. The side of his head was bashed in and he had a large wound on his back as well. He died on the spot.

The speakers in both of these instances used the metaphor of exceeding "the red line." They implicitly suggested that intoxication, like vehicular speed, can be gauged, and dangers result when drinkers exceed the limit.

This Naeaegama folk wisdom echoes scholarly research, which indicates that "Moderate doses of alcohol have been demonstrated in controlled experimental studies to have cognitive and psychomotor effects that are relevant to the risk of injury, such as reaction time, cognitive processing, coordination and vigilance" (World Health Organization 2004a, 46). In local parlance, "the red line" marks the difference between being nicely high and being out of control. Siri asserted that in the former state, drink makes one clever, but in the latter, it impairs one's judgment.

Dangerous Tipple

In addition to risking ordinary accidents while drunk, drinkers can also suffer serious consequences from drinking poisonous substances in pursuit of a high. Of the many sorts of alcohol, only ethanol (ethyl alcohol) is fit for human consumption. Other alcohols (for example, methanol and fusel oils) are toxic, and drinking methyl alcohol can lead to blindness (Ritson and Thorley 2000, 5). Over the years, a number of Naeaegama men have died from drinking something besides their usual tipple.

During an interview, I asked Charith if anyone in the village had died from drinking. Charith, a daily drinker, thought of the following two tales. He did not mention the numerous long-term village drinkers who suffered from ethanol-related diseases. Instead, he talked about the following cases where drinkers ingested the wrong sort of alcohol.

Charith said, "About fifteen years ago, a drum of liquid washed up at the beach. People opened it and it smelled like alcohol. They took it to the *kasippu* seller. The *kasippu* seller mixed the contents of the drum with *kasippu*, drank some himself, and sold the rest to his clients. The seller died, as did eight other people. A few went blind." Charith then described an incident in 1993 when two people died and several others lost or weakened their eyesight. Due to a concurrent police crack-down on *kasippu*, two men at the junction were experimenting with cheap new alcoholic drinks, hoping to find a mix that they could sell to the area drinkers at something below the going rate for a shot of arrack. They made one mixture of "wine spirits" (used to light Petromax lamps), water, lime, tomato juice, tea, sugar, and curry leaves (*karapinchaa*). Four men drank the concoction. Later, they made another mixture of methyl alcohol used for polishing iron. Both mixtures were poisonous. Of the four people who drank them, two passed away and two ended up in the hospital seriously ill, suffering from blindness, vomiting, and blood loss.

Although in the West drinking non-beverage alcohol is characteristic of severe alcoholism (Royce and Scratchley 1996), in Sri Lanka, poverty enhances the temptation to take such drinks, particularly among the group of men who rely on illicit liquor. Although richer *kasippu* drinkers switch to legal arrack for the duration of a police crack-down, many poorer men search for something cheaper to drink. *Kasippu* sellers and their loyal clients occasionally experiment with poisonous substances with ill effects. The quality of the drink, as well as the quantity imbibed, can cause great harm.

In the accidents described above, danger arises from three sources: violating commonsense safety rules while drunk, doing risky things to obtain drinks, and drinking impure substances in search of a high. Pernanen suggests that it is difficult to draw a line between harmless human folly and dangerous risk (1991, 7). Often the distinction appears in hindsight; if actions have bad outcomes, the event loses its humor. Villagers reacted to these accidental deaths with sadness or wry comments about the useless-ness of excessive and compulsive alcohol consumption.

When intoxicated people confront the realities of physics and chemis-try, the accidental consequences provide ample feedback on appropriate behavior. In contrast, when inebriated individuals tangle with each other or their sober neighbors, community members must step in to enforce the rules surrounding drunken comportment. I turn now to a darker side of intoxication in some Naeaegama villagers—the tendency toward aggression and violence.

Fights

Although people often associate alcohol with excitement, joviality, and re-laxation, alcohol can also produce gloom and sullenness, or bad temper and argumentativeness. Clinical studies link alcohol consumption with aggres-sion (Blanchard et al. 1993; Kelly and Cherek 1993, 40; Taylor and Cher-mack 1993, 78). The concept of "alcoholic myopia," in which the drinker focuses only on a few cues rather than a wider range, combined with the extremes of sentiment (including both affection and anger) induced by al-cohol can lead to an exaggerated response to circumstances (Kunitz et al. 2000, 125). If immediacies distract attention from more distant consid-erations, it can cause the drinker to ignore social controls, consequences, and punishments (Room 2001, 191). As a psychoactive substance, alcohol clearly has the power to alter a person's mood and judgment.

How a mood manifests in a drinker's behavior depends on the specific context as well as cultural norms governing drunken comportment. In Can-ada, alcohol-related violence most often takes place between drinkers at the drinking establishment or between intimates after drinking (Pernanen

1991). In Sri Lanka, alcohol use also correlates with violence. For example, a survey of patients performed at the Colombo North General Hospital in 1994 revealed that "77.2% of instances of assault were associated with alcohol ingestion, either by the assailant or by the victim" (World Health Organization 2004b, 5). In Naeaegama, one villager commented, "If you have one drunkard, you have more than enough to have a big fight." But although alcohol consumption can cause or exacerbate fights, rules still govern drunken comportment during these disputes.

A lively conversation between Lalith and his wife Janaki illustrated Naeaegama norms surrounding alcohol use and conflict. Lalith said, "Men can't fight without a drink. Without alcohol, they just have a discussion about a problem."

Janaki was fixing us tea. She called from the kitchen, "People can't scold each other if they're not drunk. When they are sober, they will think of all the good, helpful things that person has done for them, so they will not scold. After liquor, they will pick up one fault and fight about that. People drink first, then scold."

Lalith agreed, saying, "After a drink, the language gets insulting and the other side gets mad too. If the other side is also drunk, there will be a fight. But although drunken people swear a lot, they don't come to blows because they have no strength. If someone hits a drunk, he will fall down."

Janaki continued, "Being drunk is an excuse. The person can apologize later and say 'I didn't mean it! I have no memory of this! What did I say? Please excuse me.'"

"This excuse is a way to get out of the argument by blaming the drink. The drinker will meet the person he scolded the next morning and will be very humble," concurred Lalith. With these words, Lalith and Janaki disapprovingly but concisely outlined the Naeaegama rules for fighting while drunk.

Around the world, drinkers behave according to learned patterns. An altered state of consciousness that men could assume at will, drunkenness sanctioned certain behaviors in Naeaegama that would not be condoned in someone sober. Room asks, "If bad behaviour is a foreseeable consequence of drinking, why do some societies nevertheless not hold the drinker responsible?" (2001, 189). Intoxication is at best a flimsy excuse, because people could avoid bad behavior by avoiding drunkenness altogether. Furthermore, drinkers can claim to have drunk more than they actually have had in order to act with impunity. In this state of pseudointoxication, "drunkenness is feigned to take advantage of the excuse thus offered" (Room 2001, 196). In Naeaegama, some village drinkers actually suffered blackouts, but others only pretended. One informant explicitly admitted his pretence and asserted that other drinkers of his acquaintance occasionally did the same thing. "Those who wish to invoke the excuse will often take special care to advertise that they are 'drunk,'" suggests Room (2001, 190), characterizing this as a strategy of the relatively powerless.

I suggest that in Naeaegama, the solution to "the problem of responsibility for the foreseeable" (Room 2001, 194) lies in the complex social rules governing altercations involving alcohol. Villagers did not hold intoxicated individuals fully accountable for their actions—unless their behavior violated well-established and commonly recognized limits. In Naeaegama, drinkers could engage in verbal fights, which no one took seriously. Factoring the "time out" nature of drunken disputes into account, sober people usually refused to take offence at the utterances of their inebriated neighbors. Similarly, drinkers themselves carried forward no grudges from drunken disputes. One villager told me, "Friends drink together and then fight together," implying that such fights occurred frequently but signified little. Villagers took care not to let confrontations with or between drunks escalate beyond verbal exchanges. In most situations, these rules and safeguards effectively contained and constrained alcohol-related aggression. The introduction of physical violence or sober disputants marked the boundaries of unacceptable altercations. Dangerous situations could develop when drunken disputants came to blows or when sober people quarreled with inebriated neighbors, as the following case illustrates.

Spat About Pirith

A fight between Siri's and Wasantha's families discussed below illustrated how intoxication could exacerbate annoyances and lead to angry outbursts. In this case, sober people got involved in a fight started by an inebriated individual, escalating the dispute and causing serious long-term consequences.

Every morning at 4:30 a.m., the temple loudspeaker broadcasted an hour of chanting (*pirith*). Both Siri and Wasantha lived close to the temple, and the noise considerably inconvenienced their households. The day prior to this dispute, Siri, a bit drunk, had gone to the temple to request that the monks cease using the loudspeaker before dawn, or at least turn the volume down. The next day Wasantha got drunk and started shouting in front of Siri's and Telsie's gate, accusing Siri of persuading the monks to turn the speakers to face toward Wasantha's house. All the disputants later agreed that if everyone had ignored Wasantha at this stage, the conflict would have faded quickly. But Telsie yelled back to Wasantha, reminding him that his older brother had donated the loudspeaker system to the temple. Wasantha then began insulting Telsie and her family. Siri and Telsie shouted back.

Soon after Siri and Telsie legitimized the interaction by getting involved, the confrontation escalated from words to physical aggression. Stories differed on who did what to whom, but several points of commonality included that Siri and Wasantha traded blows that day, and that the following day Siri's son scuffled with Wasantha. Several neighbor women intervened to stop the physical violence, but other members of Siri's and Wasantha's families joined the shouting, including Wasantha's wife Manori and mother Padma. Later Siri got drunk, went to Padma's house, and yelled at her disrespectfully. The escalation stopped at that point, but the two families, which had associated quite closely before, ceased speaking with each other.

Confrontations started by inebriated drinkers often pass without note. But because the participants in this case used physical force and because sober and non-drinking family members on both sides got involved, the dispute escalated. An intoxicated person can explain his conduct by saying he did not mean to start a fight, but sober people have no such defense. Interestingly, when participants retold the story, they did not mention the drunken actions of the initial combatants, although liquor played a major role in starting the rift. Instead, they placed most of the blame on the sober female and male participants—those who fought without the mitigating excuse of alcohol. This case illustrates in the breach the rules that circumscribe alcohol-related altercations.

Suicide

Sri Lanka has one of the world's highest rates of suicide and suicide attempts (Marecek 1998, 69). Research suggests a strong correlation between alcohol use and self-harm in Sri Lanka. One report indicated that 84 percent of suicides in a local area were committed after consuming liquor (World Health Organization 2004b, 5). Based on a long-term study on self-inflicted pesticide poisoning (a common means of attempting suicide in Sri Lanka), Flemming Konradsen, Wim van der Hoek, and Pushpalatha Peiris conclude that "alcohol misuse was a major or important precipitant factor in 40% of the self-harm cases" (2006, 1712). They report that many boys and men drank to intoxication before their self-harm attempts, and wives and children often drank poison to protest chronic alcohol abuse of male household members.

Though violent and self-destructive, Sri Lankan suicide cases follow a cultural logic (Marecek 1998). In the United States, suicide often indicates great despair or depression. In Sri Lanka, suicide indexes badly damaged social relations. Men and women might drink poison or jump in front of a moving train because of a shame they cannot bear or an anger they cannot express in other ways (M. Gamburd 2000). Star-crossed lovers also sometimes resort to suicide when other attempts to influence their families fail (Konradsen, van der Hoek, and Peiris 2006). The shame and anger felt in these cases often denote a perception of broken cultural rules, or, in cases of thwarted love affairs, anger at the rules that keep couples apart. In male suicide attempts, alcohol may exacerbate the emotions prompting the self-harm, as the following cases suggest.

Kerosene Oil Lamp

A local drinker named Banda told me the story of his suicide attempt. This story involves issues of anger, shame, and alcohol consumption.

Banda on occasion drank with Lakshman, a heavy-drinking relative of Banda's wife Nandani. Lakshman's wife left him because he drank and hit her. Lakshman periodically visited the Naeaegama area, drinking with different men and sleeping at their houses until their wives chased him off. When his money ran out, he asked people for bus fare home. If he accumulated enough, he went drinking again.

One morning when neither Banda's wife Nandani nor son Manoj was at home, Lakshman came to Banda's house with a bottle of arrack. They drank. Banda fed Lakshman lunch. Lakshman went away saying that he would come back in the afternoon and spend the night. Because Lakshman had Rs. 5,000 or 6,000 with him, Banda knew he would return with another bottle. When Nandani came home, Banda told her that Lakshman was visiting, and asked her to prepare a special meal. Banda felt that Nandani could not refuse this request because Lakshman was her relative.

That afternoon, Lakshman arrived with a bottle. Banda and Lakshman started drinking in Banda's room. Then Banda's son Manoj came home. Manoj disapproved of Banda's drinking in general, and disliked Lakshman because he drank and got Banda drunk too. Manoj came into Banda's room, saw Lakshman, and left in silence. He stormed into the kitchen and yelled at Nandani, saying, "This house has become an open bar. Someone brings a bottle, my mother provides the 'bites,' and my father provides the restaurant to stay and drink. This place has become a brothel. People drink and sleep here." Manoj then threatened to burn the house down.

Banda was shocked that Manoj would shout and fight with his parents in front of an outsider. In addition, because Lakshman was a relative, Banda felt that Manoj was out of place for objecting to this particular person's presence.

That day there was no electricity. It was dark outside, and Nandani was cooking by the light of the kerosene lamp. Banda went to the kitchen and took the lamp. He told Manoj, "Don't burn the house down; keep it for yourself. I will burn myself."

Banda grabbed the lamp. He wanted to pour the kerosene on himself to frighten his family. He tried to keep the wick out of the way and just pour the oil on his head. But he was drunk, and the wick fell on his head. As Banda pushed the burning oil off his head, his hands also caught fire. He ran to the outside shower and opened the tap. Then he passed out.

Shame and anger motivated Banda's impulsive action. He felt that his son had overstepped socially acceptable boundaries in his expression of anger. Demonstrating his own anger and trying to scare his family into better behavior, Banda ended up burning himself badly. If Banda had not been drunk, he might not have reacted as strongly to the emotional stimulus, and his threat might have remained merely that. But had Banda been sober in the first place, his son would not have been enraged and fought with his parents in front of an outsider. In this case intoxication may have exaggerated Banda's emotional response to his son's attempt to set household limits on alcohol use.

Death by Herbicide

Banda's case ended with a long but successful recovery. Other cases have ended more tragically. In another village household, Hema's son Upul, thirty-seven, committed suicide in 2003. He drank heavily and had caused Hema considerable trouble. Hema's statements about Upul during our interview revealed both rage and grief. As in the previous example, this case deals with themes of anger, shame, and disrupted social relationships.

Several days before his suicide, the police caught Upul drinking *kasippu*. He faced a fine of Rs. 2,000 or a short jail term. Siri asserted that Hema had refused to pay the fine. Hema refuted this, and said that she had told her son that she would find a way to get the money. Then Siri suggested that Upul might have worried that his parents would be unable to raise the funds. Hema did not deny this. Siri and Hema agreed that Upul was ashamed by the thought of going to jail. Unlike the clever tricksters in the stories related above, Upul was caught and had to pay the consequences.

Upul often fought with his parents when drunk. "It was war! (*yuddha!*)," Hema exclaimed. Upul and his father had destroyed some of the kitchen chairs while fighting. Upul also fought with his mother; once he broke her elbow, an injury that sent her to the hospital for a week. Some fights took place late at night, and on several occasions Hema and her husband found themselves on their neighbor's doorstep at 1:00 a.m. This situation suggests that Upul regularly exceeded the social limits placed on drunken comportment by escalating from verbal interactions to assault and the destruction of property.

I asked what fueled Upul's anger. Hema said that his wife had gone to the Middle East without telling any of them what she planned to do. She had gone abroad to earn money for them to build a house. As described in chapter 5, female labor migration does correlate in some cases with male alcohol consumption, particularly if husbands could not earn enough to support their families. Upul may have felt angry about not having a complete family at home, and his wife's absence might have challenged his masculinity. Hema angrily blamed her daughter-in-law's migration for causing problems, and condemned the young woman's heartlessness in refusing to visit after her husband's death or to fund any funeral expenses. But I suspect that Upul's wife went abroad to escape an abusive marriage. At one point in the interview, Hema admitted that Upul's problems with alcohol started before his marriage. Hema said she "gave him a woman" to try to moderate his habit, a strategy that seems to have failed.[2]

Upul was drunk the day he poisoned himself. He fought with everyone he met and broke all the light fixtures in the house. He bought a bottle of Dramaxone (a chemical herbicide) from a nearby fertilizer factory, and told his brother's family that he planned to drink it. Hema claimed that no one told her about this. That night, after fighting with his parents and chasing them out of the house, Upul drank the poison. At eight o'clock in the evening, the neighbors heard him crying, thrashing around, yelling for help, and calling out for water. No one went to him because they had heard him fighting with his parents and knew he was badly drunk. The sounds stopped at about 2:30 in the morning.

The next morning, someone told Hema that her son was dead in the house. She thought that he had probably just passed out, so she said "Good!" But he was actually dead. They took the body to a nearby town for a postmortem. Hema gave evidence before the court that her son drank heavily

---

2. Villagers often held a man's female relatives, particularly his wife and mother, responsible for his intoxication. For example, Hema held her daughter-in-law responsible for not stopping Upul's drinking, even though her daughter-in-law was only seventeen years old when they married. In the fight described above about the temple loudspeaker, Padma held Telsie responsible for not reining in her son, and Siri held Padma responsible for not advising Wasantha. In Banda's suicide attempt, Manoj held his mother Nandani responsible for not stopping Banda and Lakshman from drinking together. Naeaegama women tried to control "their" men's drinking and fighting behaviors, often without much success.

and had broken her elbow in a past fight. The magistrate remarked that she must be glad he was dead. But Hema said she was suffering.

With tears in her eyes, Hema showed me a laminated picture of the grave and the printed burial notice. She reiterated that when Upul drank, no one else could stay in the house. But the next morning he would wake up, ask her for 5 rupees for beedies, and say, "Did I scold you last night!? No way!" Reminiscent, Hema insisted, "He was very good when he was sober. One day when I said I wanted to eat sweet potatoes, he brought a whole kilogram of them from the market. He earned money plucking coconuts and bought food for the house." After his death, Hema and her husband, a partially blind carpenter, had no income. "All our daughters are married and have problems of their own. Our surviving son won't stay in this house because he is afraid of his brother's ghost.[3] Without Upul, there is no money coming into the household."

Several themes emerge regarding broken social rules in this case. Hema called Upul "good" when he conformed to the correct filial role, bringing home money and food for the house and relating cordially with his parents. But he was a mean drunk. Upul may have had a mental illness, which he self-medicated with alcohol, or perhaps alcohol dependence created the dramatic personality shifts that Hema describes; such changes are characteristic of moderate alcoholism in the West (Royce and Scratchley 1996). His wife's employment in the Middle East may have challenged Upul's sense of self-worth, and the threat of a jail sentence for drinking illicit liquor may have enhanced his feelings of poverty and powerlessness (Konradsen, van der Hoek, and Peiris 2006, 1717). Whatever the underlying physical or psychological causes, Upul frequently broke the village rules for drunken comportment when he damaged furniture and fixtures, brawled with his father, and injured his mother. In the densely populated village, most emergencies immediately generated a crowd of supportive relatives and neighbors. But in this case, knowing Upul's character when drunk, no one stepped in to help during the hours that he shouted in pain. Had Upul received immediate medical attention, his suicide attempt might not have succeeded. The herbicide was poisonous, but the damaged social relationships were fatal.

---

3. Four months after Upul's death, the family held an exorcism ceremony. They claimed that Upul's ghost was troubling them by moving chairs around, making strange noises, and causing other problems. Although her youngest son still refused to return home, one of Hema's daughters had moved into the house with her family, providing support for her elderly parents.

Conclusion

Drinking, like other behaviors, is governed by social rules. Although inebriated individuals can get away with some conduct forbidden to sober people, well established and widely accepted rules delineate the limits of acceptable drunken comportment.

In many contexts, particularly at weddings and other celebrations, people expect and accept a certain level of intoxication. When drunken actions result in harmless or clever incidents, people laugh at the outcomes. Laughter also greets instances where drinkers exceed the norms of the celebratory "time out" state and forget standards for attire, dignity, and hygiene. Irresponsible incidents that cause inconvenience (such as urinating in a swimming pool, breaking a bed, or setting pigs loose in the cinnamon garden) are irritating at the time but make funny stories in the long term. Laughter gently polices social boundaries by ridiculing drinkers who break them, and local boys impose informal discipline by hooting at drunkards on the road.

Breaking social rules can lead to tragic as well as funny results. Villagers use the metaphor of going "over the red line" to describe obvious inebriation, particularly that which results in dangerous impairment or harm. Drinkers and non-drinkers share a common conception of these excesses. Instances that lead to alcohol-related accidents, injuries, and death fall into this category. When drinking leads to bad judgment (such as crossing the railroad track in front of a speeding train or blinding oneself by drinking methanol), the serious consequences speak for themselves. In other cases, it falls on sober people to monitor proper behavior.

Villagers in Naeaegama share a clear sense of limits on what MacAndrew and Edgerton refer to as "drunken changes-for-the-worse" (2003, 36), particularly those concerning aggression. Naeaegama villagers anticipate that drinkers will violate some social rules, but hold them strictly to others. Sober people give the inebriated some leeway with verbal invective, and social norms advise people not to take seriously anything a drunkard might say. Some drinkers take advantage of this impunity, deliberately getting intoxicated (or pretending to do so) in order to start an argument without risking serious consequences. The impunity ends at the level of verbal abuse; inebriated people should not lash out physically. For the most part, drinkers follow this rule. Drunken disputes grow serious only when drinkers introduce physical violence or when sober people get involved. With the introduction of physical blows and sober disputants, fights overflow the space reserved for drunken behavior and become serious village matters.

Like fights, suicides conform to predictable cultural patterns, with self-harm attempts often associated with alcohol use. Suicides break certain social rules. For example, strict Buddhist dictates forbid taking one's own life. At the same time, suicides also protest the breaking of social rules. Suicide expresses an individual's outrage over unfulfilled obligations, commitments, and expectations, and can indicate damaged social relationships. With alcohol exaggerating emotional highs and lows, shame or anger felt over one's own or someone else's behavior can spur self-harm. By doing physical damage, suicidal drinkers violate drinking rules, albeit injuring themselves instead of others.

In Naeaegama, most drinking takes place within well-established social limits and has few grave or lasting consequences. Yet serious mishaps, accidents, and fights sometimes spring from risky behavior. Intoxicated individuals with impaired judgment can hurt themselves and others while drunk or while trying to get drunk. Although many such cases indicate isolated instances of excess alcohol consumption, others point to serious issues of alcohol dependence. I turn to this topic in the next chapter.

8 Too Much Is Good for Nothing: Alcohol Dependence

People everywhere strike a balance between pleasure and pathology when discussing alcohol consumption (Keane 2002). Martin Plant and Douglas Cameron write, "We drink alcohol because it is good for us, and study it because it is bad for us" (2000, 237). Small quantities of alcohol are good for the body and facilitate interactions, but excess drinking can cause physical, psychological, and social problems. An anthropological approach to alcohol use explores both "normal" and "deviant" drinking within cultural frameworks (Heath 1987, 19; Room 1984). Although the majority of drinking in Naeaegama takes place in a socially accepted fashion for pleasure and camaraderie, some alcohol-dependent men display harmful drinking habits.

Naeaegama villagers tend to merge what happens when an individual drinks too much on one occasion (and gets intoxicated) with what happens when someone regularly drinks too much (and becomes addicted to liquor). Teasing apart these separate but related phenomena, I deal with issues of inebriation in other chapters by exploring the Sinhala concept of *sihiya naetuwa* (being without one's right mind, memory, or consciousness) and considering some adverse effects of intoxication, including accidents, fights, domestic violence, and suicide. Here I examine excessive regular consumption of alcohol, particularly alcohol dependence. Beginning with a discussion of the physical effects of drinking, I explore the cross-cultural validity of the concept of alcoholism as a disease. To compare Euro-American and Naeaegama concepts of "problem drinking," I examine how villagers identify and explain the physical, psychological, and social symptoms of addiction. I conclude with several case studies of heavy drinkers. The stories that drinkers, their families, and their neighbors tell to make sense of drinkers' ailments reveal how people conceptualize the meanings, stigmas, and problems associated with drinking.

Addiction

Each human develops through an interaction of genetic potential and social and physical environment (Gould 1984). Without a conducive setting, potentials cannot be fulfilled. For example, a desert dweller with potential to be a great swimmer may never set foot in a pool, and a would-be pianist who never touches the instrument will never develop the ability to play. Alcohol addiction works similarly, resulting from "the interplay of a genetic predisposition with particular environmental circumstances which act to trigger a biopsychological response that we label 'alcoholism'" (Marshall, Ames, and Bennett 2001, 159). Biomedical researchers suggest a "25–50 percent likelihood that the development of alcohol dependence may stem from genetic factors" (Acuda and Alexander 1998, 45), and Euro-American research indicates that alcoholism runs in families (Heath 1987). But without exposure to alcohol, the potential will never be realized. For example, in Sri Lanka's rural social environment, women do not drink, so women who might have become alcohol-dependent if they had been exposed to alcohol never fulfill this potential.

Even with exposure to alcohol, very few drinkers become addicts. In the United States, researchers estimate that only one in ten people have the propensity for alcohol dependence or habitual use (Royce and Scratchley 1996; Wilcox 1998). The World Health Organization suggests that globally, two billion people drink, but less than four percent of them have diagnosable alcohol disorders (2004a, 1). In the Naeaegama social environment, where men can, do, and in some contexts *must* drink, most moderate social drinkers have no problems. As mentioned in Appendix 2, 45.5 percent of Naeaegama's 277 adult men use alcohol at least occasionally. Among the 126 men over 18 who drink in Naeaegama, 34.9 percent drink occasionally, 27.8 percent drink at least once a month, and 37.3 percent (47 individuals) drink more than four times a week. At 37.3 percent, the percentage of drinkers in the heavy use category in Naeaegama exceeds both the national average (11.4 percent) and the district average (21.6 percent) (ADIC 2005, 7; see Appendix Tables 2.1 and 2.2).[1] Among the heavy drinkers, a large portion is addicted to liquor. As with the manifestation of other human potentials,

---

1. In Appendix 2, I discuss several factors that may contribute to the differences between the numbers in the Naeaegama sample and the ADIC surveys.

the causes of addiction lie in both biological predispositions and environmental contexts.

Alcohol Metabolism

The physical process of metabolizing ingestible alcohol (known technically as ethyl alcohol or ethanol) offers some clues to the nature of dependence. Once someone has ingested ethanol, the body uses several enzymes to metabolize the substance. In the liver, alcohol dehydrogenase turns ethyl alcohol into acetaldehyde, which then circulates through the body. A toxic chemical, acetaldehyde causes a number of unpleasant side effects, including flushing and nausea. But in the brain this substance forms an addictive painkiller that decreases anxiety, causing relaxation and comfort (Perez 1992, 9). Throughout the body, acetaldehyde dehydrogenase and other enzymes work to remove acetaldehyde, turning it into acetic acid and then into carbon dioxide and water.

Scientists have gathered a great deal of medical information on the metabolic and physiological processes surrounding alcohol. Each hour the liver can break down roughly one drink of alcohol (15 mg of ethanol per 100 ml of blood) (Ritson and Thorley 2000, 14). But some people (e.g., 5–10 percent of the British and 20 percent of the Swiss) have an atypical form of the alcohol dehydrogenase enzyme and can eliminate alcohol more quickly than other people. In contrast, 50 percent of some Asian groups (e.g., Japanese, Koreans, and Chinese) have a deficiency in acetaldehyde dehydrogenase that deters them from drinking (Acuda and Alexander 1998). These population-level biological differences influence regional consumption patterns.

Biological variation occurs not only at the regional level but also among individuals. Men and women process alcohol differently due to body composition and hormonal differences (Ritson and Thornley 2000, 10). Perhaps because of specific characteristics of their body chemistry, some people become adapted and addicted to liquor more easily than do others, experiencing a sense of euphoria after drinking and not experiencing hangovers the following day (Gorski 1998, 104). Studies focusing on problematic usage suggest that an alcoholic-dependent individual's liver processes alcohol differently, forming acetaldehyde at higher levels than in non-alcoholics (Royce and Scratchley 1996). An alcohol-dependent individual can tolerate more alcohol and stay high longer than a social drinker, suffering withdrawal if he does not drink. Displaying the interplay between biology and environment, these disparities may both cause and result from excess alcohol consumption.

Despite identifiable metabolic patterns, explanations of alcohol dependence remain complex. The effects of small and large doses differ, as do the effects of short- and long-term use (where tolerance and dependence occur) (Ritson and Thorley 2000, 13–15). Furthermore, addiction can arise from a variety of causes. Alcohol dependence can occur in reaction to environmental stressors, as a consequence of a psychopathology (such as an antisocial disorder or a conduct disorder), or as an independent development. Genetic causes seem most clearly connected to early onset addiction in cases of independent development of alcohol dependence (Gorski 1998, 104). In sum, the body metabolizes alcohol according to basic biological processes, but drinking leads to disparate results in different populations and individuals. A holistic explanation of alcohol dependence must incorporate both genetic and environmental variables, with an emphasis on the social context in which drinking occurs.

Debate About the Disease Concept of Alcoholism

Researchers take different perspectives on what constitutes an addiction and what addiction means in social and medical contexts. Much of the debate takes place within Europe and the United States, so I begin this discussion by exploring the western notion of "alcoholism," and consider whether this disease concept fits with Naeaegama concepts of alcohol dependence. I set up this contrast not because I wish to privilege Euro-American methods and meanings but because readers may find them a familiar and useful frame of reference.

If most Euro-Americans understand addiction as a disease of the will, how does this translate into a medical realm more concerned with mind and body (Valverde 1998, 3)? The concept of addiction that arose in the 1890s and early 1900s and is currently prevalent in the United States (Room 1984) accompanied the increased institutional control over people's bodies and the medicalization of social issues (Foucault 1978, 1979; Kleinman 1988, 26). Some addictions respond to expert intervention and medical treatment. But neither medicine nor psychiatry wholeheartedly undertakes the treatment of alcoholism (Valverde 1998, 11, 75). No specific medicine "cures" alcohol addiction. In addition, if the patient refuses to cooperate, the doctor cannot resolve anything, and if the patient willingly stops drinking, the doctor's intervention is often unneeded. These circumstances bring into question the usefulness of expert interventions in abusive drinking. For years, concerned individuals have asked, "Is drinking too much a moral vice, a bad habit, or a mental disease?" (Valverde 1998, 39). Even those who call alcoholism a disease differ as to what constitutes the problem: the mental craving or the physical effects of years of heavy drinking. Definitions of the disorder have been contradictory, controversial, and convoluted.

Several assumptions about self-control underlie the concept of addiction. Since the Enlightenment, western ideology has portrayed the individual as an autonomous, rational agent who chooses according to his or her free will. Unacceptable disruptions of this will, such as compulsions, must be controlled (Brodie and Redfield 2002). Addiction—the uncontrolled craving for a substance—corrupts the will (Melley 2002; Weinstone 2002). Although alcohol is often lumped with more addictive substances, scholars debate whether it is actually addictive or merely habit forming. People who act by habit are not under compulsions, but neither are their behaviors perfectly autonomous. Valverde calls habits "semi-conscious patterned acts that are neither fully willed nor completely automatic" (1998, 36). Habits challenge the concept of free will much less than compulsions do. In addition, alcohol seems to affect people differently, with the vast majority drinking without harm, habituation, or addiction. Although alcohol is often classified with addictive illicit drugs, considerable ambiguity surrounds the concept and condition of "alcohol addiction."

Alcoholics Anonymous (AA), a popular mutual-help organization run by and for self-identified alcoholics, firmly holds that alcoholism is a disease (Alcoholics Anonymous 2001). Often the physical dependence is easier to cure than the mental craving. Former drinkers in the United States report that even after years of sobriety, they can be tempted to drink. The rhetoric of AA reflects this by terming its members "recovering alcoholics," denoting an unending vigilance against the temptation to drink. The key to sobriety, in AA's system of thought, is admission that one is and will always be powerless over alcohol. The twelve steps of the program provide spiritual guidance, a sense of identity, and practical techniques to stay sober. AA—which some scholars perceive as an anti-scientific, unsystematic approach to a non-medical "disease"—captures the subjective experience of some addicts and supports successful habit change (Valverde 1998, 127). AA has popularized a disease concept of alcoholism with an associated cure of total abstinence, and similar twelve-step programs treat other types of addiction.

Within the cultural context of AA's powerful and pervasive "folk knowledge" about alcoholism (Antze 1987, 155), scholars debate whether alcoholism (more technically known as alcohol dependence syndrome or alcohol abuse disorder) should be treated as a disease. The wide range of alcohol-related behaviors in different social and economic contexts makes it difficult to differentiate problem drinking from other drinking patterns. In truth, alcohol misuse takes place on a continuum, though in certain studies it is considered an all-or-nothing condition (Kunitz 2006, 287). In addition, people's drinking habits change over time: "People drink in different ways at different stages in their lives, so the distinction between those who are 'problem drinkers' and those who are not is neither clear-cut nor permanent" (Plant and Cameron 2000, 236). Even in cases of what most people would call abusive or addictive drinking, not all individuals require intervention and treatment; "many dependent drinkers are able to control withdrawal symptoms with reduced amounts of alcohol until they are alcohol-free" (Bennie, McKinney, and Campbell 2000, 178). The ability of some abusive drinkers to reduce and moderate their drinking leads Audrey Kishline to question AA's assertion that alcoholism is actually a disease with no cure and only one path to remission. Instead, she contends, "Drinking too much is a behavior, something that a problem drinker *does,* not something that he or she *has*" (1998, 112). She suggests, "Alcohol abuse can and often does *lead* to real, physical diseases—but it is not, in and of itself, a disease like diabetes or malaria" (Kishline 1998, 107).

Even scholarly proponents of the disease concept of alcoholism agree that not all problem drinkers should be labeled "alcoholics." Terence Gorski contends that mild alcohol problems do not count as a disease. But, he argues, people with serious drinking problems often have a clinical syndrome with a precise cause and identifiable signs, symptoms, and impairments (1998, 99). Characterizations of alcoholism vary, but most include habituation to alcohol and the serious problems this can cause. In Euro-American society, warning signs include compulsion to drink, gulping instead of sipping drinks, drinking in secret or lying about drinking, frequent bingeing, and blackouts (Royce and Scratchley 1996). Some commonly recognized symptoms include difficulty stopping once one starts to drink despite knowing that one will regret the outcome, and alcohol's interference with one's normal role as parent, spouse, or employee (Heath and Rosovsky 1998). These symptoms emphasize personal choices and actions more than the physiological aspects that characterize most diseases.

Given that understandings of illnesses vary from society to society, Oye Gureje and colleagues (1997) undertook a study to see whether western diagnostic criteria for alcoholism hold true across cultures. They suggest that arriving at cross-culturally valid characterizations of mental disorders is difficult in general, and the concepts of alcoholism and substance dependence are no exceptions (1997, 200). The researchers examined the following criteria: "craving, loss of control, tolerance, withdrawal, progressive neglect of other pleasure, persisting use despite physical or psychological harm, and narrowing of repertoire" (1997, 204). They also examined understandings of "acute intoxication, harmful use and alcohol dependence" (1997, 207). The researchers ran into difficulties due to cultural differences in drinking patterns. For example, "'Drinking' in Greece is often taken to mean 'drinking too much' whilst social drinking or drinking with meals is not regarded as 'drinking'. In Korea, 'intoxication' denotes a state just short of coma. In these cultures, the use of alcohol is decidedly more common and tolerated. On the other hand, it was difficult to convey the idea of 'normal drinking' in Bangalore where alcohol consumption is much less common" (1997, 204). Despite these difficulties, the authors note, "The concept of certain indicators of problematic use of psychoactive substances (intoxication, hangover, craving, dependence, etc.) is recognised across cultures" (1997, 209). Areas where differences occurred reflected culturally specific drinking norms. The researchers suggest removing from cross-cultural research the concepts of "'number of drinks,' 'narrowing of repertoire'… and legal or culture-specific definitions of problematic use of psychoactive substances" (1997, 210). This research demonstrates that cross-culturally people describe alcohol addiction according to the fairly standard set of interpersonal, mental, and bodily problems portrayed in western medical systems.

Although many societies recognize the social, psychological, and physical costs of alcohol dependence, some anthropologists hesitate to use the disease concept of alcoholism. One reason is that the disease concept may not match local knowledge about alcohol abuse. Based on their research among the Navajo, Stephen Kunitz and Jerrold Levy suggest that "Because heavy drinking was the product of normal social and cultural processes and because we could not convince ourselves that in most cases it was a manifestation of psychopathology, we were unwilling to call it a disease" (2000, 176). Conceptions of the nature of the problem and appropriate curative measures differ from group to group (Kleinman 1988). In addition to ethnographic reasons not to use the disease concept of alcoholism, there is a theoretical drawback: the disease concept of alcoholism hinders a political-economic understanding of destructive drinking. Running against anthropology's fundamental concept of holism, the focus on disease takes the individual out of social context and severs analytic ties with wider systems (see Singer 1986). Despite cross-culturally observed patterns in alcohol abuse, ethnographers note the overwhelming importance of understanding drinking within local contexts and norms.

Alcohol Dependence in Naeaegama:
Disease or Character Flaw?

Naeaegama residents recognize the mental and physical ills associated with alcohol dependence, but do not see "alcoholism" as a disease. Not all drinkers become addicted, and some heavy drinkers have been able to stop.

Many villagers therefore view alcohol-dependent individuals as morally weak, and believe that their destructive drinking then causes social problems and bodily illnesses.

I had a long conversation with Siri and Bandula about the disease concept of addiction. When I asked whether someone who drinks every day is a bad person, Bandula answered, "Yes. And people don't like him when he's sober, either. They try not to associate with him because he will ask money from you, and just talking with him will give you a bad reputation. Others will assume you drink with him." Bandula then described what I refer to as syndication (see chapter 3): "If someone sees a drinking friend on the road, he'll hurry and catch up with him to get a shot with him. Giving drinks to friends is a drinking man's custom (*siritak*). Any day he has money, he will drink and give drinks to his friends." The social stigma attached to habitual drinking, combined with the financial costs, prompted Bandula's assessment of drinkers as bad people to associate with.

Siri, Bandula, and I concurred about the social problems that befell heavy drinkers: they lost their jobs, lost their connections with relatives, lied about drinking, and thought all the time about drinking. We also agreed on the physical signs of long-term excess alcohol consumption, such as liver failure and trembling hands. I suggested that these were all symptoms of alcohol dependence, and suggested that alcohol addiction was a disease. But Siri and Bandula found this confusing. They asserted that the addiction was what *caused* the disease, which they understood as the bodily ailments.

When I suggested that the habit (*puruddak*) was itself an illness, Bandula said, "The only person who can cure the habit is the drinker himself, using his own mind. If someone thinks to stop, he can stop. No one can do it for him." By this, Bandula implied that addiction was not like a regular disease, for which a doctor could intervene and make a difference. Bandula was willing to concede that one might call the habit itself an illness, but suggested that in Sri Lanka, people only try to cure the body. I said that doctors could cure a physical addiction in a week or two, but without a change in the addict's mindset, the person would start drinking again. Bandula replied that the mental explanations that heavy drinkers gave for consuming alcohol (grief, tiredness, aches, and pains) were all flimsy nonsense. I recognized his assessment of drinkers' rationalizations, and tried to portray the AA concept of alcoholics' "stinkin' thinking," such attitudes as egocentrism, resentment, envy, jealousy, insecurity, frustration, fear, dishonesty, and blaming everyone else for one's troubles (Alcoholics Anonymous 2001, chaps. 5 and 10). Of these, only dishonesty and blame shifting seemed immediately obvious to Bandula.

Trying to introduce the concept of AA, I said that in the United States a group of former drinkers could often help a drinker who wanted to stop. Echoing the sentiments voiced by several other villagers, including one doctor, Bandula thought that a group of men gathered in that way would just go out for another drink. Like most villagers, Bandula dismissed the idea that former drinkers could help each other stay sober. The fundamental concepts of AA struck villagers as both foreign and illogical, perhaps because of the impossibility of anonymity in the fishbowl context of village life, or perhaps due to the rampant hierarchy and inequality that made frank and open speech unlikely between men of different ages, castes, and classes.[2]

People in Naeaegama do have a concept of addiction, and they do think that individuals can control their minds and stop drinking. However, they view this as something an individual must do on his own. Although villagers see clearly how drinking affects families, they do not echo AA claims that an alcohol-dependent man's family members are also ill with the same disease and in some cases enable drinking behavior (Al-Anon Family Groups 2003a, 12; 2003b, 3).[3] Nor does the thought of a support group seem logical; the suggestion immediately summons up images of men syndicating money and drinking together. Because some relatively heavy village drinkers have stopped drinking, people assume that those who have not stopped choose not to, and as a result judge them to have flawed characters.

Naeaegama Social Signals of Problem Drinking

Although Naeaegama villagers do not have a concept of "alcoholism" as a disease, they do recognize a difference between drinking socially "for the jolly" (*joliyaTa*) and drinking "because of problems" (*prashnawal nisaa*). This distinction echoes one found in Euro-American contexts, where social drinking is associated with enhancing positive experiences, and solitary drinking is associated with coping with negative experiences (Mohr et al. 2001). The Naeaegama distinction also highlights the rationalization of drinking and the use of alcohol for an effect (rather than for enjoyment)

2. Some people suggest that Alcoholics Anonymous, with its emphasis on a Higher Power, does not translate well to non-Christian contexts. The emphasis on a Higher Power need not, however, preclude the use of twelve-step programs by non-Christians. For example, Pat Patton (1998) presents an intriguing adaptation of AA's twelve steps in light of Buddhist philosophy. She emphasizes meditation, mindfulness, selflessness, and loving kindness toward others (1998, 151).

3. One Al-Anon pamphlet suggests, "*It is not true that an alcoholic cannot be helped until he wants help.* It *is* true that there is almost no chance that the alcoholic will stop drinking as long as other people remove all the painful consequences for him" (Al-Anon Family Groups 2003a, 12).

that are, in the Euro-American system, signs of mild alcoholism (Royce and Scratchley 1996). In addition, villagers have a concept of addiction and a list of specific physical and social symptoms that accompany alcohol dependence. But because the Sri Lankan drinking environment differs from that in the West, the social signals of alcohol addiction differ as well. Many of the warning criteria used in Euro-American contexts, including gulping instead of sipping drinks, drinking in secret or lying about drinking, and bingeing, are typical of Naeaegama social drinking patterns, particularly for drinking *kasippu*. Certain other drinking patterns, such as drinking in the morning and drinking alone, do stand out as deviant. In the following section I discuss "problem" drinkers' rationalizations and the reactions these elicit. I then discuss Naeaegama concepts of serious physical ills that accompany prolonged heavy alcohol use.

Serious Drinkers: Drinking Because of Problems

At a certain point, drinking sociably crosses over the line into drinking to seek relief from problems, which Naeaegama residents recognized as a distinct social category. Several villagers suggested that people who drank to get rid of problems found instead that the problems had multiplied. In a Euro-American context, Joseph Perez (1992) notes that when people start rationalizing drinking and blaming others for their behavior, they are progressing into addiction. Rationalizing and blaming figure heavily in the following discussions.

The problems that villagers said spurred drinking can be physical, emotional, or social. A number of common physical conditions provided justifications for alcohol consumption. For example, many manual laborers felt that they deserved—and often needed—a drink after a day's work.[4] Men said that they drank because they were tired, cold, in pain, or unable to fall asleep. But other people offered easy alternative cures. Scoffing at such physical rationalizations, one man stated, "If someone is tired, he should have some tea and cake and rest at home! If someone is in pain, he should go to a doctor, not to a *kasippu* joint!" A drinker told me that while alcohol might relieve aches at night, in the morning the pains would return, enhanced with a hangover. Distinguishing between allowable and inexcusable justifications, Lalith said, "It's okay to drink at parties. But now people say that

---

4. Jayawardena suggests that people in Sri Lanka have recognized the pattern of manual workers using liquor "as a necessary stimulant after a hard day's labour and toil" since at least 1907 (2000, 90, quoting Wright [1907]). Other cultures report similar patterns (see Suggs 2001).

they're drinking so that they can eat well, and they need a drink before breakfast!" Siri replied, "One before breakfast, one before lunch, and five before dinner, but then you don't end up eating dinner at all!" Although many drinkers used physical excuses regularly, other members of Sri Lankan society felt that such problems did not provide solid reasons to drink.

Drinking due to emotional problems was a popular explanation for alcohol consumption in the village. Perera and his neighbor claimed that the Indian Ocean Tsunami of 26 December 2004 caused some people to drink. The neighbor felt that drinking helped men to deal with the grief of losing their children, wives, and other relatives in the tsunami. Perera shifted the causal focus from emotions to economics, saying that tsunami-affected people received ample free rice and flour rations. Women had enough food to feed the family. Men, instead of going to work, could sell some of the food aid and use the money to drink *kasippu*. The tsunami thus spurred local drinking in more than one way.

The proliferation of physical and emotional motives, some of them contradictory, led some villagers to doubt the validity of any of these excuses for drinking. Anura and his wife Chamila recited a poem that highlighted the paradoxes, adding liberal commentary along the way.

Anura said, "People drink for sorrow (*duka*) or for pain (*weedanaawa*). They also drink for happiness, for the 'jolly' [in English]. How can this be?"

Chamila added, "People drink if they want to fight and need to find some courage." This angry state is *eDitara kama* (being fearless, courageous, or arrogant).

"But," countered Anura, "Men also drink socially. They see a bottle, and then they see the people around it as friends. Some men drink because they're tired; others drink to relax and get a good night's sleep."

The plethora of paradoxes and the absence of patterns led Anura to conclude that people said they drank for all reasons, thus invalidating each one. James Royce and David Scratchley discuss similar contradictions in the western world:

> We have a drink to relax and one to pep us up; a tall cool one in the summer and one to warm us up in the winter. Which does alcohol do? We talk about being fogged up with alcohol, and taking a drink to clear our head. We have a drink because our team won or because it lost; at a wedding or at a funeral; because we are married, or divorced; happy or sad. The alcoholic can always come up with a thousand reasons to take a drink, when in reality there is not one valid reason to do so. The fact that you must use a drug because you feel hot or cold, high or low, means you need it to be "normal," and that is one definition of addiction. (1996, 96)

Although social drinkers also drink on a wide variety of occasions (Heath 2000), relying on rationalizations is characteristic of alcoholic thinking.

In addition to physical and emotional reasons for drinking, Naeaegama residents cited social causes, such as chronic and unsolvable bureaucratic problems. For example, Edward said that he drank because his army pension had gotten snarled in red tape. Edward had retired before the civil war broke out and rejoined the army for an extra fifteen years. Describing the hardships he faced, Edward said that while he was training marksmen, their camp sometimes got hit with mortar fire. He had to search bunkers, even though he was old and retired. Despite his long service and over a year of negotiating with the pension office, Edward had not gotten the correct compensation. He felt bad (*hita narak unaa*) about this problem, and it was one reason why he drank.

I asked Edward why other people drank. "You'll have to ask a psychiatrist!" he replied in English. At Siri's prompting, however, Edward speculated about why several other villagers drank. All of the men he mentioned were separated from their wives. "Mangala drinks because his wife left him and he has no place to eat. Kumaradasa's son drinks because his wife kicked him out. Neither his in-laws nor his parents will take him in or feed him." Edward also thought that men drank if their wives were working in the Middle East. Edward's own wife had recently passed away. This pattern suggests that adult men may drink if they do not have a functional family life, symbolized by a wife to keep house and cook food.

Lack of a satisfactory family life also figured into Somaratne's explanation of his drinking. Somaratne, a heavy drinker, fought continually with his wife and her family.

> From the day we married, I have been suspicious of my wife's fidelity [implying that his wife was not a virgin]. Getting drunk with friends helps me forget about family problems. I will go out drinking and I will not eat at home. The next day my body will feel awful, but I still don't want to think about my problem, so I will get drunk again. My wife knows that I'm drinking and won't talk to me. Eventually my problem will get settled or forgotten. I will talk a little with my wife, go to work, and the problem will go away. Then in a month or so I'll hear that my wife is doing something suspicious or wants to leave me, and I will drink again.

Although Somaratne blamed his wife for the marital problems that spurred his drinking, one has to wonder whether his drinking and his style of conflict resolution might not have caused or at least exacerbated some of those problems (see Seilhamer and Jacob 1990).

Although problems on the social scene can lead to drinking, drinking can also disrupt social relations. When I asked Titus what problems led people to drink, he challenged my assumption and turned my question around, asserting that drinking *caused* problems. Siri agreed, claiming that instead of helping people forget their troubles, alcohol often heightened their concerns. In addition, intoxicated people confronted others about their problems, while sober people knew better. By drinking, people made their troubles worse.

Titus was not the only villager to challenge the assumption that problems caused drinking. Manori, a drinker's wife, stated categorically that there were no real reasons to drink. Misilin, a drinker's mother, systematically eliminated possible causes: "My son Charith has a house and property. He gets three full meals every day, and there is enough food for a friend if he brings one home. There is milk for his children. His wife has a good job at a nearby garment factory. He drinks without cause. He just keeps bad company." These cases suggest that many villagers, particularly women who have had to deal with heavy drinkers, do not accept the commonly voiced social rationalizations for excessive alcohol consumption. This perspective echoes what experts have said about addiction: with addicts, there is no "other reason"; the need itself *is* the reason to drink (Brodie and Redfield 2002, 7). Manori and Misilin, like many other village women, blamed alcohol and men's drinking buddies for the troubles they faced.

Many habitual drinkers blamed someone else (usually their wife, other family members, or the government) for their drinking behavior. These patterns of excuse and denial are characteristic of alcoholism in a Euro-American context (Al-Anon Family Groups 2003a, 4), where rationalizations take on strikingly similar features (Perez 1992). Both in Naeaegama and in the West, local rationalizations seem to focus on individual problems and proximate adversaries (such as wives or stubborn bureaucrats), leaving aside the larger structural contexts (such as the overarching lack of opportunity for gainful employment and social advancement) that a political economic perspective might highlight (Singer 1986; Singer et al. 1998).

Like Euro-American therapists, Naeaegama residents recognized the irrationality of many of the excuses that people who drank "for problems" offered, and placed such drinking into a socially acknowledged category. They did not, however, recognize rationalization as a part of addiction, or draw an explicit connection between rationalizing drinking and becoming dependent on alcohol. Not until a man had physical problems did villagers deem his case "serious."

His Belly Is Finished! Serious Illnesses

When I asked Siri about men who needed a drink first thing every morning, he suggested that they would not employ the standard rationalizations discussed above.

> Even if they claim they are drinking because of a problem, the villagers know that they drink every day. Most of these men will openly admit that they cannot work without a drink because their hands are shaking. Villagers might believe it if someone who only drinks occasionally talks about a particular reason for drinking. But most people recognize the habitual drinkers. The people who drink in the morning use their shaking as a problem, without inventing other excuses. For example, some coconut pluckers ask for an advance so they can have a shot before climbing up a coconut tree.

Such habitual drinkers, commonly recognized as "drunkards" (*beebaddoo*), displayed a series of locally recognized traits.

Naeaegama villagers recognized physical symptoms of alcohol dependence, particularly trembling hands, red eyes, and swollen faces. According to Indrani, "Alcohol burns the body organs. Drinking it is like putting a flower plant in a pot of boiling water." Commonly mentioned consequences of heavy drinking included the inability to eat (malnutrition), and damage to the liver, brain, stomach, intestines, and heart. These symptoms closely correlate with biomedical symptoms recognized in Euro-American contexts (Arria and Gossop 1998; Perez 1992).

Community members also recognized that heavy alcohol use usually interfered with social relationships. In Euro-American contexts, though definitions of alcoholism vary, most include habituation to alcohol and the serious life problems this can cause. The list of symptoms used in the West emphasizes personal choice and action more than the physiological aspects that characterize most diseases. In Naeaegama, people recognized both the physical and social aspects of a drinking problem but diagnosed the social ills slightly differently. The term *leDek* refers formally to a patient with a physical disease, but in slang parlance also designates a troublemaker. Both aspects of this term apply to the heavy drinker. The main emphasis falls on the physical aspects of alcohol-related problems. The mental struggles and social ills associated with drinking are not considered a part of the disease itself, but as something that the troublesome drinker willfully causes. Despite the different weight placed on physical and social ills, villagers almost always commented on both together, including a discussion of fights, damaged social relations, and economic problems when they discussed bodily ailments caused by heavy alcohol consumption.

During an interview, Siri, Janaki, and Janaki's husband Lalith explored the fine line between drinking for pleasure and drinking to the detriment of self and others. This discussion outlined many of the criteria by which Naeaegama villagers distinguished drunkards from other drinkers. Lalith started out by suggesting that many Ayurvedic medicines contained some alcohol, implying that alcohol in moderation was not only acceptable but also healthy.[5]

Janaki replied in English, "Too much is good for nothing," then noted in Sinhala that men had to have a limit when they drank. This suggests that people recognized the inability to stop drinking at a reasonable point as a sign of dysfunction.

Siri and Janaki then listed a number of physical and social ills that arose from drinking. Siri said, "It's bad for your health. You can't eat, your eyes go bad, you get piles [hemorrhoids], and your sex drive decreases. You also go down financially."

Janaki added, "And you get skin diseases."

She nodded as Siri said, "You have fights at home. You can't even talk with the temple priest. And if you go to a doctor while drunk, the doctor won't want to treat you. If you go to a government office, they'll tell you to come back sober. They won't let you in. Your reputation and honorability go down by seventy-five percent."

"Ninety percent!" corrected Janaki.

Siri continued, "Your mouth smells like alcohol. If you're on the bus, people glare and then move away. The smell comes from the stomach."

"Some people have fainted just from smelling that smell on others!" Janaki said.

I asked if anyone had died from drinking too much. Janaki remembered a neighbor, Botin. "He drank from morning on and died. His younger brother Edward is another example!"

"Edward is at Monika's [kasippu tavern] at 6:30 a.m.," Siri elaborated.

"He drinks daily," added Janaki.

"He spends Rs. 3,000 or Rs. 4,000 a month [on alcohol]," replied Siri.

Janaki continued, "His whole pension goes to Monika, with nothing left for his family."

"Edward is Monika's best client! She lets him pay on credit, but then she waits at the post office on pension day," Siri provided.

---

5. In medical preparations, alcohol often dissolves substances not soluble in water.

Janaki exclaimed, "Just look at him, he's gotten so thin." (In Naeaegama, people often associate thinness with illness. Janaki's perception of illness proved accurate; Edward passed away in mid-2007, at age 69.)

"Is drinking hard for families?" I asked a little while later in the same conversation.

"There is a major loss of money," Janaki replied.

Lalith added, "If marriage proposals come, there are complaints about drinking. There are also fights between the husband and wife."

"After these fights, the kids get disgusted and might even take their lives through suicide from the shame of it. Or they might run away from home," Janaki said.

Lalith's and Janaki's daughter drifted in. Following up on her father's comment about marriage proposals, she said, "I would not want to marry a drinker."

"I don't like the idea of a drinking son-in-law either," agreed Janaki.

"I wouldn't like a husband who smokes, either," said the daughter.

Lalith suggested, alluding to local gender norms, "So you won't find a husband in Sri Lanka!"

Janaki retorted, "We have found two already!" referring to the husbands of their two married daughters.

The family then agreed that it would be good if the authorities could stop people from drinking in Sri Lanka, but they did not think it would be possible to achieve. Lalith continued by describing the many acceptable places for drinking: "If there's a funeral, there are drinks. You have to serve drinks at a funeral, even if there are monks coming. You need people to stay at night, and they won't stay without alcohol. And people say that a wedding is bad if there are no drinks there. They will leave without eating if there are no drinks." (Leaving a ceremony without eating implies a serious degree of social rupture.)

Janaki concluded regretfully, "Something's broken now. People used to want plain tea. Now they want liquor."

This conversation revealed a number of themes that came up in other interviews and deserve analysis. Janaki suggested that some drinkers lacked a limit, and provided the example of Edward, who drank daily on credit. Several other Naeaegama residents emphasized the pattern of daily drinking to financial detriment as pathological. For example, Virasena stated that an effect of drinking to excess was the inability to stop drinking, even if a man had to borrow money to get liquor. He associated this mental state with the physical pattern that men trembled in the morning without liquor and could not carry a plate or a cup without dropping it. Wimal also saw an association between morning drinking and other deviant drinking behaviors.

He found drinking alone to indicate a pathological pattern, which also included drinking "dirty things like *kasippu*," drinking all day long, not eating, and drinking a lot more than other people drank. Ananda Thero, a temple monk, suggested that someone who was used to drinking could not stop easily. The monk gave as an example a coconut plucker who could not peddle his bike in the morning or climb trees until he had a drink. If he stopped drinking suddenly, he would suffer incapacitating withdrawal symptoms. The combined pattern of drinking without a limit, drinking more than one could afford, drinking to stop shaking in the morning, drinking alone, and drinking disrespectable substances like *kasippu* outlines the addictive behavior of alcohol-dependent drinkers in Naeaegama.

Various informants discussed health consequences of prolonged heavy drinking. People commonly mentioned liver, heart, stomach, and kidney problems. Ananda Thero deemed drinking *kasippu* especially bad because the strong liquor was made with dubious ingredients, including, he alleged, cement. The monk exclaimed, "His belly is finished (*bokka ivarayi*), and his kidneys and liver are cemented!" Bandula stated that people got cirrhosis, vomited blood, and died. Siri told me repeatedly that many drinkers did not realize at first that their liver had been affected. They only realized once the damage grew serious. Siri maintained, "At that stage blood comes from the mouth and anus. At that stage you can take medicine and survive. But if black pieces come from mouth or anus, then you are in trouble, because those are parts of the liver." Regardless of the medical accuracy of these causes and symptoms, they illustrate a clear pattern of cultural knowledge around the consequences of alcohol dependence.

Villagers associated sexual difficulties and malnutrition with excess alcohol consumption. In addition to physical difficulties presented by hernias and what Siri called "hydro-seal" (when a man's testicles enlarge), men's wives were reluctant to have sex with their husbands when they were drunk. Describing a typical scene, Siri said, "In the evening, he's smelly and vomiting and falling asleep. To have sex you need to bathe, brush your teeth, and put on some eau de cologne. You shouldn't try to do it on a dirty sheet with a torn pillow! The next morning he's in a bad way; he has a headache and he hasn't eaten." Siri noted that in contrast to the cultural ideal of mutual satisfaction, sexual relations were not gratifying for either the drinker or his wife. Several interviewees claimed that excessive drinking led to malnutrition. As Janaki noted in the conversation above, some drinkers became very thin. Virasena suggested that daily drinkers had no strength in their bodies because they did not eat regularly. Tying malnutrition to strained marital relations, Virasena speculated that these men "Come home, fight with their wives, toss out what has been cooked, go out for another drink, and end up not having dinner." In these examples, bodily weakness and poor sexual relations indexed not only physical illness but also severe family dysfunction.

In addition to physical problems, alcohol dependence causes many social difficulties. Research in the United States suggests that three to four people are affected by each alcoholic (Wilcox 1998). Given the large family sizes and the proximity of relatives and neighbors, in Naeaegama this number is likely higher. In chapter 5, I discuss the gendered consumption struggles that result when men and women in Naeaegama have different agendas for using household finances. Because women are socially forbidden to drink, while men are in some cases almost obligated to do so, these struggles take on a very predictable pattern.

One aspect of heavy alcohol use often mentioned in Euro-American contexts is drinking to the financial detriment of the household. Many people in Naeaegama noted and worried about this pattern. For example, Aravinda said, "It is okay for people to drink to a limit, but it is wrong for a poor man who earns Rs. 350 a day to spend Rs. 600 for drink." Wimal echoed this view, saying that one of the main problems with drinking was that people spent a lot of money on it: "All the other life in the house gets upset, and people can't even plan for tomorrow. The man breaks things. All together, they probably lose three times as much as he spends on drink itself." Ananda Thero summarized the problem this way: "Men lose their jobs and the love of their kids and wives and they get illnesses and they run out of money. They could use that money for useful things." Spending money on alcohol to the detriment of household economics happened very quickly, even with only moderate drinking, in families that lived very close to the poverty line.[6] Despite the cheap price of *kasippu*, in some cases *any* expenditure on alcohol put the family's finances in jeopardy. Criticisms that men spent too much money on alcohol abounded, even with regard to moderate social drinking. The extreme consumption inherent in alcohol dependence further exacerbated this issue.

In addition to financial problems, drinkers suffered a loss of social capital. As Siri noted and Janaki seconded, drunks could not respectably travel by bus, go to a temple or a government office, or visit a doctor. In addition, as Janaki and her daughter discussed, having a heavy-drinking relative

---

6. Discussing a survey performed on 155 men, Baklien and Samarasinghe (2003, 27) suggest that "The reported expenditure on alcohol among almost half the number of daily drinkers exceeds their reported income," and speculate that over 10 percent of the total population would spend all, nearly all, or more than all of their income on alcohol.

counted against a family when they tried to arrange a marriage. Ananda Thero suggested that drunks would also do debased things like fight, womanize, shout, and scold—all activities that diminished a man's status. Interestingly, only Ananda Thero mentioned that men lost jobs due to excess alcohol consumption. This might reflect the fact that many men in the local area were self-employed laborers or cinnamon peelers and did not risk being fired if they failed to come to work or arrived drunk. Local people knew, however, which laborers were strong, reliable, and fit, and they hire accordingly. Alcohol dependent men often took on low status jobs, such as plucking coconuts, which few other villagers wished to do. Early morning hours saw garden owners trying to track down coconut pluckers before they got too drunk to climb up the trees. Because no one else wanted this job, liquor addicts were assured of an income for as long as they were fit enough to climb.

Opinions varied about whether men should consume alcohol, and how much. True to the teachings of Buddhism, Ananda Thero stood against any consumption of alcohol, asserting, "Alcohol is alcohol, be it in a bottle or a glass or a tablespoon. Any amount is too much." But in the conversation above, Lalith remarked that some medicines contained alcohol, implying that it could not be too toxic. Similarly, Bandula noted, "Some people drink a small amount every day, and that isn't bad for the body, a lot of money isn't lost, and their status isn't damaged. That is not a problem. There is no effect on the rest of their life." Lalith took this theme a little further, pointing out that in certain contexts, particularly weddings and funerals, people expected alcohol to be served. Wimal felt that people who enjoyed an occasional drink with friends were also well within their social limits. Although these villagers held different opinions on socially acceptable amounts of alcohol, they all agreed with Janaki, who summarized the secular position with her English phrase, "Too much is good for nothing." In sum, villagers saw a clear connection between the social and physical ills that accompanied regular excessive alcohol consumption, but they did not seem to see addiction itself as a disease per se.

You Can't Always Go Along in the Same Way: Heavy Drinkers

Despite recognizing the loss of health and social status associated with heavy alcohol consumption, many addicted drinkers could not break the habit. In this section, I present information from interviews with several heavy drinkers.

Mangala told Siri that he started to drink a lot after his wife ran away with another man. "What answers do you find in the bottle?" Siri asked. Mangala laughed.

"Would you marry again?" Siri enquired.

"Once was enough! (*Apoo, aeti!*)" came the quick reply. After a pause, Mangala said he planned to stop drinking at New Year time (a yearly occasion typically characterized by more, not less, drinking).

Siri replied that he too had promised on multiple occasions to stop drinking: "I think I should stop, but then I think I'll have a little bit at 10:00, and a bit more at 12:30, and then it's 5:00 again and I'm still drinking. You can't stop all at once. If you try, you get sick," Siri claimed. He and Mangala then discussed the various symptoms they had encountered with withdrawal.

Like Mangala, both Kitsiri and Sherman drank multiple times a day and experienced a variety of health troubles. Both wished and even promised to stop drinking, but had not successfully done so. Neither had access to counseling or supportive therapeutic treatment that might have made their challenge possible to meet. Family contexts clearly affected them, enabling their drinking and, for a time, their continued survival.

Little by Little I Fell into Drinking: Kitsiri

Kitsiri, thirty-eight, unmarried, and the youngest of many children, had lived with his mother in an unfinished cement house until her death in 2002. Kitsiri climbed coconut trees for a living, and he drank all day long. He said, "There's no special time for alcohol. Any time is fine." He laughed, and continued, "Last night I went home at 11:45. The guy at the railroad gate told me so; I don't remember. My brother gave me Rs. 500 four days ago. Somehow I have spent it all. I was treating my friends [to drinks]. The guy at the junction kept my bike safe. At 12:15 I went for another half bottle.[7] Sherman and I stay up late drinking because we can't sleep. Then we get up and start drinking again with *pirith*," he said, gesturing to the temple. (The monk puts the tape of *pirith* chanting tape on the loudspeaker at 4:30 a.m. and everyone in the village, including the local anthropologist, uses it as an alarm clock.) Siri said that he had seen Kitsiri that morning and gave him "a small support" of Rs. 25.

Kitsiri continued, saying, "In the morning when I get up, I have no money at all, even for a beedie. But somehow by evening I have spent Rs. 200 on

---

7. In general, drinkers take a quarter of a 625-ml bottle of *kasippu* at a time; drinking a half bottle at a time indicates a high tolerance for liquor.

alcohol."[8] Siri noted, "If you climb four coconut trees, you can earn Rs. 100."
Kitsiri elaborated,

> I used to make brooms, but now I am not doing that. I spend a certain amount
> on drinking. I would like to start doing some other sort of work. But money
> is a big problem. Whatever money I have, I drink. Otherwise I could save and
> do something. I could make good money after selling some trees on my land.
> But although many people have asked for these, I am not going to sell them.
> If I don't have money, then my friends will give me money or drinks. Of if
> I need money, I can pluck a few trees at home or from outside.

In contrast to the Rs. 6,000 Kitsiri estimated he spent on liquor a month,
he spent only Rs. 2,000 on food. He made rice and two vegetables (mixed
together into one curry), and a sambol for chili flavor. He cooked once in
the morning and ate the food three times.

I asked Kitsiri why he drank. Kitsiri shrugged with his hands. "Why do
people drink in general?" He gave the same shrug, and said, "I drink a bit.
My mind just goes to that side. I started when I was nineteen or so, drink-
ing with friends. Then it became a habit. Little by little I fell into drinking
(*Tiken Tika biimaTa vaeTunaa*). Now my mind always runs to that side.
I am talking with you now, but I am thinking about Monika's tavern."

Kitsiri asked Siri and me if there was any way to stop drinking. We mentioned a detoxification regime available from a local doctor and a rehabilitation program in Galle. Kitsiri wondered how long these would take and
how much they would cost. Siri thought that someone had to make up his
mind to stop, or be threatened with a severe punishment. Kitsiri replied,

> If I could just stay at home for one week alone, it would be enough and I
> could stop. But I can't stay at home alone. I have no wife, no mother, and no
> children. I am alone and bored, with only my dog for company. So I go to the
> junction. Then the dog eats all the food. I was expecting to stop drinking, but
> then my mother got ill and died. Now I am drinking even more than before.
> Now I don't know night from day. I can't control my brain. My relatives scold
> me, but I cannot stop drinking.

Kitsiri died of cirrhosis less than a month after our interview, at age 38. He
went to visit his brother, got sick, and passed away. I speculate that after

---

8. At Rs. 100 for a bottle of *kasippu*, if Kitsiri spent Rs. 200 drinking two bottles or 1.25 liters
a day, he spent about Rs. 6,000 and consumed roughly 37.5 liters a month, or just shy of 10 gallons of hard liquor.

the death of his mother, any semblance of normalcy in his life disappeared along with most controls on his drinking. He survived her by only seventeen months. There was a strong bond between mother and son despite the corrosive effects of alcohol addiction.

If I Drink, I Will Die: Sherman

When Siri and I interviewed Kitsiri and Sherman in late March 2004, we discussed the Naeaegama "bed tea" drinkers, a group of fifteen or twenty people (including Kitsiri and Sherman) who consumed alcohol first thing in the morning. "Don't those people get sick?" I asked. Sherman said, "I'm still fit!" and showed off his physique. A year and a half later, while I was again in Naeaegama, Sherman was diagnosed with liver damage and a hernia.

Siri and I went to visit Sherman and his wife Nilukshi soon after Sherman got home from the hospital in early August 2005. Mangala was there helping Sherman's son mow the lawn with a scythe. Sherman sat in a reclining chair (*haansipuTuwa*) and we told him not to get up. He did not look like he could, even if he had wanted to, though he did sit up straighter. He was bare-chested and wore a sarong.

Sherman showed us the hernia bulging on his belly. His wife explained, "They can't operate on it because he is too weak. He needs to get his strength back before they operate. His liver has deteriorated (*narak velaa*). The root cause is drinking." She elaborated, "The hernia started six months ago. I told him to get it checked out a bunch of times but he kept postponing it. Then it got bad and I was afraid. I forced him to go to the hospital. There are not one but two places where the intestines have come through the abdominal wall."

I asked how this hernia started. Sherman said he didn't remember. "I didn't lift anything heavy."

Nilukshi replied tartly, "You don't have a job. Of course you weren't lifting heavy things."

Sherman admitted, "I was drinking and not eating. I would drink half a bottle, which has a certain kick. If I ate, the kick would go off, and I would need to spend Rs. 50 more [for another half bottle] on drink. When the 'current' went down, I would go get another shot. I would eat at night, when I wanted to go to sleep, when I had had enough to drink for the day."

Nilukshi said that Sherman had gotten thin. He was drinking regularly. Siri and Sherman discussed in drinkers' shorthand how much Sherman drank. Siri hazarded a guess: "Five or six?"

Sherman replied, "No, ten or twelve."

"*Bottles!?*" his wife exclaimed, in a shocked voice. But the men were discussing how many times Sherman went to drink each day.[9]

"Do you plan to start drinking again?" Siri asked.

"No. I've had enough," Sherman replied.

Siri said, "I said that too, the last time I got very sick."

Nilukshi showed me the exercise book in which Sherman's doctors had written his diagnosis. In Sri Lanka, patients bring an exercise book to the doctor, and take it with them when they visit specialists and clinics. The entries were in English. True to cross-cultural doctoring norms, the handwriting was almost illegible. I could make out "Decompens…ial liver failure, Splegelian Hernia," and something "due to excess alcohol." In another place someone had written "Smoker and heavy drinker." Nilukshi showed me Sherman's medications. He was taking a stool softener to help move fecal matter past the bowel obstruction. He could eat only liquid foods. Loose, nameless pills populated a handful of paper envelopes stamped with dosage instructions. There were yellow pills that Siri identified as vitamin B supplements. There were other yellow pills. There were green pills. There were white pills.

"Did the doctors scold you?" Siri asked.

"No. But they advised me not to drink, to stop now. So now I have stopped."

Siri said, "I believe it because you can't get up to walk to the tavern."

Sherman became more animated, expanding on the tale. "The doctor asked what I drank. My wife told me not to lie to the doctor, so I told him '*kasippu*.' He said that was bad. He said that if I drink, I will die (*biiwot, maerenawaa*)." We murmured sympathetically, and Sherman elaborated: "The doctor told me that if I wanted to drink, I should first dig my own grave, then pull up a chair, have a drink, and I'll fall straight into the hole and someone could shovel some dirt in on top of me." By animating the doctor's strict warning, Sherman validated the medical reasons to stop drinking and sought to persuade Siri of the necessity. But Sherman also felt some ambivalence. He said, "I went to the hospital feeling pretty healthy, but now I feel worse. If I drink, I don't have problems. I don't feel any pain. As I got sober, the pain came on bit by bit. So now I'm stuck. I can't drink again, but I'm in pain. I haven't had a drink for a week. But I don't feel like drinking. I am afraid."

---

9. If Sherman drank a quarter bottle of *kasippu* on each visit to the tavern, in ten visits he could consume 2.5 bottles (1.6 liters). (A quarter [156 milliliters] is the equivalent of three and a half 44-milliliter "shots" in the United States.) During the prior year's interview, Sherman claimed that he could drink four bottles, or sixteen "quarters" (2.5 liters) a day.

"Will you be okay after an operation?" I asked.

"*Yes*," Sherman said emphatically. His wife's hand gesture was less sure.

Sherman was not the only villager sobered by his illness. That day, Siri's wife Telsie told me that both Siri and Wasantha were afraid for their health after seeing Sherman's state. Wasantha had a large glass of a healthy vegetable soup at the junction, and Siri ate a big lunch. Commenting on Sherman's situation, Telsie said, "You can't always go along in the same way," implying that one could not drink heavily and get away with it forever. But within less than a month, Sherman started drinking again; Siri and Wasantha started even sooner. Nearly a year later, in May 2006, Sherman was still alive, still drinking, and still too weak to have an operation to cure his hernia. He passed away in late 2006 at age 44.

Conclusion

Naeaegama tales of destructive drinking identified both the physical and the social consequences of heavy alcohol intake. In the intimate fishbowl of village life, where everyone knows everyone else's business, excess drinking and its deleterious effects were widely recognized. Examples abounded of daily drinkers who suffered, sickened, and died. Although villagers recognized mental illnesses as such, they did not see alcohol dependence in that light. Instead, they saw the drinker as a troublemaker, and held him responsible for the social consequences of his addiction. They thought that many of the rationalizations habitual drinkers gave for drinking were bogus. They believed that only the drinker himself could stop his drinking, and nobody I spoke with mentioned the possibility that a trained medical professional could help a drinker understand and control his mental craving.

In the disease concept of alcoholism commonly voiced in the United States, people discuss hitting "bottom." Bateson notes, "'Bottom' is a spell of panic which provides a favorable moment for change, but not a moment at which change is inevitable" (1972, 330). An alcoholic, according to Bateson, panics when he discovers that the system (self plus alcohol) is out of his control. Bateson sees no chance of changing an alcoholic's epistemology between "bottoms." In Naeaegama, I heard no discussion of "bottom" or a similar concept, although I spoke with Kitsiri and Sherman at moments where they were clearly receptive to change. Local understanding of alcohol dependence did not identify such turning points. Instead, commonly circulating stories illustrated the steady downward progression of alcohol-dependent men, leading, in most cases, to an early death.

Alcohol dependent men caused sorrow and irritation for their families, who had to deal with the side effects of addiction. In all the cases discussed here, family members stood by and helped addicts in times of crisis, despite their frustrations with the drinker's inability to control his cravings. Families helped drinkers sustain some sort of normalcy, providing regular food (if the drinker was willing to eat it), and taking initiative, as Sherman's wife did, to get the man to a doctor. As part of their family responsibilities, these individuals protected men from some of the consequences of their drinking, thus enabling them to both live and to continue to drink. Men without wives or mothers, such as Kitsiri and Edward, were more vulnerable.

Like many addicts, families seemed at a loss for how to stop a man's drinking. The available sources of help, such as a doctor's regimen of medications or a government-sponsored rehabilitation camp, seemed expensive and scary. Doctors could provide relief for the physical symptoms associated with withdrawal, but other health complications (hernia, malnutrition, liver failure) tended to usurp the focus on addiction. Though few, options did exist to support people struggling with alcohol cravings. In the next chapter I discuss community-administered correctives for heavy drinking, and explore more formal medical, religious, and social programs for addicts and their families.

9 A Goddess of Wrath: Treatments

"There's a shrink on every corner in the USA," asserted Titus.

"There's a *kasippu* tavern on every corner in Naeaegama," Siri replied. He continued, "Those are the mental hospitals here!"

Siri's claim that *kasippu* taverns replace mental hospitals in Sri Lanka reflects simultaneously the dearth of actual facilities supplying psychological and psychiatric aid, and the rationalizing fiction that drinking can help people forget their troubles. In this chapter, I examine the resources villagers draw upon for help with dependence and other sorts of abusive drinking. Drinkers' family members and neighbors often impose informal but surprisingly effective sanctions against destructive drinking. These sanctions work against drunken comportment that exceeds the local within-limits rules and against long-term heavy drinking that threatens family respectability. When informal sanctions fail, people turn to other authorities, particularly medical and religious practitioners. Here I consider community-administered correctives and medical and spiritual cures, exploring their strengths in changing drinking behavior and habits.

Community-Administered Correctives

Although many societies allow people to drink and get drunk, social constraints can and do control drinking, especially when drinkers threaten to do harm to themselves or others. People in Naeaegama recognized the problems caused by both occasional intoxication and long-term heavy drinking. For the most part, the community policed drinking behaviors on its own, drawing on a number of possible correctives. Some correctives villagers administered themselves, including humiliation, family pressure, and the threat of physical punishment. Others they hoped that doctors, monks, or police officers would deliver. These correctives varied in suitability and effectiveness, with some of the seemingly weaker ones being quite potent (Heath and Rosovsky 1998). In this section I consider some of the informal sanctions and semi-formal preventative measures that people in the Naeaegama area employed against destructive drinking behaviors.

Local community members, especially young boys, administered informal social sanctions on inappropriate intoxicated behavior. Most local drinkers conformed to social expectations of drunken comportment, but occasionally intoxicated changes for the worse exceeded acceptable limits (MacAndrew and Edgerton 2003). As discussed in other chapters, teenage boys restrained deviant drinking behaviors by hooting at intoxicated neighbors and playing pranks on them when they passed out. Young men chastised drunkards with mild physical inconvenience and considerable public humiliation. Freely circulating stories of creative punishments warned drinkers of the risks of excess.

Although Naeaegama rules governing allowable drunken comportment generally discouraged physical violence, villagers did consider hitting obstreperous drinkers an effective disciplinary option. On the topic of alcohol, villagers considered Buddhist monk Ananda Thero strict (*saerayi*, literally strong, cruel, or rough). When I mentioned that I had heard he chased intoxicated people out of his temple compound, the monk affirmed, "I chase them out the gate and hit them too! Drinkers disturb the sober people." Ananda Thero claimed that despite being intoxicated, drinkers still had enough volition to control their aggressive behaviors. If they learned that they would face punishment for their actions, they would not trouble other people when they took liquor. "Drinking alcohol is an excuse to go out and act like that. This is some sort of pride for the drinker. The only medicine is to hit the man," the monk concluded. But he only resorted to physical discipline when his advice was ignored, and he never recommended it to others. He stated, "A monk can't tell women or men to hit anyone; it is against our religion." By inflicting public humiliation and promising violence, Ananda Thero sent a clear message to the community that he did not condone any liquor-associated anti-social behaviors on temple grounds.[1]

---

1. Samarasinghe discusses the bad effects that follow from community acceptance of drunken misbehavior (2005, 7, 18, 33). He suggests that community-level interventions can change local perceptions about drunken behavior. "Allegedly alcohol-induced aggression declines, despite

Villagers tacitly approved of physical punishment and imprisonment for known heavy drinkers. The police caught Mangala at Amarapala's *kasippu* tavern in early April 2006. Because he had several prior cases against him, Mangala received a Rs. 5,000 fine [Rs. 4,113 in 2004 figures]. He could not pay, and none of his relatives bailed him out, so Mangala spent nine days in jail. Telling me this story, Siri opined, "They should put drinkers in prison for six months so they can't drink. If they drink again, they should put them in jail for a year and then only let them out with bus fare."

Siri's strict dictates corresponded with a cure Perera suggested. When I asked how to stop a habitual drinker from drinking, Perera dramatically said, "Cut off a leg so he can't walk; otherwise he won't stop." Siri cynically replied, "You'd have to cut off *both* legs, because the man would hop to the tavern on one!" But treatments for heavy drinking such as imprisonment or (more fancifully) amputation require external structures that eradicate the drinker's access to alcohol. Although effective while administered, such techniques usually fail to control drinking when access is reestablished.

Authoritarian and condemnatory approaches to excess drinking often create ill will and resistance. In contrast, methods that motivate drinkers to stop on their own can be more effective. Ananda Thero mobilized the students in his Buddhism classes to control excess drinking. "I tell the children not to do sinful things (*paw vaeDa*). Now the local children think alcohol is disgusting (*apriyayi*). They don't like drinking, even the sixteen- and seventeen-year-old boys. I get the children to correct their parents as well. For example, if a father drinks, I tell his kids to go in the morning and be kind and loving with him, tweak his ears and suggest that the father not drink that night, but that they should all eat dinner together." The monk claimed that this method had worked well in the area around his temple. Many men had reduced the amounts they drank. Alcohol-related problems had also decreased, especially *kasippu* production, fights, and domestic violence, as had thefts, robberies, molestations, and cases of men harassing women bathing at the public well. To corroborate his assertion, Ananda Thero showed us a certificate from the Officer in Charge at the local police station stating that the number of complaints from the temple area had greatly diminished because of the monk's activities. In this case children, seemingly the most helpless of society's members, proved very effective in moderating paternal drinking.

---

alcohol consumption remaining unchanged, when communities become less accepting of it" (Samarasinghe 2006, 627).

Other villagers agreed that pressure from children could change men's drinking patterns. Bandula claimed that he stopped drinking because his daughters scolded him. "They are afraid of the effects drinking could have on my health. They said they'd stop going to school if I drank," he remembered. Because educating children is one of the primary duties of a Sri Lankan parent, threatening to stop going to school (something that children can control) unless their father stops drinking (something that children cannot control) is an effective strategy of protest. Another man stopped selling *kasippu* to protect his daughters' reputations. Arranging good marriages is an important parental duty, and family status figures heavily in the process. In some cases a man who cannot stop drinking to save his own health and social standing might stop drinking to protect his daughter's education or reputation.

A new social role can also modify a man's behavior, presenting him with a compelling reason to stop or moderate his drinking. People hoped that when a man married, his wife or the responsibility of having a family would sober him up. For example, Hema (whose son's suicide is described in chapter 7) tried to control her son's heavy drinking by "giving him a woman," a strategy that failed. Some men stopped drinking when their children were born. Siri promised to stop drinking when his son got married and brought home his bride, but that date came and went without a perceptible change in Siri's behavior. Siri's father, Martin, stopped drinking after he retired from public service and took on local responsibilities as principal of the Buddhist Sunday School and justice of the peace. In all these cases, heavy drinking conflicted with the perceived requirements of the man's new social role.

Collectively, these cases suggest that pressure from neighbors, family members, and clergy does affect drinking behavior. Public humiliation and the threat of force can limit intoxicated changes for the worse. Long-term drinking patterns are more difficult to change. Although local men suggested that jail terms and physical punishments might work, gentler measures often accomplished the same goals more effectively. Changes in social roles often prompted a reduction in drinking, and daughters' pleas seemed quite effective in influencing a father's habits. But even though family and community pressure did achieve the desired goal in some cases, in other cases such pressure merely led to stress, tension, and fights.

Medical Treatments

Many people recover from alcohol problems without entering treatment. In dealing with problem drinking, it is useful to distinguish between intoxication and alcohol dependence. Naeaegama rules governing intoxicated changes for the worse are fairly effective in regulating drunken comportment. In many instances, social pressures also work to regulate and reduce habitual heavy drinking. Around the world, people display a range of drinking behaviors during their lifespan, and many youth "age out" of heavy drinking, particularly when they enter new social roles. Bingers can go a long time without drinking, and many stop binging as they mature. Some alcohol dependent people can reduce their consumption of alcohol, control withdrawal symptoms, and free themselves of dependence (Bennie, McKinney, and Campbell 2000, 178). In their examination of factors that influenced self-initiated "natural recoveries" in the United States, Linda Sobell et al. (1993) identified different patterns depending on age and gender. Other important factors included having support from spouses, family, and friends; changes in social life and leisure activities; changes in health and diet; and changes in self-control (Sobell et al. 1993, 55). In Naeaegama, several village men who drank heavily in the past were known to have stopped completely. Many men, however, continued to drink in increasingly inappropriate ways.

Most problem drinkers do not seek treatment, either in Naeaegama or in Euro-American contexts. In developed countries, "the ratio of untreated to treated alcohol abusers is estimated to range from a conservative 3:1 to a liberal 13:1 ratio" (Sobell et al. 1993, 35). In Euro-American contexts, people do not take advantage of available treatment for a variety of reasons. They may be in denial about their problem or not want to stop drinking; they may know they have a problem but think they can handle it alone; they may not want to face the stigma of going into treatment; they might not trust the system or think it will be effective; or they might not have the needed funds or childcare to go into treatment (Grant 1997). In Naeaegama area, drinkers are equally reluctant to seek treatment, and treatment options are scarcer, more expensive, and less widely accepted than in Euro-American contexts.

Because many people were able to control their own drinking, there was some dispute in Naeaegama about the role of medical interventions in treating alcohol dependence. Bandula suggested, "A drinker needs to use his mind to cure his habit. There are no other cures, even the ones offered on TV. Not even doctors can do it. Sometimes people in the drinker's family want him to stop, so they believe all the publicity and try those false ways and spend a lot of money uselessly. If a drinker's family takes him to the hospital, he might get better there, then come home and start drinking again." Naeaegama residents recognized the constellation of physical, social, and psychological problems that accompany alcohol dependence. But, as discussed in chapter 8, villagers did not hold a disease concept of alcoholism. They recognized the concept of mental illness, but did not see alcohol dependence in this light. Instead, they saw continued heavy drinking as a question of flawed moral character and lack of motivation. Many felt that if a drinker wanted to stop, he could do so on his own; if he did not want to stop, no doctor could help him. Despite this, doctors were called in to help with alcohol-related problems. Although persistent drinkers could and did ignore social and legal sanctions, they often took notice if they developed a serious physical illness.

Naeaegama villagers could choose from an array of treatment when they fell ill. For physical ills they often consulted a doctor trained in western medicine or a traditional Ayurvedic healer. For mental problems, a monk or village priest (*kapu-mahattayaa*) could mediate between the patient and various powerful deities, and an exorcist could bargain with and cure illnesses caused by demons and ghosts (Carbine 2000; Kapferer 1983; Wirz 1954). Nothing besides financial constraint prohibited seeking simultaneous treatment from any number of these experts. With the exception of western-trained doctors, healers respected each other's skills and often referred patients to each other, depending on the nature of the illness. In the following sections, I examine how these different practitioners dealt with the problem of alcohol dependence. Here I present data gathered from the local allopathic (western) and Ayurvedic (indigenous) doctors in the Naeaegama area regarding their approach to alcohol dependence and alcohol-related illnesses.

Western Approaches

Community members and health practitioners agreed that an effective cure required the drinker's cooperation. A mother of two addicted sons, Misilin talked about medical cures available to help treat alcohol dependence. She said, "There are medicines, but most guys won't take them." Misilin would willingly have paid for medical treatment for her sons, but they refused. Misilin's perception of reluctance was echoed by Dr. Mendis, who said that in his experience, drinkers had no interest in stopping; they wanted a cure for their immediate problem and did not want to hear about the larger picture. Nevertheless, people continued to hope that medical doctors could help with problem drinking. Misilin remembered one man cured by his physician: "He got this medicine from the doctor. The doctor said, 'Use this; but if you drink, you will die.' He hasn't drunk in two years." In this she echoes Dr. Priyanka, who felt that an explanation of the health effects of alcohol sobered up many of his patients. Medical doctors often provided both advice and prescriptions for problem drinkers, although they placed more emphasis on physical cures. No local organizations provided western-style therapy or counseling.

Dr. Mendis

Dr. Mendis's small office smelled of disinfectant. To the left of the door sat a large desk. Fifteen years of written records graced the bookcases, and cabinet tops held boxes of medicine. Dr. Mendis, a fit and alert-looking man in his early seventies, had silvery hair and a nice smile. Retired from government service, he opened his private dispensary at 9:00 or 9:30 a.m. and stayed until 7:00 p.m.

When I said we wanted to ask him about local alcohol use, Dr. Mendis immediately opined in English, "Regarding alcoholism, these people don't want to get out of it, even with the help of drugs. I have only found one or two drinkers who say they want to stop. Usually they come in with other complaints. I tell them that the condition will get worse if they keep smoking or drinking. But most are not interested in stopping." I asked if these patients understood that they were sick from alcohol. Dr. Mendis answered, "I don't know. Often they come in drunk, so I can't tell what they understand. They come in for another complaint. They think that they can just get some medicine and go home and drink and they will be okay even if they continue [drinking] alcohol. For example, if someone comes in with an infection from a wound, I will prescribe antibiotics. I tell the person that this won't work as well as it should unless he stops alcohol [intake]. These people just take the medicine and go."

In Dr. Mendis's experience, although drinking men did not want to quit, their wives wished they would stop drinking. Dr. Mendis said that he was especially concerned about how liquor affected the family. "Ours is a poor economy. When the husband takes alcohol, the family economics are badly hit." Women desperate for cures for their husbands came to see Dr. Mendis for help. "Recently one woman came. She has an incorrigible husband. The household finances are very bad and the children are suffering. She was close to committing suicide. She had no other resort. She came to me pleading for help. I told her that her husband needed institutional care."

In the past, Dr. Mendis gave wives prescriptions for Antabuse (disulfiram), a drug that causes vomiting if taken in conjunction with alcohol.

These women put the Antabuse in their husband's tea or food without his knowledge. In a few instances this has been enough to cure the man of the problem. But sometimes men take the pill, and then drink, and it makes them seriously ill. They arrive back at my dispensary in a bad way. This scares the

wife, and that is the end of the treatment. The drinking person wonders what
has happened. If he suspects he was given Antabuse, he might get mad at me.
If I prescribed the drug to the husband, his compliance with the Antabuse
would be very poor.

Because of his misgivings about the interaction of Antabuse and alcohol,
Dr. Mendis no longer treated alcohol-dependent men or gave their wives prescriptions for Antabuse. Instead, he sent patients to the local hospital or the
psychiatrist in Unawatuna, a town thirty miles to the south. "Unfortunately,
only a few people go all the way to Unawatuna. They just stay here in this area
without treatment. If there are other complications from alcohol, I treat them
separately." Dr. Mendis recognized the need to address alcohol-related social
problems, but conceded that he could not handle them with medicine alone.

Dr. Priyanka

The other local doctor, Dr. Priyanka, was a tall and confident man in his
early forties. He worked at the local hospital during the days and ran a private dispensary early in the morning and after work in the evening. Unlike
Dr. Mendis, Dr. Priyanka was ready, even eager, to treat alcohol-dependent
patients, and had a good local reputation for success in this endeavor. He
launched into an enthusiastic technical description of his treatment program, and seemed disappointed when he learned that I held a doctorate in
anthropology, not medicine.

Dr. Priyanka said that if patients had liver failure and central nervous system complications such as coma, seizures, hallucinations, or vomit stained
with blood, then he suggested "in-ward treatment" at the area hospital.
Otherwise he could deal with people at his dispensary. Education formed
a main element of Dr. Priyanka's dispensary treatment program. He talked
for a half hour with his patient. Siri emphasized that most doctors did not
take this much time; Dr. Priyanka's cures were effective because he explained the situation thoroughly. He counseled people about alcohol dependence and what would happen to them in five years if they continued
to drink heavily. "I talk about their kidneys, liver, and nervous system. I also
talk about impotence, which really gets to the men. I have a different lecture for the educated people, because they already know some of the effects
of heavy drinking." Dr. Priyanka found educated drinkers harder to cure,
and cited Siri as an example; these men drank despite knowing the consequences, so he could not scare them into stopping.

During his two-week treatment, Dr. Priyanka insisted that people stay
home from work and abstain from alcohol. The treatment got patients

through withdrawal, during which they might be bedridden and sleep all day. The exact length of the treatment depended on the withdrawal symptoms suffered. Symptoms included trembling, aches, loss of appetite, insomnia, and *delirium tremens* with confusion, agitation, auditory and visual hallucinations (some with a touch of paranoia). Some patients bled from the rectum because withdrawal aggravated hemorrhoids. Sometimes they vomited and had gastritis, or got peripheral neuropathy (numbness of the hands and feet). Dr. Priyanka prescribed a series of medications including benzodiazepines and vitamin supplements to reduce these withdrawal symptoms. After treatment for withdrawal, he started patients on Antabuse, prescribing one tablet daily for one month.

Well-known for the success of his cures, Dr. Priyanka had treated many alcohol patients in the local area and from nearby towns. Dr. Priyanka emphasized the importance of counseling alcohol patients and persuading them to stop. He said, "Many drinkers—ninety-nine percent of them—want to stop! But they can't because they're addicted. They get withdrawal symptoms, so they can't stop. I can help them over those. I can cure fifty percent of the people just by talking with them! That's why people come to me." He claimed that only three patients out of the 200–300 he had treated had relapsed in the prior three years.[2] When I asked if I could send interviewees to him if they asked about treatment, he said he would be happy to care for anyone I referred to him in the course of my research.

With his positive attitude and his comprehensive outpatient treatment for withdrawal symptoms, Dr. Priyanka crafted a successful approach to treating alcohol dependence. Research on alcohol interventions suggests that "confrontation is counterproductive in the attempt to motivate the client for treatment and that a non-confrontational approach should be preferred" (Heather 2000, 169). Dr. Priyanka's method matches those deemed most successful by Euro-American researchers. Colin Bennie, Iain McKinney, and David Campbell suggest that "'Brief interventions' consisting of assessment, advice about drinking and follow-up, proved to be effective in encouraging positive changes in drinking behavior for many problem drinkers" (2000, 179). General practitioners like Dr. Priyanka are ideally situated to provide these interventions. In addition, research suggests the effectiveness of motivational enhancement therapy. Instead of confronting a patient in an authoritarian or hostile manner, therapists who adopt this

2. The two men I met who had gone through Dr. Priyanka's detoxification program had both stayed sober for several months before starting to drink regularly again. I do not know whether Dr. Priyanka kept official track of long-term relapse rates among his patients.

strategy encourage patients to initiate changes on their own. The therapist provides advice, suggests a range of alternative options, and offers empathy and feedback, but leaves the responsibility for the change up to the client (Heather 2000, 169). This approach is particularly effective for patients with less serious problems who are already contemplating the need for change but feel ambivalent about taking the first steps. Dr. Priyanka reached out directly to this demographic. This Sri Lankan practitioner of western medicine developed a technique quite similar to that judged most effective by researchers working in Euro-American contexts. But western medicine was only one of several locally available forms of treatment.

Indigenous Approaches: Dr. Sepali

The indigenous Ayurvedic medical tradition has a long history in South Asia. Increasingly, Euro-American researchers recognize that complementary and alternative medicine can offer holistic approaches to treating alcohol addiction. Ayurvedic techniques can be helpful in treating dependence by restoring energy balance, strengthening the immune system, and treating liver disorders (Sukul 2000, 194). Sri Lankans often turn to Ayurvedic practitioners to cure a number of ills. Dr. Sepali was a cheerful woman in her late twenties who worked at an Ayurvedic center in a nearby town. Siri and I spoke with her about Ayurvedic perspectives on alcohol at her village home on several occasions.

The Ayurvedic tradition does not completely condemn alcohol. Dr. Sepali suggested that a little bit of alcohol is good for the body; consumed in the right quantity, alcohol is medicinal. For example, a popular Ayurvedic drink called "Arishta" contains 8 percent alcohol. "Different sorts of alcohol have different effects on the body. The stronger stuff is worse and harms the body more quickly. And drinking above the limit isn't good," she warned. In this she echoed other medical practitioners who assert that "the poison is in the dose rather than in the substance" (Heath 2000, 125).

Dr. Sepali explained that when people drink, poisons are produced in the body. There are three humors (*tundos*) in the body: air or wind (*waata*), fire or bile (*pita*), and water or phlegm (*kapa*). Drinking upsets the balance between them. To treat the effects of drinking, an Ayurvedic physician strives to balance the humors. Because alcohol causes the fire humor to increase in the body, Dr. Sepali's treatments were all cooling in nature. One cure, oil mixed with lime juice, would sober an intoxicated person when applied to his head. A drink made with acidic fruits and a special salt reduced intoxication and cleaned the stomach. Several of the remedies induced vomiting, including salt water, mustard water, and water with honey.

Other concoctions reduced the concentration of alcohol in the drinker's system. Dr. Sepali listed over a dozen herbs, including coriander, to consume or to spread on the palms of the hands and soles of the feet. She said that drunken people and alcohol addicts should reduce the fire humor by drinking cooling fluids (like young coconut water [*kurumba*]), doing cooling activities (like bathing in cool water), and using cooling herbs.

In caring for an addict, Dr. Sepali talked with the drinker and his family, giving advice and then treatment. Advice plays a major role in the Ayurvedic system, whereas allopathic doctors in Sri Lanka seem to dispense pills and dismiss patients as quickly as possible. (This context makes Dr. Priyanka's communicative approach to alcohol-dependent patients especially noteworthy.) Dr. Sepali suggested that her treatments would help someone who was intoxicated and someone who drank heavily on a regular basis, implying that the two were often the same. According to the Ayurvedic system, withdrawal symptoms such as trembling hands come from mental, not physical causes. She could prescribe some nerve system medicine to help. In addition to the cures she outlined earlier, she sometimes gave patients placebo pills, which worked especially well for smokers, drug addicts, and insomniacs. She saw no problems with patients taking both eastern and western medicines at the same time, and mentioned that Antabuse could effectively discourage relapses. Dr. Sepali also recommended meditation and rehabilitation programs, but noted that rural areas had few such facilities.

Rehabilitation

In this book, I deal almost exclusively with alcohol use and make only infrequent mention of other drugs. Historian K. M. de Silva (2002, 6) suggests that Sri Lanka is not a major player in the international drug trade. But locals and tourists do indulge in prohibited substances, particularly in the coastal areas. Heroin and marijuana (*ganja*) are the most common drugs used in Sri Lanka. "Heroin, the brown variety also known as the brown sugar, is used for inhalation, a method preferred by the users in our country to that of the method of injecting, which requires a more soluble variety known as white sugar" (Jeyanathan 2006, A9). Sri Lanka's few rehabilitation and treatment programs focus mostly on curing addictions to illicit drugs, not alcohol.

Both governmental and non-governmental organizations (NGOs) run rehabilitation programs in Sri Lanka.[3] There are roughly thirty such pro-

3. Sri Lanka has a variety of rehabilitation programs. The National Dangerous Drugs Control Board (NDDCB) runs four drug rehabilitation centers in the more populous areas of

grams on the island, and all but four deal principally with drug addiction. My sources uniformly agreed that demand for treatment exceeds availability; efficacy "fluctuates" (as one informant delicately put it); more alcohol programs are needed; and expense and location make programs inaccessible to many addicts. In this section I provide information on the Mel Medura alcohol and drug abuse program in Colombo, discuss the challenges faced by a monk involved with the Prevention of Substance Abuse and Rehabilitation (Sarvodaya Samodaya Sewa) program associated with the famous Sri Lankan NGO Sarvodaya, and relate the experiences of a village man who went through the government's drug rehabilitation program at the Pallekale Open Prison Camp.

Mel Medura: Dr. Fernando

Mel Medura, the Sumithrayo Drug Demand Reduction Programme, occupied a large colonial-era house in one of Colombo's most prestigious neighborhoods. Sumithrayo, a branch of Befrienders International, has run this program since 1984 (Ellawala 2005, 2). I interviewed Dr. Manoj Fernando, the Executive Director of Mel Medura (interview with author, June 29, 2006). We spoke in English. Dr. Fernando was a fit, energetic, and friendly man in his thirties.

Mel Medura assisted about 350 clients a year for alcohol abuse and 50–100 for heroin addiction. Most of Mel Medura's clients were middle class and came from the Colombo area and its suburbs. In contrast to the high fees charged by other facilities, Mel Medura only took Rs. 1,000 (Rs. 827 in 2004 figures) from each person. Dr. Fernando felt the fee necessary, citing that it enhanced people's perception of the program's value while covering charges for building upkeep, refreshments, and treatment follow-up activities. Dr. Fernando evaluated new clients. If a man exhibited symptoms of withdrawal or mental illness, Dr. Fernando referred him to the medical

---

the country (Police Narcotics Bureau 2006). The prison system also runs drug rehabilitation camps for convicts. In addition, Reverend Kuppiyawatte Bodhananda Thero heads the Mithuru Mithuro Movement—an NGO that runs nine rehabilitation centers, again in the more populous southwestern areas of Sri Lanka (Police Narcotics Bureau 2006; World Health Organization 2003). The famous Sri Lankan NGO Sarvodaya also works in conjunction with Reverend Bodhananda Thero. The Sumithrayo organization runs the Mel Medura alcohol and drug abuse program in Colombo, and the Alcohol and Drug Information Centre (ADIC) runs an experimental program in Negombo. Several international NGOs run programs in conjunction with local branch offices, including the United Nations and the International Organization of Good Templars (United Nations 2003). Two Alcoholics Anonymous groups meet in Sri Lanka. With the exception of Mel Medura, AA, and ADIC, these resources deal mainly with heroin addiction.

or psychiatric branches of the Colombo National Hospital. For the most part, however, Mel Medura sought to demedicalize and deinstitutionalize treatment.

Until 2004, Mel Medura operated an in-house treatment program. A shift in philosophy and a re-evaluation of cost-effectiveness prompted a change; in 2006, Mel Medura operated only a day care program. Clients came daily for two weeks, attending morning and afternoon treatment sessions. Dr. Fernando disapproved of programs that kept a client in an alcohol-free environment for months on end. He stated, "Of course he stops drinking in that case; the stuff isn't around so he has to. When you put him back in his usual environment, he starts again. Ninety percent of the people drink again in those cases." In contrast to the costly and artificial environment of a residential rehabilitation center, Mel Medura encouraged clients "to gain control while remaining in their own environment" (Ellawala 2005, 14). Mel Medura's practice conforms to a trend away from in-patient treatment around the world (Bennie, McKinney, and Campbell 2000, 179). Research suggests that outpatient care achieves the same outcomes for considerably less money.

The two-stage Mel Medura treatment program focused on skill development and relapse prevention. Activities included psychotherapy, relaxation techniques, and individual and group counseling. Lifestyle modification formed a part of the cognitive behavioral therapy offered (Acuda and Alexander 1998; Heather 2000). The program developed skills such as time- and money-management, repairing family relationships, coping with urges for sex or drugs, and the ability to understand and dismiss harmful advertising promotions (Ellawala 2005, 15, 18). Counselors helped clients work toward a goal, such as finding a job. The treatment sought to empower both individuals and their peer and family groups to change harmful habits and avoid relapse. Mel Medura also offered a program to encourage and enlighten family members. The program strove to "'release' the person taking the responsibility for the client's conduct," particularly the wives and mothers who "have to be weaned off the 'enabler' role" (Ellawala 2005, 16). Mel Medura encouraged family members to support the client's efforts without either supervising his activities or raking up unpleasant family history. After the initial intervention, the staff periodically followed up with clients over two years. They provided what Dr. Fernando referred to as "booster doses" of counseling, visiting a client at home and bringing him back to treatment if he had relapsed. Seventy to 80 percent of their clients stopped drinking following the program, but after a month only 35 to 50 percent were still sober—a percentage that Mel Medura hoped to improve in the future.

Extending the program beyond their Colombo facility, Mel Medura organized half-day community treatment modules during which the staff members entered high-risk communities and worked to change alcohol and drug use patterns using the techniques employed at the center. Their message suggested that "The chemical effect of most psychoactive drugs is not in itself pleasant," and tried to create "awareness in the community regarding the unhealthy influence of promotions by commercial groups[,]" which suggest that drinking will enhance social standing or pleasure (Ellawala 2005, 10). Given prevailing social norms, this endeavor was an uphill battle. In addition, local *kasippu* sellers in one community reportedly threatened staff members for undermining their livelihood, a pattern also observed in other instances of community interventions (Samarasinghe 2005, 40).

The Sarvodaya Samodaya Sewa Program:
Suddhamma Thero

While studying for his degree at a local university, Suddhamma Thero led a temperance organization called the Anti-Alcohol Association (Amadyapa Vyaapaaraya). Because of his experience with the subject, Sarvodaya selected him to direct their Prevention of Substance Abuse and Rehabilitation (Sarvodaya Samodaya Sewa) program. Suddhama Thero served as the project director in Kalutara and Galle districts for about ten years.

One of the program's main objectives was to rehabilitate drug addicts. The program did not bring people in by force. According to Suddhamma Thero, the Sarvodaya drug rehabilitation center used Ayurvedic and western medicines and counseling. They found medicines especially useful during the first week, when many clients experienced withdrawal symptoms. After withdrawal, addiction became a mental problem. Keeping the mind in one place through meditation helped the rehabilitation process. "If you are always thinking about and looking for drugs and alcohol, you have no mental peace or freedom," Suddhamma Thero asserted. The monk claimed that the program successfully cured 6 or 7 percent of its clients.

Another objective of the Sarvodaya program was to educate youth about drugs, alcohol, and tobacco in order to prevent addiction. Suddhamma Thero felt that overall, educated youth were drinking less. Many campaigns successfully targeted university students and schoolboys. But these campaigns had not taken place as often or been as successful in the rural areas. In addition, the local drug dealers resented the campaigns. During the last month Suddhamma Thero directed the Sarvodaya program, villagers staged a poster campaign against him, alleging that he secretly supported the drug business and that he called the police to tell them to let the drug dealers out of jail. The posters asserted that he ran the counseling program as a cover. Denying these charges as pure fabrication, Suddhamma Thero lamented that at several locations around his town monastery, people sold drugs and *kasippu*. Despite police raids and court fines, these businesses thrived uninterrupted.

Information from the Mel Medura and Sarvodaya program suggests that Sri Lanka has developed indigenous methods of dealing with drug and alcohol addiction. Although similar to (and indeed drawing on) such programs in the west, the Sri Lankan programs use unique, culturally appropriate methods and approaches. These cases also illustrate that drug dealers and *kasippu* businesspeople actively oppose public information campaigns.

Pallekale Open Prison Camp: Janith

Although many men drank daily in the Naeaegama village, I only heard of one individual who had attended a treatment program. Cravings for mind-altering substances drove men to break social rules and neglect their household duties. In return, family members felt torn between loyalty to kin and the need for help with dysfunctional relationships. Misilin, the mother of two addicts, took radical steps to keep her sons from using and selling illegal substances. While her daughter-in-law was abroad, Misilin turned in her son Janith, a heroin user and smalltime dealer, to the police. From the court, he went to a drug rehabilitation program in the upcountry town of Pallekale.

Soon after Janith's release from the program, Siri and I interviewed him about the Pallekale Open Prison Camp rehabilitation center. According to Janith, inmates arrived from the prison system, and approximately a hundred men lived in four wards inside a barbed-wired compound. Like schoolboys, they wore white shirts and blue shorts. The inmates ate good food—perhaps better than what they would have eaten at home. Three times a day, they took western medicine for the joint pains caused by the drugs they had taken. They also received medical and dental treatment as needed. The daily program included work and study. Each morning they exercised for an hour and then went to work. Janith made brooms from coconut fiber. Other inmates grew vegetables, welded metal to make gates, or trained in masonry. On some afternoons a man came and taught them about drugs. On other afternoons they studied English or learned about religion. They meditated and observed *pansil* (recited the five Buddhist precepts) three times a day. On Poya Days (full moon holidays sacred in the Buddhist religion) the Buddhist inmates observed *sil* (a standard religious practice followed by many older village women and some men).[4] The program combined medical approaches with educational, employment, and religious elements to rehabilitate drug users.

Curious about how effective the program had been in changing Janith's lifestyle, I asked if Janith still meditated and observed *sil* on Poya Days. He laughed at the idea. "I have to earn money. I have no time to take Poya off. I need to find food." Janith did not recall receiving any individual or group therapy while in the rehabilitation program. I asked if anyone followed up with Janith after he returned from the rehabilitation program. "No," Janith answered. "They said not to do it again. We know not to." Janith asserted that when he got out of the rehabilitation program he was fit and healthy. He neither drank nor took drugs. "Now," he told us, "I take some *kasippu* but no drugs (*kuDu*, literally powder)."

"What would you do if someone invited you to use some drugs?" Siri asked.

"I would tell him I have stopped," Janith replied.

"What would you do if someone asked you if he should start taking drugs?" I asked.

"Don't! (*epaa!*)" Janith replied passionately. "Take anything else, but not that! If a man takes drugs, he will be ruined [literally 'break into powder'] (*minihaa kuDu biwot kuDu wenawaa*). The man's name is *kuDu* too.[5] Drugs are the end! They are the worst thing someone can do. It is worse than drinking. If you drink, you just fall in a ditch. Drugs are worse. You can't get enough of them, and you're afraid."

Janith used drugs for ten years, supporting a Rs. 300 a day habit by the time he went into treatment. If he did not have his fix, he started to ache. Siri asked, "Did you want to stop taking drugs when you went into rehab?"

"Even if I had wanted to, I couldn't have," Janith replied. He asserted, "You can't not take drugs (*nobii baeae*). You compulsorily have to take them (*anivaaryeen bonDa onaeae*). A man is a madman if he doesn't take them (*miniha pisseek biiwe naetnam.*) It would have been better to hang on a gallows (*ellumgaha*) than to stop. People can stop taking arrack on their

---

4. The Five Precepts forbid devotees to kill, steal, be unchaste, tell lies, and take intoxicating substances. On Poya days, people observing *sil* observe the first five precepts plus several more. The precept forbidding unchaste behaviors is modified so devotees renounce sexual activities for the day. In addition, the devotee will not sit on high chairs or beds, will not eat after noon, will not partake in dancing and music making, and will abstain from putting on perfume or flower garlands.

5. Janith's statement that a drug user's name will be "*KuDu*" refers to a village nicknaming habit; for example, a drug user named Lal would be called "KuDu-Lal."

own, but not drugs. I had tried before to get off drugs. There was a place in Colombo that gave pills to help. I went a dozen times but I always started taking drugs again after the effect of the pills wore off." Janith had not translated his training to extend to other addictive substances, such as alcohol and cigarettes. But he seemed convinced and convincing about not using drugs, and to this end his rehabilitation was clearly successful. Though effective, such treatments reached few, if any, of the alcohol-dependent men in the village.

Spiritual Treatments

Both western (allopathic) and indigenous (Ayurvedic) medical approaches focus on physical aspects of alcohol dependence. Although clearly aware of the mental and social sides of addiction, medical practitioners did not deal with these areas directly. Rehabilitation programs addressed these aspects, but such treatment centers, rare in general, were lacking entirely in most rural areas. Villagers turned elsewhere for mental and moral support. In this section, I examine the spiritual resources available to families of alcohol-dependent men and drinkers who tried to quit or who had quit and wished to stay sober.

Although Buddhism provides a consistent message not to indulge in intoxicating substances, some drinkers used religious arguments to challenge advice to stop drinking. Complex systems of knowledge, religions can provide support for almost any position. Consider the following interaction between Siri and Dr. Sepali, the Ayurvedic physician. Dr. Sepali said, "Drinking shortens your life." Siri replied, "The Lord Buddha predestines death. Some kids die at birth. I have been lucky to have sixty-one years. Whether I drink or not, go to the temple or not, it won't change my death date." In this Siri referred to a common local conception of karma and fate.[6] Implicitly defending his desire to drink as long as he lived, Siri defiantly continued, "When I die, I'll take four bottles of arrack and a small glass with me in my coffin!" Drawing on common concepts of karma, Siri used the authority of Buddhism to undermine both Buddhist teaching and medical advice.

As Wilcox (1998, 40) observes about alcoholics in the United States, drinkers in Sri Lanka often rejected the authority of law enforcement, medical professionals, and religious leaders. Yet by this very rejection the drinker acknowledged the specialists' cultural right to advise individuals

6. Army soldiers also refer to the theory that the Lord Buddha predestines people's deaths when they talk about the risks they face during wartime (M. Gamburd 2004b).

on health and behavior (Foucault 1994). While police, judges, and doctors held only scientific and legal authority, religious practitioners had supernatural backing. Drinkers unwilling to give up their habit rejected this authority, leading some villagers to fear that religious intervention could not cure addiction. One village laborer said, "Religion can't help. Drinking men don't believe in religion. And the monks will chase people off for coming to the temple drunk. Then the person will scold the priests in filth [a sign of deep social dysfunction]." Hema, whose alcohol-dependent son committed suicide, noted despondently, "The monks say to stop but the boys don't listen." Indeed, religious authorities had little success in reforming unreceptive drinkers. Drinkers who wished to stop, however, could turn to spiritual powers for support in their decision. In some instances, sacred and supernatural prohibitions brought about changes that secular authority could not achieve (Heath 1987).

Charmings

In some cases, a combination of medical knowledge and spiritual authority could effectively guide a believer to sobriety. Dr. Devika, a newly certified Ayurvedic practitioner in Naeaegama, mentioned that her training covered supernatural topics. Some practitioners charmed bananas, king coconuts (*taembili*), or oil to help people stop drinking and to cure other illnesses. Dr. Devika, however, feared to talk with spirits and devils to attempt such cures. She felt these techniques could work, but the few true practitioners were judged along with the many charlatans. Most important in these treatments was the drinker's cooperation. "If they believe in the cure, it can help. But some people don't realize that drinking is bad for them, and they don't think they should stop. So then they won't stop." Efficacy depended on the patient's belief and cooperation.

Spiritual practitioners agreed that a drinker ought to assent to his cure. Indeed, a drinker who took this step might require no further treatment. Ananda Thero asserted, "If a man decides not to drink, he can stop without any aid, and no one can get him to start again, not for friendship or pride or anger. It all depends on the mind (*hita*)." Drinkers and their families nevertheless sometimes searched for assistance. Much admired for his skill, Ananda Thero administered cures for a wide range of mental, physical, and social problems, including headaches, back pains, high fevers, financial worries, and divorce cases. He emphasized the power of *pirith*, the Pali verses containing the Buddha's sermons: "At one time the Lord Buddha's enemies sent an elephant to kill him. They gave the elephant sixteen pots of toddy [coconut beer]. The elephant charged. The Lord Buddha recited *pirith* and *gaataa* [prayers], and the elephant became sober. He stopped his charge and worshipped the Lord Buddha." Ananda Thero used this set of *pirith* verses to treat alcohol dependence.

Ananda Thero's techniques varied depending on the attitude of the drinker. For a man ready and willing to give up liquor, Ananda Thero charmed a series of king coconuts by chanting the appropriate *pirith* verses 108 times over each coconut, a forty-five-minute process. When he charmed coconuts for pregnant women or sick elders, Ananda Thero let family members take the fruit to the patient. But he required drinkers to come to the temple every morning for seven days to drink the coconut in his presence. "Otherwise all my hard work is in the forest," Ananda Thero asserted with a laugh, gesturing as if tossing a coconut over his shoulder. For a drinker unwilling to stop, Ananda Thero gave remedies that wives and mothers could use in secret. For example, he chanted *pirith* verses over golden coconut oil and instructed women to put three drops in the drinker's rice at lunch and dinner. Over a month, this cure would gradually reduce the man's alcohol consumption. Women could also mix one teaspoon of pig's milk with a quarter bottle of cow's milk; served every day for three days, this folk cure would cause a drinker to vomit at the smell of alcohol. The monk emphasized that all cures worked better and quicker if the drinker said he wanted to stop. "But if a person drinks regularly, he won't want to stop suddenly. So I tell him to reduce gradually, going from one bottle to three quarters to a half to a quarter. In a month he can reduce what he drinks. But the problem is that people want the whole bottle," he said, glaring and pointing at Siri, who smiled sheepishly.

Anticipating community needs, Ananda Thero prepared supplies in advance. In the corner of the temple relic room where junior monks recited *pirith* every morning and evening, on a narrow table behind a heavy red curtain, sat over a hundred bottles of coconut oil and Ayurvedic medicines. White holy thread (*pirith nuul*) connected all the bottles, dipping into the oil under each bottle cap. Large plastic canisters of water and a basin of untrodden beach sand mixed with mustard seeds sat under the table, similarly linked by white thread. These supplies served a variety of purposes; for example, a small amount of *pirith* water could bless a new well, and a sprinkling of sand would fend off demons. *Pirith* verses enhanced the Ayurvedic medicines and gave spiritual power to the coconut oil. Ananda Thero provided these items and services to the community free of charge, but people often made donations to the temple if pleased with the results.

Not all spiritual cures worked out, particularly those given to drinkers unwilling to quit. Hema once took her son's horoscope to a ritual specialist

Fig. 5. Ananda Thero's supply of charmed oil. *Pirith nuul* runs from bottle to bottle under the caps. Photograph by author.

who put some medicine in a king coconut to stop him from drinking. Her son stayed sober for three weeks, then took up his old habits. Hema lamented, "I spent a lot of money for him." She had considered using Antabuse tablets but had heard they were dangerous if someone took them in conjunction with liquor. Hema concluded, "No doctor or monk can help. People just have to decide in their own heart to stop drinking." Her refrain echoed the words of medical and spiritual practitioners alike.

Vows: The Kali Temple

If alcohol addiction is an illness, it is a strange one, highly dependent on the drinker's volition. Religious treatments can help someone acknowledge a problem and reinforce his effort to quit. For example, Medicine writes of the Yuwipi ceremony among the Lakota Sioux, in which someone may ask for supernatural aid in curbing drinking problems (2007, 124). Similarly, the Native American Church has helped many Navajo cease drinking (Kunitz 2006, 291). In Sri Lanka, people find religious cures particularly effective for treating mental illnesses.

Kali, a wrathful and uncontrollable Hindu goddess, is both feared and respected. Many Sri Lankans, both Hindu and Buddhist, turn to her in moments of crisis. For example, Patricia Lawrence (1997) suggests that Sri Lanka's ethnic conflict has revitalized the cults of territorial Hindu goddesses in eastern Sri Lanka. Oracles at the Amman temples help victims of violence come to terms with the trauma and injury of war. In some cases, torture victims who have made vows to Kali-amman in moments of extreme duress fulfill those vows by engaging in what Euro-Americans might consider radical forms of worship—including piercing their cheeks with metal rods, walking over hot coals, and suspending themselves on flesh hooks. The rituals offer an opportunity for a far-reaching remaking of self. Supplicants offer their injured bodies and suffering minds to the goddess, receiving whole minds and bodies back at the end of the experience. By turning to the goddess and her rituals, people seek control over a situation that they cannot manage in other ways. Alcohol-dependent individuals seeking spiritual assistance choose the kind of help they need. While an American alcoholic might choose a God of mercy (Antze 1987), a Sri Lankan *beebaddeek* might choose a Goddess of wrath.

Men seeking radical self-transformation vowed to stop drinking, and faced dire consequences if they broke their promise to Kali. In 2004, Bernard, who had recently stopped drinking, told us,

> I make a good salary. When I'm drinking, it all goes to alcohol. I wanted to stop drinking, so I got treatments from Dr. Priyanka. It costs me Rs. 200 for each intravenous drip, and I took eight of these treatments. After that I stopped drinking for three or four months. Then I drank again, and I was afraid I would go back to my old habits. So I made a vow at the Kali temple (*Kaali maeaenii deevaalaya*) that I would not drink. Bad things happen to you if you break this sort of vow. The first and only time I started to have a drink after making that vow, I was at a wedding. A glass fell and cut my foot so badly that I couldn't walk.

Bernard showed us the scab on his foot. Since that incident a month prior to our conversation, Bernard claimed he had not taken liquor.

Bernard waxed passionate about the Kali temple. "People go there and promise to stop drinking. Even foreigners come to this temple! They know that the goddess will punish them physically if they break their vows. They will break an arm or get paralyzed with their tongue sticking out, or they will have a fight or an accident," Bernard warned. Then he told a story of a businessman who drank after vowing not to. "He was going somewhere in his van. He got boils and blisters on the bottoms of his feet. Someone else had to drive! He went back to the temple (*koovila*) and apologized, and then he was cured." Bernard also told a story of a man who spent Rs. 30,000 a month on alcohol. "He gave a table worth Rs. 15,000 to the Kali temple when he promised to stop drinking. The people who are cured there give free food to the people coming for treatment. They spend the money they used to use for drinking for a good purpose instead." Both the stories and the service provided to others seeking sobriety play a role in the process.

Men risked punishment if they broke their vows. Supervising supernaturally, the omniscient goddess administered the punishment. Those seeking a secular account might say an individual had internalized the supervision and administered his own discipline (Foucault 1979). By circulating stories regarding the misery of their lives before they stopped drinking, the effectiveness of their vows, and the severity of the goddess's punishments for relapses, Bernard and other Kali devotees repeated the stories that help them resist liquor. This process bears some similarity to the personal narratives recited by recovering alcoholics in Alcoholics Anonymous. As one scholar suggests, "Recovery in AA can be seen as a triumph of the discursive over the bodily: the recovering alcoholic keeps telling the story and, in doing so, finds a way not to swallow another alcoholic drink" (Warhol 2002, 108).[7] By Bernard's account, at the Kali temple men reinforced their collective determination to stay sober.

On a Saturday morning a year and a half after this conversation, Siri and I set out with Bernard to visit the Kali temple, picking up a ritual specialist, Mattius, along the way. By trishaw we traveled ten miles, the last three on unpaved paths muddy from recent rain. Amid secluded paddy fields and cinnamon gardens, we found a dozen vehicles and a considerable crowd. Six small buildings, one for the Lord Buddha and the rest for the goddess Kali, huddled under tall trees populated by fruit bats. Devotees used a sheltered area in front of the main temple for preparing baskets of offerings (*puujaa waTTi*).[8] The smaller shrines lacked porches. The two structures I visited each had two rooms. In the anteroom of the main temple, a table

---

7. Common American folk narratives suggest that after a moment of radical despair or "hitting bottom," the drinker understands the need for change (Perez 1992). The healing process includes recognizing that self-directed attempts to control drinking have been fruitless, surrendering oneself to a Higher Power, and committing oneself to a humble life of helping other problem drinkers (Alcoholics Anonymous 2001). Many recovering alcoholics regularly attend Alcoholics Anonymous meetings, where they tell their individual stories (termed by various scholars as "drunkologues" [Warhol 2002] or "surrender myths" [Antze 1987]. These stories follow a similar three-part pattern of depression, illness, or other crisis, followed by a sense of helplessness and a reaching out toward and surrender to a Higher Power, which brings a feeling of comfort and release. These stories present a powerful transformation in individual subjectivity, akin to a rebirth with a transformed relationship to alcohol.

8. An offering basket for Kali should include seven sorts of sweets and seven sorts of fruits. The offering must include two "Tamil" foods: boiled chickpeas and deep fried lentil balls (*waDee*). People also often include an egg and some curd and treacle in their offerings.

held a tray with clay oil lamps and a metal triton covered with coins tied in red cloth strips. In the shrine room, flowers, oil lamps, and various other ritual instruments were placed in front of a statue and colorful pictures of the goddess.

Mattius and the priest (*kapu-mahattayaa*) of the main temple each told us the myth of the site's establishment. During the Portuguese colonial period, a surveyor came to measure the land. His horse cart got stuck in mud. Unable to move the vehicle, the surveyor spent the night in the forest. In the morning an old lady appeared. She promised to move the cart if the surveyor gave her a small bit of the land, to which he agreed. A manifestation of the goddess, the old woman magically moved the cart and promptly disappeared. Devotees set up a temple to Kali on that site. The temple fell out of use when the Tamil villagers left the area. About forty-five years ago, a Sinhala priest reestablished the temple, and now there are five small worship sites on the land.

Another important story, related by the priest of the main temple, explained the nature of Kali's power. "The gods were beating the demons in the ongoing war between good and evil. The chief demon, a shape-shifter, appeared to Kali in the guise of her husband Ishwara, who has a third eye in the middle of his forehead. The demon sought Kali's blessing, with which the demons could win the war. Kali detected the imposter." Showing us a standard iconographic picture of many-armed Kali standing on a demon, the priest explained, "Kali kicked, stepped on, and killed the demon." Although neither my informants nor the literature on Kali made the comparison, when Kali faced a demon who looked like her husband, her case paralleled a village woman facing a drunken spouse under the influence of a mind-altering substance. Unlike most local women, however, Kali had the power and the prerogative to name and expel the intruder. Perhaps this enhanced her appeal to female supplicants.

The priest at the second temple (a schoolteacher during the week) provided a printed list of thirty services, including making talismans to protect people working overseas, cure diabetes, help with interviews, and nullify malefic planetary influences. His intercession with Kali could also help women get married, get pregnant, and protect their babies. The list mentioned techniques to settle marital disputes, solve land problems, and help businesses develop. Sandwiched between ceremonies for weak students and curses for thieves was the service rendered to wives and mothers of drinkers to cure men of alcohol problems.

To achieve their desired ends, people engaged in one of several general processes. One path was for a supplicant to make a vow presenting a basket

Fig. 6. In this mass-market image, the goddess Kali tramples the demon who impersonated her husband.

of offerings, tying a coin in a cloth, or smashing a coconut adorned with a piece of burning camphor. The supplicant fulfilled the vow if and when the goddess did as the supplicant asked. Supplicants fulfilled vows by presenting offerings, breaking coconuts, giving money or other valuables to the temple, or hanging a flag on a nearby tree. A second path entailed having a ritual specialist like Mattius compose benevolent verses (*seth kavi,* blessing poems). The supplicant presented an offering basket to the goddess and the priest chanted a summoning followed by the verses. The supplicant might repeat the chanting and prestations for several days.

Mattius and the two priests all said that they could help a man stop drinking. In one scenario, the man did not want to stop, and his relatives (often his wife or mother) came unbeknownst to him to ask for help. The priest made offerings to the goddess and then charmed some water, which the woman could secretly put into the man's food or tea. Some women came for seven days, bringing seven baskets of offerings—no small investment of time and money. In addition, a ritual specialist like Mattius could prepare verses for chanting. In a second scenario, the drinker came in person, made an offering, had some verses chanted, and vowed not to drink. All the ritual specialists agreed that they got better results if the drinker himself requested their services.

The priests reported that men rarely drank after making vows, but sometimes continued after their relatives performed ceremonies in secret. Both Mattius and Siri related stories about a Naeaegama man, Jayasekera, who died after his wife went to the Kali temple. Mattius said that Jayasekera's family wanted him to stop drinking. They came to Mattius secretly for help. Mattius wrote some benevolent verses, which a priest chanted. Jayasekera, who knew nothing of this, continued to drink. Soon after the rituals, he got a bad case of diarrhea. Mattius stopped the verse recitations; he felt that the combination of ritual and alcohol use was killing the man. Later Siri asserted that a long period of heavy drinking had weakened Jayasekera's health. When Jayasekera started defecating black feces, his family took him to the hospital, where he died. Dismissing ritual influence as a cause, Siri saw the death as the result of chronic alcohol abuse.

As our trishaw bounced over rutted roads on our way home, I asked Bernard whether he had stuck to the vow that he had taken a year and a half earlier. To my surprise, Bernard denied ever making such a vow. Although Bernard seemed sober while accompanying us on our visit to the Kali temple, Siri told me later that Bernard had recently resumed daily drinking after a year of sobriety. I found Bernard's about-face puzzling. Because he had participated that day in several short rituals at the Kali temple, I felt that his faith in the goddess remained unchanged. Rather than doubt Kali's powers, perhaps he had selectively edited his memory of his own past actions, thus protecting himself from the mental effects of breaking his vow. Kali lost none of her authority, but a rewriting of history allowed Bernard to escape her wrath.

Vows, like charmed coconuts, took their power from the patient's belief. Janith, the recovering drug addict, spoke of spiritual cures with disdain. He said impatiently, "That's all lies." Then, implicitly admitting that he previously gave some credence to the method, he continued, "One time I went to Kande Vihara [a famous Buddhist temple with associated shrines for various gods and goddesses]. I promised not to drink. I didn't drink for a month. Then I started again." Showing that he was not alone in relapsing after such treatment, Janith related the following story: "One man went and promised not to drink. Then he got desperate for alcohol, so he soaked some bread with arrack and ate it. That's not 'drinking,' right!?" Janith's vignettes portrayed believers caught between the letter of the law and the power of compulsion. Because no punishments befell the vow breakers, Janith's examples challenged the logic of the system. But Siri implicitly affirmed the effectiveness of supernatural power with a countertale about another local man. "He went to [a nearby Buddhist temple] and promised not to drink. But then he drank arrack. He fell and broke his leg and was laid up in bed for eight months. That was his punishment for breaking his promise." No one took deities lightly. But their powers could not help addicts who chose not to stop drinking, broke their vows and recognized no bad consequences, or selectively forgot what they had promised.

Conclusion

Naeaegama treatments for alcohol abuse included methods that forcibly kept drinkers away from alcohol, scared them, ridiculed or shamed them, and supported them in their endeavors to quit. More effective than the formal negative sanctions administered by the police were the informal sanctions applied by family members and community representatives. Some people exerted pressure more effectively than others. Men often defied their wives, but daughters could sometimes persuade their fathers to modify their habits, claiming that the fathers' excess drinking damaged their reputations. Preventative education in schools and temples reached youth, but conflicted with the positive information that children received about alcohol from the media and the community. As long as hosts serve alcohol at ceremonies and men drink to demonstrate their manliness, youngsters will view messages of abstinence with ambivalence.

Naeaegama residents chose from a variety of resources when confronting alcohol dependence. Although approaches varied, practitioners uniformly agreed that treatments worked best when the drinker himself wished to stop. Both western and Ayurvedic medical practitioners dealt more with the body and its physical addiction than with the mind. They referred the remaining work to rehabilitation centers. Unfortunately, the few such programs available dealt mainly with drugs rather than with alcohol, had limited capacities, and offered little follow-up. Like most programs of their sort, they had low success rates. Local treatments shared elements with Euro-American techniques of motivational enhancement therapy and cognitive behavioral therapy but also revealed culturally specific characteristics drawing on Buddhist philosophy and spiritually based treatments for mental illness.

Some addicts turned to charismatic religious leaders and popular deities to treat their dependence on liquor. Religious treatments administered through temples and rehabilitation programs sought to address mental issues of craving and lack of willpower. A charismatic Buddhist monk, Ayurvedic healer, or priest could help a drinker change his habits. For those who respected religious traditions, taking a vow not to drink gave the supplicant access to informal support and counseling at the temple. Those who broke their promises to Kali brought upon themselves the wrath of the goddess, which for some drinkers proved more effective than the admonitions of family, friends, clergy, doctors, and the police.

Conclusion

Having read this lengthy discussion of alcohol use in Sri Lanka, the reader may ask what contribution it makes to the literature. I hope this work will illustrate the value of holism in the study of alcohol. In the past, many anthropologists have focused on the functional, integrative roles that drinking plays in society. Indeed, drinking can solidify group identity, enforce kinship links, and allow cliques and communities to differentiate themselves from others. In Naeaegama, drinking serves these functions at village ceremonies and in local taverns. Through specific drinking patterns, people enact identities of family membership, gender, age, class, and profession. But concluding the discussion of alcohol use with the cultural construction of identity would tell only part of the story.

In this ethnography, I move beyond issues of individual and community identity to examine the political economics of alcohol. This allows me to look at power dynamics in a series of concentric settings. At the household level, I explore negotiations over how to spend scarce resources. These consumption struggles reveal valuable insights into spousal relations and gender roles in local families. A political economic perspective also illuminates issues around the manufacture and sale of illicit liquor, the status of bootleggers within the community, and relationships between *kasippu* businesspeople and local police and politicians. This orientation situates alcohol as a commodity within the economy, and shows how its production, distribution, and consumption are deeply embedded within local, national, and international relations of power and inequality.

In addition to talking about identity and political economics, this book also focuses on issues of problem drinking. "We drink alcohol because it is good for us, and study it because it is bad for us," write Plant and Cameron (2000, 237). Similarly, Heath notes, "Part of the fascination of the subject of alcohol is its double-edged capacity to induce euphoria and sociability on the one hand, and, on the other, to lead to serious personal and social problems" (2000, xiii). All too often in the past, scholars have separated the functional and dysfunctional in their discussions of ingested substances. But a study focusing solely on functional drinking would leave the reader asking why anyone would consider alcohol use bad, and a study focusing only on problem drinking would raise the query of why anyone would drink or allow others to do so. In this study of alcohol use in Naeaegama, I hope that I have demonstrated both the positive and the negative aspects of drinking, neither inflating nor deflating the problem (Room 1984) but presented drinking in a holistic context by talking about its many roles in the village community. Within alcohol studies, much of the research on abusive drinking comes from the clinical literature on treatment. This area would benefit from an integration of interdisciplinary insights and a greater attention to wider contexts within which destructive drinking takes place. Simultaneously presenting both edges of the proverbial sword helps make sense of why people drink, why some drink to excess, and how community members approach the issue of problem drinking. My holistic perspective sets both the functional and the dysfunctional aspects of alcohol use into dialog with one another within the framework of a community ethnography.

Where Next?

In light of this historical and contemporary discussion of alcohol use in Naeaegama, one might ask what the future will bring to the village and to the island of Sri Lanka. This book describes the micro-politics of alcohol use in a village context. Although I have tried to tie local dynamics to a wider social context, the larger system deserves fuller attention.

Various scholars contend that integration into a cash-based market economy increases the availability of alcohol and the number of people who drink heavily (Dietler 2006; Kunitz 2006; Singer 1986; Suggs 2001). Over the past fifty years, Sri Lanka has grown evermore integrated into the global economy and life for many people has gotten harder. The International Monetary Fund has implemented Structural Adjustment Programs, tourism has expanded, the export of garments has grown, and international labor migration continues to rise. During this same time period, Naeaegama elders have noted an increase in male drinking, with more men drinking, drinking at younger ages, and drinking in less respectful and less circumspect ways. With the current escalation in Sri Lanka's ongoing ethnic conflict, possibilities for economic growth and development remain dim; and such development would in all likelihood exacerbate the inequalities between rich elites and the mass of poor laborers. Given the correlation between poverty and the use of psychotropic substances, one might predict that changes in problem drinking will reflect the country's economic health. These trends should be examined through the lens of both qualitative and quantitative data.

Although alcohol use can reflect social marginalization on a large scale, within communities drinking indicates full adult status. Those who are not deemed sufficiently in charge of themselves are often not allowed to drink (Valverde 1998, 145). Ongoing social changes in Naeaegama suggest that young men now drink, regardless of whether their elders deem it appropriate. Increasingly, women have also begun to drink, though they only drink beer and only consume it in the newly allowable context of weddings and other celebrations. In the future, local norms surrounding gender and age will continue to evolve. Men and women may proceed to drink more, at earlier ages, or women's current agendas to decrease spending on alcohol and prioritize other domestic needs may prevail. If women continue to fight against male alcohol use, their struggle could grow politicized (Eber 2001). If women organized a temperance movement, they might frame their objections within Sinhala-Buddhist rhetoric, or they could adopt an explicitly feminist or Marxist point of view emphasizing ties between gender, family, private property, capitalism, human rights, and the state (Engels 1972; Stephens 1995). Whatever route local women's initiatives take, scholars should continue to consider these questions.

As gendered power struggles change alcohol-related practices at the grassroots level, state regulatory interventions are likely to do so from the top down. Administrative initiatives may serve covert agendas. Government policies often rely on and reinforce powerful ideologies and stereotypes as they exercise power over a population through regulations, surveillance, and interventions (Foucault 1991). As an example of the links between institutional initiatives and ideology, Robert Elias (1997) considers state policies within a larger discussion of the international drug trade. Elias argues that in the United States, the "war on drugs" has distinct class- and race-based elements. Over the past forty years, increasing inequalities on the global scale have lead to resistance and rebellion. Elias argues that states can suppress dissent by using force masked as progressive interventions for the good of the population. Under the surface justification of eradicating the trade in dangerous substances, the U.S. government implements policies that amount to an undeclared war on African American men in U.S. inner cities and on "communist" insurgents in other countries. Overseas, Structural Adjustment Programs and military aid to repressive governments often block progressive change and combat challenges to the capitalist system. In both the developed and the developing world, such interventions target the most disempowered people using paternalistic arguments, disciplining the disaffected "for their own good and the good of society." Discourse about legitimate problems can easily mask the use of force and violence to maintain and enhance existing power relations.

The state's regulation of space and substance will affect people's lived experiences as Sri Lanka grows ever more embedded in the neo-imperial global economy. Future research on alcohol should focus on relationships between international liquor conglomerates and government policy. Scholars could fruitfully investigate how legal liquor manufacturers in Sri Lanka articulate with the international industry as transnational corporations expand rapidly into the developing world. The global trend in food manufacturing runs toward centralization and consolidation, as relatively few decision makers control ever-vaster amounts of resources (Hendrickson and Heffernan 2002). In the future, legal liquor companies with international links are likely to reach more efficiently into village life, bringing different alcoholic products to poor drinkers. Anti-competitive forces will seek to drive out small, local producers, and advertising ventures designed to expand the market for alcoholic beverages into the female and youth population will influence how people drink legal liquor and its illicit counterpart.

As a challenge to global corporate monopolies and to state power, the production and consumption of *kasippu* will likely face increased scrutiny. Although respectable villagers scorn the local production of *kasippu* as a disreputable undertaking, illicit distillation sets grassroots businesspeople against the transnational corporations that now manufacture and market the lion's share of alcoholic beverages around the world. The *kasippu* business is one of few that still operate outside the scrutiny of the state. What sorts of resistance will people in Naeaegama put up against the homogenization, consolidation, and regulation of the alcohol industry (Singer 1986, 126)? If the government were to initiate a coordinated program to stamp out the illicit alcohol industry, the measures would have different effects on people depending on their ethnicity, class, and area of residence. Naeaegama men consume legal liquor at important occasions, but many people rely on *kasippu* for their informal and regular drinking. Current laws criminalize the ordinary drinking activities of a large segment of the poor male population, but in practice the surreptitious consumption of *kasippu* does not challenge the state (Marcus 2005, 267). Changes in regulations and law enforcement could politicize *kasippu* consumption in new and different ways.

Policies can regulate everyday practices not only through criminalization but also through medicalization. The government is slowly developing the newly established National Authority on Tobacco and Alcohol. This organization will ideally mobilize and coordinate the efforts of experts in the fields of health, justice, education, media, trade, and youth affairs. One might ask what political and ideological dynamics will be folded into this institution's approaches to the prevention and treatment of problem drinking. The Authority might encourage the development of Euro-American techniques, or it could support indigenous medical and religious modalities. The experts might promote a view of alcohol abuse as an individual pathology, or they could recognize the role of family, local, national, and international contexts. If the government's experts take a stand on the role of family in treatment, their views could have repercussions on local gender roles, particularly in discussions of enabling and co-dependency (Borovoy 2005). Equally important, will the government experts politicize the systemic nature of substance abuse by recognizing as part of its cause the inequality and lack of opportunity in the national and global economy (Singer 1986, 125)? And will they strive to address the discrimination and oppression that may lead some men to drink? Consumption choices are embedded within concentric contexts, and treatments and interventions that acknowledge all of these layers will be more effective than those that focus on the individual alone. An approach to problem drinking that addresses the underlying socio-economic issues that lead to global inequality and local despair would be innovative, effective, and welcome.

Finding a Solution

I want to conclude on a personal note. As I performed the research for this book, villagers in Naeaegama shared with me both the joy and the pain surrounding local use of alcohol. I witnessed the alcohol-enhanced conviviality at weddings and coming-of-age celebrations, and in Monika's *kasippu* tavern I caught a glimpse of the warm social dynamics that drew men to her establishment. I also shared the frustrations of wives and mothers who struggled to rein in their heavy-drinking husbands and sons. I talked with a number of alcohol-dependent men about their drinking habits; sadly, several of them have since passed away. I also interviewed practitioners passionate about their curative efforts. I owe a debt of gratitude to all the people who spoke openly and frankly with me, and I hope that I have adequately conveyed their eloquent voices in this book.

Problem drinking in Naeaegama is very real to me because of Siri's alcohol habit. Without Siri's in-depth knowledge of alcohol use, I would never have thought to write this book and could never have gathered the data I have presented here. A respected and well-connected man, Siri moves fluidly in Naeaegama. He served as my mother's research associate in the late 1960s, and since 1992 he has worked closely with me, so he also understands the curiosities of anthropologists. With forty years of experience, he can clearly and insightfully explain the workings of Naeaegama society. Siri is my interpreter, my guide, my mentor, and my protector. He knows how to tell a joke in troubled times, and his enthusiasm has often sparked mine when my spirits drooped. He and Telsie have opened their house to me on numerous occasions for lengthy periods of time, meeting me half way in the task of bridging cultural divides. Within the village kinship system, Siri is my father's younger brother (*bappa*). I respect him as an associate, I honor him as a kinsman, and I love him as a friend. And therefore my fears and frustrations over Siri's smoking and drinking lend a personal element to this study, especially the search for effective treatments for alcohol dependence.

In July 2006, I fully expected Siri to smoke and drink himself to his grave. Armed with two inhalers and the advice of several doctors to stop smoking, Siri faced a growing asthma problem. Usually a firm believer in western science and medical knowledge, in this case Siri found other healing modalities preferable. He concocted elaborate rationalizations of which heating and cooling drinks, fruits, and vegetables he could and could not consume at which times of the day to minimize his coughing and wheezing. A decade ago, my father died of lung cancer after fifty years of smoking, and I did not want to lose my *bappa* in the same way. But Siri met my occasional suggestion to "Stop smoking for a few days and see what happens to the cough" with a toothy smile and complete non-compliance.

Siri's drinking also made me fear for his health. After our visit to the Kali temple in July 2006, I asked Siri if taking a vow would help him stop drinking.

"No. Nor did Dr. Priyanka's medicine a few years back. I must feel like that about my own life. If I decide to, I will stop. Other measures are all temporary. Most people give 'small boy' advice as opposed to talking to the interior of the heart. The doctors, the vows to Kali—they are trying to make people afraid."

After a thoughtful pause, Siri added, "The tavern is also a kind of temple. A lot of people come and worship in the afternoon."

Fig. 7. Alcohol: both pleasure and need.
Photograph by author.

"Is alcohol a god?" I asked.

"Yes, a kind of god," Siri agreed. "You have to control it by yourself. No medicines can help."

Implicitly acknowledging the harm his drinking had done to his body, Siri returned to a theme he mentioned periodically. "Black diarrhea is bad. That is a sign that the liver is in its last stages. I check my feces each morning to make sure it's light colored instead of black." He gestured as if holding a flashlight and looking between his legs into a squat toilet. "If it's black," he said, "I must find a solution."

I asked hopefully, "Quit?"

"No. It's too late for that by then," he told me, impatient because he knew I knew that already.

New Beginnings

Humans are creatures with the habit of habit change. Despite the addictive properties of alcohol, sometimes a person who wants to stop drinking reaches a turning point where he can make a change with the support of family members, representatives of the state, and members of the medical profession. One Sunday in August 2006, a little before sunrise, the police raided a *kasippu* tavern at the junction. Word reached Telsie and me minutes later that our clever trickster had for once failed to outwit the law. Dressed in our best and bearing cash to bail Siri out, we went to the police station. After two hours and a stern lecture from the Officer in Charge, we all came home. That afternoon Dr. Priyanka prescribed a dose of diazepam and several other medicines, and gave Siri an injection of thiamine to help him through withdrawal symptoms.

Two weeks later, sober and by his account loving it, Siri glanced up at me with a big grin as I set out on my morning walk to fetch the paper. "Look," he said, pointing to the tiny plant in front of him. "The rose I brought from my aunt's garden is flowering." One fragrant, pale pink blossom graced the bush, fragile but promising.

Appendix 1
Glossary

I here provide a list of Sinhala and English terms used frequently in the book. The words are also defined in the text at first usage

arrack Hard liquor distilled from toddy, the fermented sap of the coconut flower

Ayurvedic medicine Indigenous medical system, in contrast to allopathic (western) medicine

beebaddoo Habitual drunkards

beedie A cheap smoke made of tobacco rolled in the leaf of the Diospyros Melanoxylon or Diospyros Ebinum tree. Cigars are rolled in tobacco leaves, and tobacco wrapped in anything else is called a cigarette (Tobacco Tax Act No. 8 of 1999, 13).

bites Snack food such as fried fish and boiled chickpeas eaten while drinking liquor

daana An almsgiving or a gift of food for Buddhist monks, often followed by a large family feast

"eight" A 5-liter can of *kasippu* containing eight .625 liter bottles of liquor

Fifth Precept The fifth of five injunctions about lay behavior, directing Buddhists not to take intoxicating substances

Five Buddhist Precepts Akin to the Ten Commandments in Christianity, the Five Precepts forbid devotees to kill, steal, be unchaste, tell lies, or take intoxicating substances

"forty-five" A 28-liter can of *kasippu* containing forty-five .625-liter bottles of liquor

***gooDa* (rhymes with "soda")** Raw fermented mixture from which *kasippu* is distilled

Jaffna Main city in the war-torn Tamil-dominated Northern Province of Sri Lanka

kaala kanniyaa Literally a "time eater," figuratively an idler or useless person

kapu-mahattayaa Village priest or officiant at the temple (*deevaalaya*) of a god or goddess

kasippu Cheap local moonshine, an illicit distillate and hard liquor much like arrack in potency, roughly 33 percent alcohol by volume

kiribath Milk rice, a mix of rice and coconut milk patted flat, cut into squares, and eaten on auspicious occasions

kuDu Drugs, heroin

laejja baya naetuwa Without shame and fear

laejjayi Ashamed or shy

leDek A patient with a physical disease; in slang the term designates a troublemaker

mat kuDu or *kuDu* Drugs (literally powder)

mat paen Alcohol

mat venDa To get dizzy or high

nibbaana Nirvana

pampooriya kiyenawaa Boasting by listing one's good deeds, qualifications, and important relatives

pancha silaya See Five Buddhist Precepts

pansil Five Buddhist Precepts

pawu Sin, the opposite of *pin*, merit

pin Merit, the opposite of *pawu*, sin

pirith Pali verses containing the Buddha's teachings, usually chanted

Poya Days Full moon holidays sacred in the Buddhist religion

quarter A quarter bottle or 156 ml. of *kasippu*, the standard unit of measure for drinking illicit liquor in Naeaegama. The equivalent of three and a half 44-milliliter "shots" of hard liquor in the United States.

sansaaraya Samsara, the cycle of reincarnation

sihiya naetuwa Without memory, right mind, conscience, or consciousness

sil A standard religious practice followed by many older village women and some men, particularly on Poya days. People observing *sil* observe eight instead of five Precepts. The precept forbidding unchaste behaviors is modified so devotees renounce sexual activities for the day. In addition, the devotee will not sit on high chairs or beds, will not eat after noon, will not partake in dancing and music making, and will abstain from putting on perfume or flower garlands.

syndicating (*hawule gevanavaa*, literally contributing and paying) Local men pool their money with their peers to buy alcohol. Someone who has money today will provide drinks for others who are broke; on another day he will receive free drinks in return.

taanhaawa Greed or craving, a shortcoming in the Buddhist tradition

tap A large container of *kasippu*, e.g., a "forty-five" or a "sixty" bottle container

teetotaler Someone who does not drink alcohol

Thero Respectful form of address for a Buddhist monk; akin to the English term Reverend

toddy A beer-like beverage made from fermented sap of the coconut flower

trishaw A covered, three-wheeled motorcycle with a two- or four-stroke engine and seating for three in the back

veaddo Veddas, autochthonous hunter-gatherers viewed as the uncivilized original inhabitants of Sri Lanka

veda-mahattayaa Ayurvedic physician, indigenous healer

Appendix 2

Village and National Statistics on Alcohol Use

Statistical information about alcohol use provides an important context for the study of drinking in Naeaegama. Officially, Sri Lanka has a low rate of per capita alcohol consumption estimated at only 0.18 liters of pure alcohol per adult per year in 2000 (World Health Organization [WHO] 2004a, 11). This figure places Sri Lanka as number 195 of the 213 countries surveyed—within the lowest 10 percent in terms of "recorded" alcohol consumption. Even including the WHO estimate of a further 0.5 liters of pure alcohol per adult per year in "unrecorded" or illicit consumption, Sri Lankan consumption still falls well below the means of Europe (about 10 liters) and the United States (about 6 liters) (2004a, 10, 16). WHO's estimate of illicit liquor consumption may, however, fall short of the actual level.

The official figures contrast starkly with village perceptions of local drinking. Naeaegama residents estimated that 80 percent of men drank, nearly 20 percent of them on a daily basis. In search of collaborating quantitative data, in 2006 Siri and I counted drinking men in the immediate village area. The results are displayed in Appendix Table 2.1. Using the official election list, we rated the 567 Naeaegama area residents over the age of eighteen into four categories according to Siri's knowledge of their drinking habits. We borrowed the categories (listed in the table) from "spot surveys" conducted biannually by the Alcohol and Drug Information Centre (ADIC). If Siri did not know how much someone drank, we listed him as not drinking at all. Siri automatically assumed that none of the women drank, even though several women we interviewed said that they sometimes sipped beer at weddings. This list may also underestimate

Appendix Table 2.1. Drinking Statistics in Naeaegama, April 2006

Level	Men	%	Women	%	Total	%
0 (does not drink)	151	54.5	290	100	441	77.8
1 (drinks occasionally, at ceremonies)	44	15.9	0	0	44	7.8
2 (drinks more than once or twice a month)	35	12.6	0	0	35	6.2
3 (drinks more than four times a week or daily)	47	17.0	0	0	47	8.3
Total:	277	100	290	100	567	100.1

the number of men who drink occasionally at weddings and other ceremonies, because Siri listed several men as teetotalers whom I personally witnessed indulging moderately at village events. Overall, however, I trust Siri's ability to peer into the fishbowl of village life and present an accurate profile of the drinking community.

It is illuminating to compare the Naeaegama data with results from ADIC's July 2005 spot survey of 1,541 men over the age of fifteen in six Sri Lankan districts (ADIC 2005). The ADIC data suggests that in the Galle District (which encompasses the village of Naeaegama), 60.1 percent of the men surveyed used alcohol at least occasionally (compared to 61 percent nationally). The gender disaggregated data from Naeaegama suggest that a smaller proportion of men, 45.5 percent, drink at least occasionally.

As illustrated in Appendix Table 2.2, the ADIC spot survey suggests that among drinkers nationally, 60.6 percent drink on special occasions, 28.0 percent drink a few times a month, and 11.4 percent drink daily (2005, 7). In the Naeaegama data, out of the 126 drinkers, 34.9 percent drink occasionally, 27.8 percent drink at least once a month, and 37.3 percent drink more than four times a week. Comparing the two surveys, Naeaegama has proportionally fewer drinkers overall. Among the drinkers, the Naeaegama survey reveals fewer occasional drinkers and more daily drinkers than the national average. Interestingly, the ADIC survey found a higher proportion of daily drinkers (21.6 percent) in the Galle district than in the nation on average (11.4 percent) (2005, 7). Such patterns warrant further quantitative investigation.

Several factors may explain the differences between the numbers in the Naeaegama and ADIC surveys. First, the Naeaegama sample is substantially smaller than the ADIC sample. Second, the ADIC data includes men between the ages of fifteen and eighteen, which the Naeaegama sample did not count

Appendix Table 2.2. Comparison of Naeaegama and
National Distribution of Drinkers

Level	Naeaegama	National
1	34.9	60.6
2	27.8	28.0
3	37.3	11.4

Source: ADIC (2005).
Note: Levels indicate frequency of drinking as in table 2.1.

as they did not appear on the election list.[1] The ADIC survey also sampled
men under forty at twice the rate that they sampled men over that age, even
though the highest percentage of drinkers occurred in the older age bracket
(ADIC 2005, 2, 7; World Health Organization 2004b, 1). Siri and I did not
weigh the Naeaegama sample in the same manner. Third, in Naeaegama Siri
and I included people who frequently drank heavily but did not necessarily
drink every day in level 3. The ADIC Spot Survey does not discuss how they
classified such drinkers; the researchers may have included them in level 2
instead. Fourth, the nature of the two surveys differs. ADIC drew its subjects from an anonymous sample and gathered self-reported information on
drinking levels. Siri and I took a sample of the whole with a third party's
educated best guess at consumption levels. These methodological differences
could affect outcomes in various ways. For example, people notoriously
underreport alcohol consumption (Abeyasinghe 2002; World Health Organization 2004a, 4), so the ADIC survey could report artificially lower numbers. In addition, Siri could perhaps have overestimated both the number of
non-drinkers and the number of heavy drinkers in Naeaegama. Fifth, ADIC
conducts their survey in public locations such as bus stations. This sampling
approach may influence the age and drinking profile of respondents; for
example, many of the older and heavier Naeaegama drinkers do not often
travel by bus. Further quantitative research could clarify these issues.

Despite the differences in numbers achieved, both the ADIC and the
Naeaegama surveys concur in their general assumption of female abstinence; ADIC did not survey women, and Siri assumed that no village women
drank. Both surveys show relatively high male alcohol consumption and a
relatively large number of daily drinkers. Other sources also reveal a high

---

1. Youth aged 15–18 drink heavily in some cultures. Although local informants suggested
that some Naeaegama boys experimented with liquor at this age, neither Siri nor I heard of
repeated heavy drinking by boys in their early teens.

number of daily drinking and/or alcohol-dependent men in Sri Lanka. For example, WHO reports that a 2002 study among 1,027 individuals revealed heavy episodic drinking (13.3 percent) and heavy and hazardous drinking (15.6 percent) among males, with no instances of such drinking among females (2004b, 2). These numbers correspond closely to the Naeaegama data that suggest 17.0 percent of men drink more than four times a week. Abeyasinghe (2002, 32) claims that in the Colombo slum where he did his research, 15 to 20 percent of men were dependent on alcohol, only 1 or 2 percent abstained totally from liquor, and the rest were social drinkers. He also found that 4 or 5 percent of the women were dependent on alcohol and 10 percent drank socially, numbers much higher than reported by ADIC or found in Naeaegama. Drinking habits clearly vary from place to place, with identity factors influencing consumption. These data demonstrate the importance of understanding local drinking patterns and setting official per capita consumption figures into cultural context.

Appendix 3

Calculating Inflation in Sri Lanka

Rampant inflation in Sri Lanka makes comparing prices from different years difficult. Throughout most of the book, unless otherwise noted, monetary figures have been adjusted for inflation and are stated in 2004 rupees. In these calculations, I have used the Consumers' Price Index (CPI) (see Appendix Table 3.1). This index measures the prices of consumer items, and suggests the changing purchasing power of wages.

To calculate what Rs. 1000 in 1998 would be worth in 2004, divide the CPI number for 2004 (161.9) by the CPI number for 1998 (120.8), and multiply the result (1.34) by Rs. 1,000, to obtain the figure of Rs. 1,340. This means that a consumer would spend Rs. 1,340 in 2004 to buy what he or she could have purchased with Rs. 1,000 in 1998.

Occasionally, as noted in the text, I give both nominal values (rupee values informants report) and real values (equivalents in 2004 figures, adjusted for inflation). In these special cases I have done this to show how dramatically inflation has affected the value of the Sri Lankan rupee over the years. In other instances, particularly when quoting informants, I have left nominal values in the text to preserve the flow of the narrative, especially if, for example, modifying a round figure would seem awkward. In cases where exact figures matter to the argument and the interview did not take place in 2004, I mention 2004 values in square brackets in the sentence.

To avoid encumbering the text, I have only noted US$ equivalents for particularly salient figures. Between 2004 and 2006, when most of the ethnographic information used in this book was gathered, US$1 was roughly equivalent to Rs. 100 (Institute of Policy Studies 2005, 22), and all dollar equivalents are calculated at that rate.

Appendix Table 3.1. Sri Lanka Consumers' Price Index

Year	SLCPI (January)
[1992]	[68.3]
[1993]	[77.5]
1995–97	100
1998	120.8
1999	126.8
2000	122.1
2001	134.1
2002	152.4
2003	163.4
2004	161.9
2005	191.0
2006	197.2

Sources: Figures for 1992 and 1993 reflect the Greater Colombo Consumers' Price Index as reported by the Department of Census and Statistics 2007. All other figures reflect the Sri Lanka Consumer's Price Index as reported by the Department of Census and Statistics 2006.

Bibliography

Abeyasinghe, Ranil. 2002. *Illicit Alcohol: Drinking Culture in Colombo—A Study of Alcohol Consumption Among the Urban Poor in a South Asian Capitol.* Colombo, Sri Lanka: Vijitha Yapa.

Acuda, Wilson, and Barton Alexander. 1998. "Individual Characteristics and Drinking Problems." In *Drinking Patterns and Their Consequences,* edited by Marcus Grant and Jorge Litvak, 43–62. Washington, DC: Taylor and Francis.

Afflitto, Frank M. 2000. "The Homogenizing Effects of State-Sponsored Terrorism: The Case of Guatemala." In *Death Squad: The Anthropology of State Terror,* edited by Jeffrey A. Sluka, 114–26. Philadelphia: University of Pennsylvania Press.

Ahearn, Laura M. 1999. "Agency." *Journal of Linguistic Anthropology* 9, nos. 1–2: 12–15.

——. 2001. "Language and Agency." *Annual Review of Anthropology* 30: 109–37.

Alcohol and Drug Information Centre (ADIC). 1994. "Impact of Alcohol Use on Family Well-Being." Research and Evaluation Division, ADIC: Colombo, Sri Lanka.

——. 1999. "Summary of the National Level Situation Regarding Alcohol, Tobacco, and Other Drugs." ADIC and FORUT: Colombo, Sri Lanka.

——. 2003. "Spot Survey on Tobacco and Alcohol Use (July)." Research and Evaluation Division, ADIC: Colombo, Sri Lanka.

——. 2004. "Parental Survey on Drug Use." Research and Evaluation Division, ADIC: Colombo, Sri Lanka.

——. 2005. "Spot Survey July 2005." Research and Evaluation Division, ADIC: Colombo, Sri Lanka.

Al-Anon Family Groups. 2003a. "Alcoholism, A Merry-Go-Round Named Denial." World Service Office, Al-Anon Family Groups.

——. 2003b. "Understanding Ourselves and Alcoholism." World Service Office, Al-Anon Family Groups.

Alcoholics Anonymous. 2001. *Alcoholics Anonymous: The Story of How Many Thousands of Men and Women Have Recovered from Alcoholism.* 4th ed. New York: Alcoholics Anonymous World Services. http://www.aa.org/bigbookonline/index.cfm (accessed May 17, 2004).

Antze, Paul. 1987. "Symbolic Action in Alcoholics Anonymous." In *Constructive Drinking: Perspectives on Drink from Anthropology,* ed. Mary Douglas, 149–81. Cambridge: Cambridge University Press.

Arria, Amelia M., and Michael Gossop. 1998. "Health Issues and Drinking Patterns." In *Drinking Patterns and Their Consequences,* edited by Marcus Grant and Jorge Litvak, 63–87. Washington, DC: Taylor and Francis.

Babor, Thomas, Raul Caetano, Sally Casswell, Griffith Edwards, Norman Giesbrecht, Kathryn Graham, Joel Grube, Paul Gruenewald, Linda Hill, Harold Holder, Ross Homel, Esa Osterberg, Jurgen Rehm, Robin Room, and Ingeborg Rossow. 2003. *Alcohol: No Ordinary Commodity: Research and Public Policy.* Oxford: Oxford University Press.

Baer, Hans A., Merrill Singer, and Ida Susser. 2003. *Medical Anthropology and the World System.* 2nd ed. Westport, CT: Praeger.

Baklien, Bergljot, and Diyanath Samarasinghe. 2003. *Alcohol and Poverty in Sri Lanka.* Dehiwala, Sri Lanka: Norwegian Institute for Urban and Regional Research (NIBR)/ Solidaritetsakjonen for utvikling (FORUT), Sridevi Printers.

Bandara, Kelum, Yohan Perera, and Gagani Weerakoon. 2006. "Strive for Peace in New Year, Say Political Leaders." *Daily Mirror,* 13 April, 1.

Bass, Daniel. 2004. "A Place on the Plantations: Up-Country Tamil Ethnicity in Sri Lanka." Ph.D. diss., University of Michigan.

Bateson, Gregory. 1972. "The Cybernetics of 'Self': A Theory of Alcoholism." In *Steps to an Ecology of Mind: A Revolutionary Approach to Man's Understanding of Himself,* 309–37. New York: Ballantine Books.

Baudrillard, Jean. 1981. *For a Critique of the Political Economy of the Sign.* St. Louis: Telos Press.

Bennie, Colin, Iain McKinney, and David Campbell. 2000. "Home Detoxification for Problem Drinkers." In *The Alcohol Report,* edited by Martin Plant and Douglas Cameron, 178–88. London: Free Association Books.

Blanchard, D. Caroline, Rosemary Veniegas, Irene Elloran, and Robert J. Blanchard. 1993. "Alcohol and Anxiety: Effects on Offensive and Defensive Aggression." *Journal of Studies on Alcohol,* Supplement 11: 9–19.

Boddy, Janice. 2005. "Spirit Possession and Gender Complementarity: Zar in Rural Northern Sudan." In *Gender in Cross-Cultural Perspective,* edited by Caroline B. Brettell and Carolyn F. Sargent, 397–407. 4th ed. Upper Saddle River, NJ: Prentice Hall.

Borovoy, Amy. 2005. *The Too-Good Wife: Alcohol, Codependency, and the Politics of Nurturance in Postwar Japan.* Berkeley: University of California Press.

Bourdieu, Pierre. 1977. *Outline of a Theory of Practice.* Translated by Richard Nice. Cambridge: Cambridge University Press.

———. 1984. *Distinction: A Social Critique of the Judgment of Taste.* London: Routledge & Kegan Paul.

Brodie, Janet Farrell, and Marc Redfield. 2002. "Introduction." In *High Anxieties: Cultural Studies in Addiction,* edited by Janet Farrell Brodie and Marc Redfield, 1–15. Berkeley: University of California Press.

Brown, Karen McCarthy. 2001. *Mama Lola: A Vodou Priestess in Brooklyn.* Rev. ed. Berkeley: University of California Press.

Budget Speech 2006. 2006. 2006 Budget Speech. 8 December 2005. http://www.treasury.gov.lk/FPPFM/fpd/pdfdocs/budget2006dec/budget2006English.pdf (accessed June 26, 2006).

Cameron, Douglas, and Martin Plant. 2000. "Drinking and Problem Drinking." In *The Alcohol Report,* ed. Martin Plant and Douglas Cameron, 1–4. London: Free Association Books.

Carbine, Jason A. 2000. "Yaktovil: The Role of the Buddha and Dhamma." In *The Life of Buddhism,* edited by Frank E. Reynolds and Jason A. Carbine, 160–76. Berkeley: University of California Press.

Carby, Hazel. 1985. "'On the Threshold of Women's Era': Lynching, Empire and Sexuality in Black Feminist Theory." *Critical Inquiry* 12, no. 1: 262–77.

Carrier, James G., and Josiah McC. Heyman. 1997. "Consumption and Political Economy." *Journal of the Royal Anthropological Institute* 3, no. 2: 355–73.

"Censorship and Cacophony." *Sunday Times,* 20 August, 10.

Central Bank. 2003. "Central Bank of Sri Lanka Annual Report 2002." Central Bank of Sri Lanka, Colombo. http://www.lanka.net/centralbank/Annual_index-2002.html (accessed March 3, 2004).

——. 2006. "Central Bank of Sri Lanka Annual Report of the Monetary Board to the Hon. Minister of Finance for the Year 2005." Central Bank of Sri Lanka, Colombo.

Central Intelligence Agency. 2006. *The World Factbook.* http://www.odci.gov/cia/publi cations/factbook/index.html(accessed September 20, 2006).

Chatterjee, Piya. 2003. "An Empire of Drink: Gender, Labor and the Historical Economies of Alcohol." *Journal of Historical Sociology* 16, no 2: 183–208.

Clifford, James, and George E. Marcus, eds. 1986. *Writing Culture: The Poetics and Politics of Ethnography.* Berkeley: University of California Press.

Colapietro, Vincent M. 1989. *Peirce's Approach to the Self: A Semiotic Perspective on Human Subjectivity.* Albany: State University of New York Press.

Commissioner General of Excise. 2005. "Administrative Report of the Excise Commissioner General for the Year 2004." Excise Department, Colombo, Sri Lanka.

Crump, Thomas. 1987. "The Alternative Economy of Alcohol in the Chiapas Highlands." In *Constructive Drinking: Perspectives on Drink from Anthropology,* edited by Mary Douglas, 239–49. Cambridge: Cambridge University Press.

Das, Veena. 1997. "Language and Body: Transactions in the Construction of Pain." In *Social Suffering,* edited by Arthur Kleinman, Veena Das, and Margaret Lock, 67–91. Berkeley: University of California Press.

de Munck, Victor C. 1996. "Love and Marriage in a Sri Lankan Muslim Community: Toward a Reevaluation of Dravidian Marriage Practices." *American Ethnologist* 23, no. 4: 698–716.

de Silva, Kingsley M. 1981. *A History of Sri Lanka.* Berkeley: University of California Press.

——. 2002. "Corruption in Sri Lanka: The National Legislature, 1938–2001." In *Corruption in South Asia: India, Pakistan and Sri Lanka,* edited by Kingsley M. de Silva, G. H. Peiris, and S. W. R. de A. Samarasinghe, 303–68. Kandy, Sri Lanka: International Centre for Ethnic Studies.

de Silva, Senaka. 2006a. "Over 1000 Cops Deployed for New Year Duty." *Daily Mirror,* 7 April, 2.

——. 2006b. "Police Log." *Daily Mirror,* 9 May, 2.

de Silva, Wimala. 2002. "The Family: Continuity and Change." In *Women in Post-Independence Sri Lanka,* edited by Swarna Jayaweera, 211–44. New Delhi: Sage.

Department of Census and Statistics. 2001. "Literacy Rates by Sector and Sex." http://www.statistics.gov.lk/social/literacy_tbl.htm(accessed September 28, 2004).

———. 2006. "The Sri Lanka Consumers' Price Index—SLCPI (1995—1997 = 100)." http://www.statistics.gov.lk/price/slcpi/slcpi_monthly.pdf (accessed June 26, 2006).

———. 2007. "Movements of the Current CCPI, GCPI and SLCPI." http://www.statistics.gov.lk/price/ccpi/Movements%20of%20the%20current%20CCPI%20and%20SLCPI.pdf (accessed September 5, 2007).

Dietler, Michael. 2006. "Alcohol: Anthropological/Archaeological Perspectives." *Annual Review of Anthropology* 35: 229–49.

Douglas, Mary. 1966. *Purity and Danger: An Analysis of the Concepts of Pollution and Taboo.* London: Ark Paperbacks.

———. 1987. "A Distinctive Anthropological Perspective." In *Constructive Drinking: Perspectives on Drink from Anthropology,* edited by Mary Douglas, 3–15. Cambridge: Cambridge University Press.

Eber, Christine. 2000 [1995]. *Women and Alcohol in a Highland Maya Town: Water of Hope, Water of Sorrow.* Rev. ed. Austin: University of Texas Press.

———. 2001. "'Take My water': Liberation Through Prohibition in San Pedro Chenalho, Chiapas, Mexico." *Social Science and Medicine* 53: 251–62.

Ehrenreich, Barbara, and Arlie Hochschild. 2002. *Global Women: Nannies, Maids, and Sex Workers in the New Economy.* New York: Metropolitan Books.

Elias, Robert. 1997. "A Culture of Violent Solutions." In *The Web of Violence: From Interpersonal to Global,* edited by Jennifer Turpin and Lester R. Kurtz, 117–47. Chicago: University of Illinois Press.

Ellawala, Nalini. 2005. *The Mel Medura Modality: Helping People with Problems Relating to Drug Use.* Colombo, Sri Lanka: Mel Medura.

Eller, Jack David. 1999. *From Culture to Ethnicity to Conflict: An Anthropological Perspective on International Ethnic Conflict.* Ann Arbor: University of Michigan Press.

Engels, Friedrich. 1972. *The Origin of the Family, Private Property, and the State.* New York: Pathfinder Press.

Excise Ordinance. 1956. Government of Ceylon Legislative Enactments: Excise Ordinance. Reprinted 1998. Colombo, Sri Lanka: Department of Government Printing.

Feddema, J. P. 1997. "The Cursing Practice in Sri Lanka as a Religious Channel for Keeping Physical Violence in Control: The Case of Seenigama." *Journal of Asian and African Studies* 32, nos. 3–4: 202–22.

Fekjaer, Hans Olav. 1993. *Alcohol and Illicit Drugs: Myths and Realities.* Colombo, Sri Lanka: Alcohol and Drug Information Centre.

Fernandez-Armesto, Felipe. 2002. *Near a Thousand Tables: A History of Food.* New York: Free Press.

Foucault, Michel. 1978. *The History of Sexuality,* vol. I. New York: Vintage.

———. 1979. *Discipline and Punish.* Translated by Alan Sheridan. New York: Vintage.

———. 1991. "Governmentality." In *The Foucault Effect: Studies in Governmentality,* edited by Graham Burchell, Colin Gordor, and Peter Miller, 87–104. Chicago: University of Chicago Press.

———. 1994. "Two Lectures." In *Culture/Power/History: A Reader in Contemporary Social Theory,* edited by Nicholas B. Dirks, Geoff Eley, and Sherry B. Ortner, 200–221. Princeton: Princeton University Press.

Frederick, M. A. 2006. "How to Attract More Tourists, Sri Lankan Style." Letter to the editor. *Daily Mirror,* 28 July, A10.

Gamburd, Geraldine E. 1972. "The Seven Grandparents: Locality and Lineality in Sinhalese Kinship and Caste." PhD diss., Columbia University.

Gamburd, Michele Ruth. 1995. "Sri Lanka's 'Army of Housemaids': Control of Remittances and Gender Transformations." *Anthropologica* 37, no. 1: 49–88.

——. 1998. "Absent Women and Their Extended Families: Sri Lanka's Migrant Housemaids." In *Negotiation and Social Space: A Gendered Analysis of Changing Kin and Security Networks in South Asia and Sub-Saharan Africa,* edited by Carla I. Risseeuw and Kamala Ganesh, 276–91. New Delhi: Sage.

——. 1999. "Wearing a Dead Man's Jacket: State Symbols in Troubled Places." In *Conflict and Community in Contemporary Sri Lanka,* edited by Siri Gamage and Bruce Watson, 165–77. New Delhi: Sage.

——. 2000. *The Kitchen Spoon's Handle: Transnationalism and Sri Lanka's Migrant Housemaids.* Ithaca: Cornell University Press.

——. 2002. "Breadwinners No More: Identities in Flux." In *Global Women: Nannies, Maids, and Sex Workers in the New Economy,* edited by Arlie Hochschild and Barbara Ehrenreich, 190–206. New York: Metropolitan Books.

——. 2003. "In the Wake of the Gulf War: Assessing Family Spending of Compensation Money in Sri Lanka." *International Journal of Population Geography* 9, no. 6: 503–15.

——. 2004a. "Money That Burns Like Oil: A Sri Lankan Cultural Logic of Morality and Agency." *Ethnology* 43, no. 2: 167–84.

——. 2004b. "The Economics of Enlisting: A Village View of Armed Service." In *Economy and Ethnic Conflict in Sri Lanka,* edited by Deborah Winslow and Michael Woost, 151–67. Bloomington: Indiana University Press.

——. 2005. "Lentils There, Lentils Here: Sri Lankan Domestic Labour in the Middle East." In *Asian Women as Transnational Domestic Workers,* edited by Shirlena Huang, Brenda S. A. Yeoh, and Noor Abdul Rahman, 92–114. Singapore: Marshall Cavendish.

——. 2008. "Milk Teeth and Jet Planes: Kin Relations in Families of Sri Lanka's Transnational Domestic Servants." *City and Society* 20, no. 1: 5–34.

——. n.d. "Corruption and Complicity: State Regulations and Sri Lanka's Illicit Liquor Industry."

"GL: Women's Status in Lankan Society Much Change." 2003. *Daily Mirror,* 30 October, 4.

Gomez, Shyamala, and Mario Gomez. 2004. "Sri Lanka: The Law's Response to Women Victims of Violence." In *Violence, Law and Women's Rights in South Asia,* edited by Savitri Goonesekere, 207–67. New Delhi: Sage.

Goonesekere, Savitri. 2002. "Constitutions, Governance and Laws." In *Women in Post-independence Sri Lanka,* edited by Swarna Jayaweera, 41–78. New Delhi: Sage.

——. 2004. "Overview: Reflections on Violence Against Women and the Legal Systems of Some South Asian Countries." In *Violence, Law and Women's Rights in South Asia,* edited by Savitri Goonesekere, 13–76. New Delhi: Sage.

Gorski, Terence T. 1998. "Alcoholism Should Be Treated as a Disease." In *Alcohol: Opposing Viewpoints,* edited by Scott Barbour, 98–104. San Diego: Greenhaven Press.

Gould, Steven Jay. 1984. "Singapore's Patrimony (and Matrimony): The Illogic of Eugenics Knows Neither the Boundaries of Time nor Geography." *Natural History* 93, no 5: 22–29.

Government Gazette. 1995. Part I: Section I, Gazette Extraordinary of the Democratic Socialist Republic of Sri Lanka No. 865/7, 04 April 1995. Excise Ordinance, Excise

Notification No. 823. Ministry of Finance and Planning. Colombo, Sri Lanka: Department of Government Printing.

———. 1997. Part I: Section I, Gazette Extraordinary of the Democratic Socialist Republic of Sri Lanka No. 1001/20, 13 November 1997. Excise Ordinance, Excise Notification No. 833. Ministry of Finance and Planning. Colombo, Sri Lanka: Department of Government Printing.

———. 1998. Part I: Section I, Gazette Extraordinary of the Democratic Socialist Republic of Sri Lanka No. 1026/14, 7 May 1998. Excise Ordinance, Excise Notification No. 834. Ministry of Finance and Planning. Colombo, Sri Lanka: Department of Government Printing.

———. 2005a. Part I: Section I, Gazette Extraordinary of the Democratic Socialist Republic of Sri Lanka No. 1422/17, 8 December 2005. Excise Ordinance, Excise Notification No. 883. Ministry of Finance and Planning. Colombo, Sri Lanka: Department of Government Printing.

———. 2005b. Part I: Section I, Gazette Extraordinary of the Democratic Socialist Republic of Sri Lanka No. 1422/18, 8 December 2005. Excise (Special Provisions) Act No. 13 of 1989. Ministry of Finance and Planning. Colombo, Sri Lanka: Department of Government Printing.

———. 2005c. Part I: Section I, Gazette Extraordinary of the Democratic Socialist Republic of Sri Lanka No. 1424/7, 19 December 2005. Excise Ordinance, Excise Notification No. 887. Ministry of Finance and Planning. Colombo, Sri Lanka: Department of Government Printing.

———. 2006. Part II of May 05, 2006. The Gazette of the Democratic Socialist Republic of Sri Lanka. Supplement. National Authority on Tobacco and Alcohol. Ministry of Healthcare and Nutrition. Colombo, Sri Lanka: Department of Government Printing.

Grant, Bridget F. 1997. "Barriers to Alcoholism Treatment: Reasons for Not Seeking Treatment in a General Population Sample." *Journal of Studies on Alcohol* 58: 365–71.

Grant, Marcus, and Jorge Litvak, eds. 1998. *Drinking Patterns and Their Consequences.* Washington, DC: Taylor and Francis.

Gureje, Oye, Venos Mavreas, J. L. Vazquez-Barquero, and Aleksandar Janca. 1997. "Problems Related to Alcohol Use: A Cross-Cultural Perspective." *Culture, Medicine and Psychiatry* 21: 199–211.

Gusfield, Joseph. 1987. "Passage to Play: Rituals of Drinking Time in American Society." In *Constructive Drinking: Perspectives on Drink from Anthropology,* edited by Mary Douglas, 73–90. Cambridge: Cambridge University Press.

Harvey, Penelope. 1994. "Domestic Violence in the Peruvian Andes." In *Sex and Violence: Issues in Representation and Experience,* edited by Penelope Harvey and Peter Gow, 66–89. New York: Routledge.

Heath, Dwight B. 1987. "A Decade of Development in the Anthropological Study of Alcohol Use, 1970–1980." In *Constructive Drinking: Perspectives on Drink from Anthropology,* edited by Mary Douglas, 16–69. Cambridge: Cambridge University Press.

———. 1998a. "Cultural Variations among Drinking Patterns." In *Drinking Patterns and Their Consequences,* edited by Marcus Grant and Jorge Litvak, 103–25. Washington, DC: Taylor and Francis.

———. 1998b. "Raising Alcohol Taxes Would Not Reduce Alcohol-Related Problems." In *Alcohol: Opposing Viewpoints,* edited by Scott Barbour, 165–67. San Diego: Greenhaven Press.

———. 2000. *Drinking Occasions: Comparative Perspectives on Alcohol and Culture.* Philadelphia: Taylor and Francis.

Heath, Dwight B., and Haydee Rosovsky. 1998. "Community Reactions to Alcohol Policies." In *Drinking Patterns and Their Consequences,* edited by Marcus Grant and Jorge Litvak, 205–20. Washington, DC: Taylor and Francis.

Heather, Nick. 2000. "Psychosocial Treatment Approaches and the Findings of Project MATCH." In *The Alcohol Report,* edited by Martin Plant and Douglas Cameron, 154–78. London: Free Association Books.

Hendrickson, Mary K., and William D. Heffernan. 2002. "Opening Spaces Through Relocalization: Locating Potential Resistance in the Weaknesses of the Global Food System." *Sociologia Ruralis* 42, no. 4: 347–69.

Hettige, Siri T. 1991. "Administration Reports of the Excise Commissioner." Colombo, Sri Lanka: Government of Sri Lanka.

Hunt, Geoffrey, and Judith C. Barker. 2001. "Socio-Cultural Anthropology and Alcohol and Drug Research: Towards a Unified Theory." *Social Science and Medicine* 53:165–88.

Hunt, Geoffrey P., Kathleen MacKenzie and Karen Joe-Laidler. 2005. "Alcohol and Masculinity: The Case of Ethnic Youth Gangs." In *Drinking Cultures: Alcohol and Identity,* edited by Thomas M. Wilson, 225–54. Oxford: Berg.

Hussein, Ameena. 2000. *Sometimes There Is No Blood: Domestic Violence and Rape in Rural Sri Lanka.* Colombo, Sri Lanka: International Centre for Ethnic Studies.

Institute of Policy Studies. 2003. *Sri Lanka: State of the Economy.* Colombo, Sri Lanka: Institute of Policy Studies.

———. 2005. *Sri Lanka: State of the Economy 2005.* Colombo, Sri Lanka: Institute of Policy Studies.

Jayawardena, Kumari. 2000. *Nobodies to Somebodies: The Rise of the Colonial Bourgeoisie in Sri Lanka.* New Delhi: Leftword Books.

Jayaweera, Swarna, Malsiri Dias, and Leelangi Wanasundera. 2002. *Returnee Migrant Women in Two Locations in Sri Lanka.* Colombo, Sri Lanka: CENWOR.

Jeyanathan, Anton B. 2006. "Give Priority to Drug Law Enforcement." *Daily Mirror,* 24 June, A9.

Kapferer, Bruce. 1983. *A Celebration of Demons.* Bloomington: University of Indiana Press.

Kariyakarawana, Kurulu. 2006. "The Devil's Brew in Muthurajawela: How Excise Officials Raided an Illicit Brewery in the Marshes of Ja-ela." *Daily Mirror,* 29 July, A10.

Kariyakarawana, Kurulu, and Shane Senewiratne. 2006. "Heavy Fines for Selling Liquor." *Daily Mirror,* 11 May, 4.

Keane, Helen. 2002. "Smoking, Addiction, and the Making of Time." In *High Anxieties: Cultural Studies in Addiction,* edited by Janet Farrell Brodie and Marc Redfield, 119–33. Berkeley: University of California Press.

Kelly, Thomas H., and Don R. Cherek. 1993. "Alcohol and Anxiety: The Effects of Alcohol on Free-Operant Aggressive Behavior." *Journal of Studies on Alcohol,* Supplement 11: 40–52.

Kenkel, Donald S. 1998. "Raising Alcohol Taxes Could Reduce Alcohol-Related Problems." In *Alcohol: Opposing Viewpoints,* edited by Scott Barbour, 160–64. San Diego: Greenhaven Press.

Kirch, Patrick V. 2001. "Polynesian Feasting in Ethnohistoric, Ethnographic, and Archaeological Contexts." In *Feasts: Archaeological and Ethnographic Perspectives on*

Food, Politics, and Power, edited by Michael Dietler and Brian Hayden, 168–84. Washington, DC: Smithsonian Institution Press.

Kishline, Audrey. 1998. "Alcoholism Should Not Be Treated As a Disease." In *Alcohol: Opposing Viewpoints,* edited by Scott Barbour, 105–12. San Diego: Greenhaven Press.

Kleinman, Arthur. 1988. *The Illness Narratives: Suffering, Healing, and the Human Condition.* London: Basic Books.

Konradsen, Flemming, Wim van der Hoek, and Pushpalatha Peiris. 2006. "Reaching for the Bottle of Pesticide—A Cry for Help. Self-Inflicted Poisonings in Sri Lanka." *Social Science and Medicine* 62: 1710–719.

Kunitz, Stephen J. 2006. "Life-Course Observations of Alcohol Use Among Navajo Indians: Natural History or Careers?" *Medical Anthropology Quarterly* 20, no. 3: 279–96.

Kunitz, Stephen J., and Jerrold E. Levy, with K. Ruben Gabriel, Gilbert Qintero, Eric Henderson, Joanne McCloskey, and Scott Russell. 2000. *Drinking, Conduct Disorder, and Social Change: Navajo Experiences.* Oxford: Oxford University Press.

Lawrence, Patricia. 1997. "Violence, Suffering, Amman: The Work of Oracles in Sri Lanka's Eastern War Zone." In *Violence and Subjectivity,* edited by Veena Das, Arthur Kleinman, Mamphela Ramphele, and Pamela Reynolds, 171–204. Berkeley: University of California Press.

Leonard, Kenneth E., and Marilyn Senchak. 1993. "Alcohol and Premarital Aggression Among Newlywed Couples." *Journal of Studies on Alcohol,* Supplement 11: 96–108.

Levine, Hillel. 1987. "Alcohol Monopoly to Protect the Non-Commercial Sector of Eighteenth-Century Poland." In *Constructive Drinking: Perspectives on Drink from Anthropology,* edited by Mary Douglas, 250–69. Cambridge: Cambridge University Press.

Limon, José E. 1989. "'Carne, Carnales,' and the Carnivalesque: Bakhtinian 'Batos,' Disorder, and Narrative Discourses." *American Ethnologist* 16, no. 3: 471–86.

"Liquor Shop Near Asgiriya Viharaya a Nuisance." 2006. *Daily Mirror,* 24 April, 1.

Lynch, Caitrin. 2002. "The Politics of White Women's Underwear in Sri Lanka's Open Economy." *Social Politics: International Studies in Gender, State, and Society* 9, no. 1: 87–125.

———. 2007. *Juki Girls, Good Girls: Gender and Cultural Politics in Sri Lanka's Global Garment Industry.* Ithaca: Cornell University Press.

MacAndrew, Craig, and Robert B. Edgerton. 2003 [1969]. *Drunken Comportment: A Social Explanation.* Clinton Corners, NY: Percheron Press.

Marcus, Anthony. 2005. "Drinking Politics: Alcohol, Drugs and the Problem of US Civil Society." In *Drinking Cultures: Alcohol and Identity,* Thomas M. Wilson, 255–76. Oxford: Berg.

Marecek, Jeanne. 1998. "Culture, Gender, and Suicidal Behavior in Sri Lanka." *Suicide and Life Threatening Behavior* 28, no. 1: 69–81.

Margolis, Stacey. 2002. "Addiction and the Ends of Desire." In *High Anxieties: Cultural Studies in Addiction,* edited by Janet Farrell Brodie and Marc Redfield, 19–37. Berkeley: University of California Press.

Mars, Gerald. 1987. "Longshore Drinking, Economic Security and Union Politics in Newfoundland." In *Constructive Drinking: Perspectives on Drink from Anthropology,* edited by Mary Douglas, 91–101. Cambridge: Cambridge University Press.

Mars, Gerald, and Yochanan Altman. 1987. "Alternative Mechanism of Distribution in a Soviet Economy." In *Constructive Drinking: Perspectives on Drink from Anthropology,* edited by Mary Douglas, 270–79. Cambridge: Cambridge University Press.

Marshall, Mac. 1979. *Weekend Warriors: Alcohol in a Micronesian Culture.* Palo Alto, CA: Mayfield.

Marshall, Mac, and Leanne Riley. 1999. "Introduction." In *Alcohol and Public Health in 8 Developing Countries*, edited by Leanne Riley and Mac Marshall, 5–12. Geneva: World Health Organization.

Marshall, Mac, Genevieve M. Ames, and Linda A. Bennett. 2001. "Anthropological Perspectives on Alcohol and Drugs at the Turn of the New Millennium." *Social Science and Medicine* 53: 153–64.

McClelland, David C., William N. Davis, Rudolf Kalin, and Eric Wanner. 1972. *The Drinking Man: Alcohol and Human Motivation*. Toronto: Collier-Macmillan.

McKechnie, Ron, and Douglas Cameron. 2000. "Drinking at Cross Purposes." In *The Alcohol Report*, edited by Martin Plant and Douglas Cameron, 39–55. London: Free Association Books.

McKnight, David. 2002. *From Hunting to Drinking: The Devastating Effects of Alcohol on an Australian Aboriginal Community*. London: Routledge.

Medicine, Beatrice. 2007. *Drinking and Sobriety Among the Lakota Sioux*. Lanham, MD: Altamira Press.

Melley, Timothy. 2002. "A Terminal Case: William Burroughs and the Logic of Addiction." In *High Anxieties: Cultural Studies in Addiction*, edited by Janet Farrell Brodie and Marc Redfield, 38–60. Berkeley: University of California Press.

Milgram, Gail Gleason. 1993. "Adolescents, Alcohol and Aggression." *Journal of Studies on Alcohol*, Supplement 11: 53–61.

Miller, Daniel. 1995. "Consumption and Commodities." *Annual Review of Anthropology* 24: 141–61.

Mintz, Sidney M. 1997. "Time, Sugar, and Sweetness." In *Food and Culture: A Reader*, edited by Carole Counihan and Penny Van Esterrick, 357–69. New York: Routledge.

Mitchell, Jon P., and Gary Armstrong. 2005. "Cheers and Booze: Football and *Festa* Drinking in Malta." In *Drinking Cultures: Alcohol and Identity*, edited by Thomas M. Wilson, 179–200. Oxford: Berg.

Mohan, Davinder, and H. K. Sharma. 1995. "India." In *International Handbook on Alcohol and Culture*, edited by Dwight B. Heath, 128–41. Westport, CT: Greenwood Press.

Mohr, Cynthia D., Stephen Armeli, Howard Tennen, Margaret Anne Carney, Glenn Affleck, and Amber Hromi. 2001. "Daily Interpersonal Experiences, Context, and Alcohol Consumption: Crying in Your Beer and Toasting Good Times." *Journal of Personality and Social Psychology* 80, no. 3: 489–500.

Nanda, Serena. 1992. "Arranging a Marriage in India." In *The Naked Anthropologist*, edited by Philip R. Devita, 34–45. Belmont, CA: Wadsworth.

Ngokwey, Ndolamb. 1987. "Varieties of Palm Wine Among the Lele of the Kasai." In *Constructive Drinking: Perspectives on Drink from Anthropology*, edited by Mary Douglas, 113–21. Cambridge: Cambridge University Press.

Nicholson, Melanie. 2006. "Without Their Children: Rethinking Motherhood Among Transnational Migrant Women." *Social Text* 24, no. 3: 13–33.

Ong, Aihwa. 1988. "The Production of Possession: Spirits and the Multinational Corporation in Malaysia." *American Ethnologist* 15, no. 1: 29–42.

——. 1999. *Flexible Citizenship: The Cultural Logics of Transnationality*. Durham: Duke University Press.

Ortner, Sherry B. 1989. *High Religion: A Cultural and Political History of Sherpa Buddhism*. Princeton: Princeton University Press.

——. 2006. *Anthropology and Social Theory: Culture, Power, and the Acting Subject*. Durham: Duke University Press.

Patton, Pat. 1998. "Buddhism Can Help Alcoholics Stay Sober." In *Alcohol: Opposing Viewpoints*, edited by Scott Barbour, 149–56. San Diego: Greenhaven Press.

Peebles, Patrick. 1986. "Profits from Arrack Renting in Nineteenth Century Sri Lanka." *Modern Sri Lanka Studies* 1, no. 1: 65–83.

———. 1995. *Social Change in Nineteenth Century Ceylon*. New Delhi: Navrang.

Perez, Joseph F. 1992. *Alcoholism: Causes, Effects, and Treatment*. Muncie, IN: Accelerated Development.

Pernanen, Kai. 1991. *Alcohol in Human Violence*. New York: Guilford Press.

Plange, Nii-K. 1998. "Social and Behavior Issues Related to Drinking Patterns." In *Drinking Patterns and Their Consequences*, edited by Marcus Grant and Jorge Litvak, 89–102. Washington, DC: Taylor and Francis.

Plant, Martin, and Douglas Cameron. 2000. "Summary and Conclusions." In *The Alcohol Report*, edited by Martin Plant and Douglas Cameron, 235–38. London: Free Association Books.

Police Narcotic Bureau. 2006. Police Narcotic Bureau. http://www.police.lk/divisions/pnb.asp (accessed June 27, 2006).

Popp, Sharon. 2001. "An Ethnographic Study of Occupationally-Related Drinking in the Skilled Building Trades." *Anthropology of Work Review* 22, no. 4: 17–21.

Quintero, Gilbert. 2002. "Nostalgia and Degeneration: The Moral Economy of Drinking in Navajo Society." *Medical Anthropology Quarterly* 16, no. 1: 3–21.

Rahula, Walpole. 1959. *What the Buddha Taught*. London: Gordon Fraser.

Ritson, Bruce, and Anthony Thorley. 2000. "Alcohol and Its Effects: General Effects." In *The Alcohol Report*, edited by Martin Plant and Douglas Cameron, 5–34. London: Free Association Books.

Roberts, Michael W. 1982. *Caste Conflict and Elite Formation: The Rise of a Karava Elite in Sri Lanka, 1500–931*. Cambridge: Cambridge University Press.

Rogers, John D. 1989. "Cultural Nationalism and Social Reform: The 1904 Temperance Movement in Sri Lanka." *Indian Economic and Social History Review* 26, no. 3: 319–41.

Room, Robin. 1984. "Alcohol and Ethnography: A Case of Problem Deflation?" *Current Anthropology* 25, no. 2: 169–78.

———. 1999. "Preface." In *Alcohol and Public Health in 8 Developing Countries*, edited by Leanne Riley and Mac Marshall, 1–3. Geneva: World Health Organization.

———. 2001. "Intoxication and Bad Behaviour: Understanding Cultural Differences in the Link." *Social Sciences and Medicine* 53: 189–98.

Royce, James E., and David Scratchley. 1996. *Alcoholism and Other Drug Problems*. New York: Free Press.

Ruwanpura, Kanchana N. 2000. *Structural Adjustment, Gender and Employment: The Sri Lankan Experience*. Geneva: ILO.

Said, Edward. 1986. "Orientalism Reconsidered." In *Literature, Politics, and Theory*, edited by Francis Barker, 210–29. London: Methuen.

Samarasinghe, Diyanath. 1995. "Sri Lanka." In *International Handbook on Alcohol and Culture*, edited by Dwight B. Heath, 270–79. Westport, CT: Greenwood Press.

———. 2005. *Strategies to Address Alcohol Problems*. Colombo, Sri Lanka: FORUT.

———. 2006. "Sri Lanka: Alcohol Now and Then." *Addiction* 101: 626–28.

Sampson, Steven. 2005. "Integrity Warriors: Global Morality and the Anti-Corruption Movement in the Balkans." In *Corruption: Anthropological Perspectives*, edited by Dieter Haller and Cris Shore, 103–30. London: Pluto Press.

Saunders, John B., and Simon de Burgh. 1998. "The Distribution of Alcohol Consumption." In *Drinking Patterns and Their Consequences,* edited by Marcus Grant and Jorge Litvak, 129–52. Washington, DC: Taylor and Francis.

Saxena, Shekhar. 1999. "Country Profile on Alcohol in India." In *Alcohol and Public Health in 8 Developing Countries,* edited by Leanne Riley and Mac Marshall, 37–60. Geneva: World Health Organization.

Schmandt-Besserat, Denise. 2001. "Feasting in the Ancient Near East." In *Feasts: Archaeological and Ethnographic Perspectives on Food, Politics, and Power,* edited by Michael Dietler and Brian Hayden, 391–403. Washington, DC: Smithsonian Institution Press.

Schneider, Jane, and Peter Schneider. 2005. "The Sack of Two Cities: Organized Crime and Political Corruption in Youngstown and Palermo." In *Corruption: Anthropological Perspectives,* edited by Dieter Haller and Cris Shore, 29–46. London: Pluto Press.

Scott, Joan. 1988. *Gender and the Politics of History.* New York: Columbia University Press.

Sedgwick, Eve Kosofsky. 1993. *Tendencies.* Durham: Duke University Press.

Seilhamer, Ruth Ann, and Theodore Jacob. 1990. "Family Factors and Adjustment of Children of Alcoholics." In *Children of Alcoholics: Critical Perspectives,* edited by Michael Windle and John S. Searles, 168–86. New York: Guilford Press.

Singer, Merrill. 1986. "Toward a Political-Economy of Alcoholism: The Missing Link in the Anthropology of Drinking." *Social Science and Medicine* 23, no. 2: 113–30.

———. 2001. "Toward a Bio-Cultural and Political Economic Integration of Alcohol, Tobacco and Drug Studies in the Coming Century." *Social Science and Medicine* 53: 199–213.

Singer, Merrill, Freddie Valentin, Hans Baer, and Zhongke Jia. 1998. "Why Does Juan Garcia Have a Drinking Problem? The Perspective of Critical Medical Anthropology." In *Understanding and Applying Medical Anthropology,* edited by Peter J. Brown, 286–302. Mountain View, CA: Mayfield.

Single, Eric. 2000. "The Positive and Negative Impacts of Alcohol Use." In *The Alcohol Report,* edited by Martin Plant and Douglas Cameron, 123–29. London: Free Association Books.

Single, Eric, and Victor E. Leino. 1998. "The Levels, Patterns, and Consequences of Drinking." In *Drinking Patterns and Their Consequences,* edited by Marcus Grant and Jorge Litvak, 7–24. Washington, DC: Taylor and Francis.

Smart, Josephine. 2005. "Cognac, Beer, Red Wine or Soft Drinks? Hong Kong Identity and Wedding Banquets." In *Drinking Cultures: Alcohol and Identity,* edited by Thomas M. Wilson, 107–28. Oxford: Berg.

Smart, Reginald G. 1998. "Trends in Drinking and Patterns of Drinking." In *Drinking Patterns and Their Consequences,* edited by Marcus Grant and Jorge Litvak, 25–41. Washington, DC: Taylor and Francis.

Sobell, Linda C., John A Cunningham, Mark B. Sobell, and Tony Toneatto. 1993. "A Life-Span Perspective on Natural Recovery (Self-Change) From Alcohol Problems." In *Addictive Behaviors Across the Life Span: Prevention, Treatment and Policy Issues,* edited by John S. Baer, G. Alan Marlatt, and Robert J. McMahon, 34–66. Newbury Park, CA: Sage.

Spicer, Paul. 1997. "Toward a (Dys)functional Anthropology of Drinking: Ambivalence and the American Indian Experience with Alcohol." *Medical Anthropology Quarterly* 11, no. 3: 306–23.

Spivak, Gayatri C. 1985. "Can the Subaltern Speak? Speculations on Widow Sacrifice." *Wedge* 7–8: 120–30.

Sri Lanka Bureau of Foreign Employment (SLBFE). 2006. "Annual Statistical Report of Foreign Employment—2005." Research Division, Battaramulla.

Stabenow, Dana. 2002. *Better to Rest.* New York: Signet.

Stacey, Judith. 1990. *Brave New Families.* London: Basic Books.

Stephens, Lynn. 1995. "Women's Rights are Human Rights: The Merging of Feminine and Feminist Interests Among El Salvador's Mothers of the Disappeared (Co-Madres)." *American Ethnologist* 22, no. 4: 807–27.

Stone, Linda. 1997. *Kinship and Gender: An Introduction.* Boulder, CO: Westview Press.

Strunin, Lee. 2001. "Assessing Alcohol Consumption: Developments from Qualitative Research Methods." *Social Science and Medicine* 53: 215–26.

"Sugar, Booze and Fags." 2006. *Sunday Island,* 9 July 9, 8.

Suggs, David N. 1996. "Mosadi Tshwene: The Construction of Gender and the Consumption of Alcohol in Botswana." *American Ethnologist* 23, no. 3: 597–610.

——. 2001. "'These Young Chaps Think They Are Just Men, Too': Redistributing Masculinity in Kgatleng Bars." *Social Science and Medicine* 53: 241–50.

Sukul, Diwakar. 2000. "Complementary Therapies for the Treatment of Alcohol Dependence." In *The Alcohol Report,* edited by Martin Plant and Douglas Cameron, 189–205. London: Free Association Books.

Taylor, Stuart P., and Stephen T. Chermack. 1993. "Alcohol, Drugs and Human Physical Aggression." *Journal of Studies on Alcohol,* Supplement 11: 78–88.

Tax Information at a Glance. 2005 http://www.fpd.gov.lk/pdf/revenue/Taxinformation_2005n.pdf (accessed June 26, 2006).

Thornton, Mary Anna. 1987. "Sekt Versus Schnapps in an Austrian Village." In *Constructive Drinking: Perspectives on Drink from Anthropology,* edited by Mary Douglas, 102–12. Cambridge: Cambridge University Press.

Thurman, Christopher. 2000. "Alcoholic Drinks: Supply and Demand." In *The Alcohol Report,* edited by Martin Plant and Douglas Cameron, 79–122. London: Free Association Books.

Travel Lanka: Monthly Tourist Guide. 2003. "Activities and Attractions" 9, no. 8: 45.

United Nations. 2003. "Directory: Non-Governmental Organizations and Drug Abuse Prevention, Treatment and Rehabilitation." United Nations Office on Drugs and Crime, Vienna.

Valverde, Mariana. 1998. *Diseases of the Will: Alcohol and the Dilemmas of Freedom.* New York: Cambridge University Press.

Vijesandiran, Sangaran. 2004. *Alcoholism in the Sri Lankan Plantation Community.* Kandy, Sri Lanka: Satyodaya.

Warhol, Robyn R. 2002. "The Rhetoric of Addiction: From Victorian Novels to AA." In *High Anxieties: Cultural Studies in Addiction,* edited by Janet Farrell Brodie and Marc Redfield, 97–108. Berkeley: University of California Press.

Weerakoon, Nedra. 1998. "Sri Lanka: A Case Study of International Female Labour Migration." In *Legal Protection for Asian Women Migrant Workers: Strategies for Action,* edited by S. Sta. Maria Amparita, J. J. Balisnono, R. Plaetevoet, and R. Selwyn, 97–118. Makati City, Philippines: Ateneo Human Rights Center.

Weinstone, Ann. 2002. "Welcome to the Pharmacy: Addiction, Transcendence, and Virtual Reality." In *High Anxieties: Cultural Studies in Addiction,* edited by Janet Farrell Brodie and Marc Redfield, 161–74. Berkeley: University of California Press.

Whitehead, Stephen. 1998. "The Impact of Alcohol Control Measures on Drinking Patterns." In *Drinking Patterns and Their Consequences,* edited by Marcus Grant and Jorge Litvak, 153–67. Washington, DC: Taylor and Francis.

Wilcox, Danny M. 1998. *Alcoholic Thinking: Language, Culture and Belief in Alcoholics Anonymous.* Westport, CT: Praeger.

Williams, Raymond. 1977. *Marxism and Literature.* Oxford: Oxford University Press.

Wilson, Douglas C., and William L. Rathje. 2001. "Garbage and the Modern American Feast." In *Feasts: Archaeological and Ethnographic Perspectives on Food, Politics, and Power,* edited by Michael Dietler and Brian Hayden, 404–21. Washington, DC: Smithsonian Institution.

Wilson, Thomas M. 2005. "Drinking Cultures: Sites and Practices in the Production and Expression of Identity." In *Drinking Cultures: Alcohol and Identity,* edited by Thomas M. Wilson, 1–24. Oxford: Berg.

Winslow, Deborah. 1980. "Rituals of First Menstruation in Sri Lanka." *Man,* New Series 15, no. 4: 603–25.

Wirz, Paul. 1954. *Exorcism and the Art of Healing in Ceylon.* Leiden: E. J. Brill.

World Health Organization. 2003. "Directory of Health Related NGOs: Sri Lanka." Colombo, Sri Lanka: World Health Organization.

——. 2004a. "Global Status Report on Alcohol 2004, pt. I." Geneva: World Health Organization, Department of Mental Health and Substance Abuse.

——. 2004b. "Global Status Report on Alcohol 2004, pt. II. Country Profiles, South-East Asia Region: Sri Lanka." Geneva: World Health Organization, Department of Mental Health and Substance Abuse.

Wright, Linda. 2000. "Evidence-Based Alcohol Education in Schools." In *The Alcohol Report,* edited by Martin Plant and Douglas Cameron, 206–34. London: Free Association Books.

Yalman, Nur. 1967. *Under the Bo Tree.* Berkeley: University of California Press.

Index

Abeyasinghe, Ranil, 15–16, 18–19, 21, 70–71, 93, 100, 112, 136
abstinence, 6, 21, 26, 32–34, 71, 79–82, 95, 180, 242
accidents, 25, 35, 85, 162–66, 176
acetaldehyde, 178
addiction
  behavior vs. disease, 54, 179–84, 189, 205–6
  cravings, 6, 27, 51, 179–82, 215
  cultural differences, 181–82
  Euro-American perspectives, 17, 49–51, 54, 127, 177, 179–81, 185, 188–89, 193, 205
  vs. habit, 50–51, 180–81
  physical consequences, 41, 183, 189–93, 197–98
  social consequences, 183–85, 188–91, 193–94
  statistical data, 17
  withdrawal, 54, 62, 178, 181, 192, 195, 205, 209, 211, 214
  See also *sihiya naetuwa*
adolescent drinking, 19, 72, 83
agency, 6, 46, 48–54, 60, 62, 65, 67
aggression, 20, 53, 61, 120, 126, 166–69
alcohol, types of
  arrack, 15, 19, 29–30, 35, 60, 88, 92, 100, 132–36, 166
  beer, 35, 71–72, 88, 100
  foreign liquor, 3, 32, 35, 38, 99
  offered at ceremonies, 92–99

preference based on occupation, 76
preference based on status, 35, 60–61, 76, 87, 100, 105
toddy, 33, 35, 71, 100, 134, 147, 156
Very Special Old Arrack (VSOA), 35
See also *kasippu*
Alcohol and Drug Information Center (ADIC), 15, 20–21, 71, 85–86, 177, 240–43
Alcoholics Anonymous (AA), 127, 180, 183–84, 222
alcoholism, 17, 49–50, 165–66, 173, 176–89, 206–7
almsgivings. See *daanas*
Altman, Yochanan, 92
Ames, Genevieve, 3, 177
Antabuse, 207–9, 211, 220
Anti-Alcohol Association (*Amadyapa Vyaapaaraya*), 214
Arishta, 210
Armstrong, Gary, 82–83
arrack, 15, 19, 29–30, 35, 60, 88, 92, 100, 132–36, 166
Ayurvedic treatment method, 206, 210–11

Baklien, Bergljot, 15, 32, 53–54, 64, 76–78, 92, 100, 105, 107, 113, 126
Barker, Judith, 2–4, 6
bars, 35, 38, 61, 76, 87–88, 99–103
Bateson, Gregory, 47–48, 116, 122, 129, 199
beebaddoo, 62–64, 189–90, 221
beer, 35, 71–72, 88, 100

Befrienders International, 212
behavior. *See* social norms
Bennett, Linda, 3, 177
Bennie, Colin, 181, 205, 209, 213
Bentota Beach Hotel, 161
binge drinking, 6, 41–42, 76, 85, 181, 205
biological effects of alcohol, 41, 47–48, 56,
    164, 178–79, 210
Bodhisattva, 57–58
bonDa, 16
Borovoy, Amy, 126–28, 233
boundaries, 3, 68–69, 87, 168, 171, 174
Bourdieu, Pierre, 48–50, 69, 129, 150
Buddhism, 9, 15–16, 25–28, 43–44, 51, 81,
    91, 159, 217–19

Cameron, Douglas, 49, 176, 180–81, 230
Campbell, David, 181, 205, 209, 213
capitalism, 5–6, 18, 30, 231–32
Carrier, James, 75, 109, 129
Cartesian dualism, 48, 50
celebrations. *See* ceremonies
Central Bank, 9, 39
ceremonies
    coming-of-age, 11–12, 97–98
    daanas, 92, 96, 152, 159
    effect of social norms, 4, 60, 88, 91,
        94–95
    funerals, 11–12, 92, 96–97, 151–52,
        191, 194
    gifts, 22, 92–93, 97
    New Year holiday, 9, 21–23, 32–33, 89–91,
        102, 195
    role of alcohol, 26, 91–92, 95–97
    spending on alcohol, 97–99
    weddings, 11–12, 61, 92–96, 98–99,
        161, 194
charmings, 218–20
Chatterjee, Piya, 32, 110, 118
Christianity, 9, 26, 29, 31–32, 71, 91
codependence, 127. *See also* enabling
Colombo North General Hospital, 119,
    167, 213
colonial period, 5–6, 25, 28–34, 44, 110,
    118, 131
Consumer Price Index (CPI), 244–45
consumption
    adolescents, 19, 83
    annual cycles, 89–91, 108
    associated with eating meat, 32–34, 87, 92
    changing patterns, 18–20, 82
    colonial period, 30–34

deadly results, 112, 165–66, 190, 192,
    199, 225
extreme intoxication, 160–66
justification, 185–88
legal vs. illicit liquor, 36, 41, 101,
    105, 132
medical purposes, 32, 62, 194, 210
for pleasure, 14, 88–108
stages of intoxication, 55–62
statistical data, 15, 20–21, 35–36, 71,
    177, 240–42
struggles over, 11, 83, 109–15, 119–20
time of day, 62–63, 66, 96, 106, 195, 197
corruption, 5, 40–41, 43, 132, 141–44
cravings, 6, 27, 51, 179–82, 215
craziness, 53, 161
cultural construction of identity, 6, 31,
    49–51, 68–70, 75–76, 113, 116–18
cure rates, 209
Customs Department, 38

daanas, 92, 96, 152, 159
Daily Mirror, 90
deaths, alcohol-related, 112, 165–66, 190,
    192, 199, 225
debt burden, 9
Department of Census and Statistics, 9, 245
dependency. *See* addiction
de Silva, K.M., 29, 31, 211
Dietler, Michael, 3–5, 18, 28–29, 68, 91,
    131, 230
disease concept of alcoholism, 54, 179–84,
    189, 205–6
distillation, 42, 134–38, 232
Distilleries Company of Sri Lanka, 36
divorce, 107, 126–29, 218
domestic violence, 5, 20, 24–25, 118–27,
    176, 203
Dramaxone, 172
drinkers, types of
    adolescents, 19, 72, 83
    beebaddoo, 62–64, 189–90, 221
    binge, 6, 41–42, 76, 85, 181, 205
    habitual drunkards, 62–63, 189–90, 221
    pleasure/jolly, 14, 55, 88–108, 184, 186
    problem, 5–7, 51, 128, 180–99, 204–6,
        209, 229–30
    tricksters, 158–59, 162
drinking establishments
    bars, 35, 38, 61, 76, 87–88, 99–103
    hotels, 3, 35, 38, 93, 98, 100, 161–62
    segregation by social status, 100

taverns, 7, 35, 88, 99–107, 136, 141–44, 147, 149–50
drunken comportment, 6, 47, 60, 64, 156–62, 166–69, 172–73, 202

Eber, Christine, 5, 26, 34, 70, 124, 231
economics. *See* political economics
Edgerton, Robert, 6, 47, 60, 156, 174, 202
educational programs, 84–86, 208, 216, 226
Education Department, 85
Elias, Robert, 231–32
enabling, 127, 129, 184, 195, 200, 213, 233
ethanol (ethyl alcohol), 3, 165, 178
ethnography, 4–8, 13–14, 16, 54, 156, 182
Excise Department, 25–26, 37–40, 132, 135, 145
excise taxes, 37–40, 42, 132, 147
expenditures on alcohol, 78, 111–12, 195–96

families
    bonds created by drinking together, 77, 88
    divorce, 107, 126–29, 218
    domestic harmony, 41
    domestic violence, 5, 20, 24–25, 118–27, 176, 203
    effect of female migration, 110, 113–18, 129
    household financial strategies, 27, 81, 109, 111–12, 119, 193, 207
    household relations, 22–23, 41, 53, 111, 207
    role in treatments, 213
    socialization into drinking, 84
    See also gender roles
female migration, effect on families, 110, 113–18, 129
fermentation, 28, 134–36
Fernandez-Armesto, Felipe, 28, 91
festivals. *See* ceremonies
fighting, 23, 61, 110, 118–27, 166–69
Five Precepts, 26–28, 43, 81, 85, 153, 159, 215–16
foreign exchange, 9
foreign liquor, 3, 32, 35, 38, 99
Freud, Sigmund, 49
funerals, 11–12, 92, 96–97, 151–52, 191, 194

gambling, 21–23, 27, 89
Gamburd, Michele, 7, 27, 32, 110, 114–15, 122, 141, 170

ganja, 51, 211
gender roles
    conflicts over alcohol consumption, 110, 115, 119–20
    differences, 16, 21, 55, 81
    division of labor, 115
    females, 66, 69–74, 82, 93, 100–102, 110–11, 115, 127, 231, 242–43
    males, 69–72, 74–83, 93, 110, 112–13, 242–43
    non-drinking males, 74–75, 79–82
    See also families
globalization, 5, 18–19, 110, 115, 230–33
gooDa, 134–37
Goonesekere, Savitri, 124
Gorski, Terence, 178–79, 181
government policies, 5, 25, 27, 29–30, 36–45, 91, 124, 132, 155, 231–33
Gulf Cooperation Council, 114
Gureje, Oye, 181–82
Gusfield, Joseph, 89

habitual drunkards, 62–63, 189–90
Heath, Dwight, 6, 13, 42–43, 54–55, 67–68, 72–73, 82, 84–88, 131, 156–57, 181, 230
hegemony, 69
heroin, 211–12
Heyman, Josiah, 75, 109, 129
Hinduism, 9, 26, 71, 91, 220
HIV/AIDS, 16
hooting, 161–62, 174, 202
hotels as drinking establishments, 3, 35, 38, 93, 98, 100, 161–62
household financial strategies, 27, 81, 109, 111–12, 119, 193, 207
household relations, 22–23, 41, 53, 111, 207. *See also* families
Hunt, Geoffrey, 2–4, 6, 70, 77
Hussein, Ameena, 119, 127

identity
    age, 82–86
    categorization, 68–69
    cultural construction of, 6, 31, 49–51, 68–70, 75–76, 113, 116–18
    education, 82–84
    group dynamics, 68, 87
    mind-body split, 2, 47–50
    occupation, 75–77, 112
    personhood, 6, 46, 54n
    rank/status, 76–77, 94–95
    See also gender roles

illicit liquor. See *kasippu*
imprisonment, 145, 203–4, 215–17
Indian Ocean tsunami (2004), 10,
    152–53, 186
inflation, 17, 244–45
Institute of Policy Studies, 9, 114, 244
International Distillers Limited, 36
International Monetary Fund, 9, 230
intoxication, 6, 26–29, 46–66, 72, 81–82,
    122–26, 157–76, 181–82, 204–5. See
    also *sihiya naetuwa*

Jayawardena, Kumari, 5, 30–32, 92, 118, 152
joliyaTa, 88, 184

Kali, 220–25, 234
Kande Vihara, 225
Karaava caste, 29
karma, 27, 43, 153, 217
kasippu
    consumption, 15, 35–36, 103, 132
    costs, 17, 60–61, 99–101
    distribution, 132–33, 139–40
    family enterprise, 148–50
    gooDa, 134–37
    government regulations, 132, 134–35, 155
    ingredients, 56, 103, 134–35
    kooD, 135–36
    law enforcement, 132, 135, 137–38,
        140–46, 149–50, 155
    production, 133–38, 147–48
    retailers, 101–4, 132, 136, 138–46,
        148–50, 154, 202
    social acceptance, 132, 134, 150
    transportation, 133–34, 138–39, 142
Kenkel, Donald, 42
Kishline, Audrey, 181
Konradsen, Fleming, 169–70, 173
kooD, 135–36
Kunitz, Stephen, 18, 70, 112, 166, 180, 182,
    220, 230

laejjayi, 64, 157n
law enforcement, 5, 90–91, 132, 134–38,
    140–46, 149–50, 155, 158–59,
    165–66, 215
Lawrence, Patricia, 220–21
leDek, 189
Leino, Victor, 41–42, 60
Leonard, Kenneth, 118–19
Levine, Hillel, 132
Levy, Jerrold, 112, 182

Lion Brewery, 36
literacy, 9

MacAndrew, Craig, 6, 47, 60, 156, 174, 202
malnutrition, 189, 192, 200
manufacture. See production of alcohol
marijuana. See *ganja*
Marriage Registration Ordinance, 128
Mars, Gerald, 75, 92
Marshall, Mac, 3, 35, 55, 177
masculinity, 55, 69–71, 74–76, 110–13,
    115–19, 127, 129, 172
mat kudu, 85
mat paen, 16, 85
McKinney, Iain, 181, 205, 209, 213
McKnight, David, 34, 80, 110
Medicine, Beatrice, 26, 34, 55, 57, 79,
    103, 220
Melley, Timothy, 49, 180
Mel Medura, 212–15
metabolism, 54, 178–79
methanol (methyl alcohol), 135n, 165, 174
Middle East, 10–11, 19, 28, 44, 105–10,
    113–16, 131, 173
military, 7–8, 32, 76–77, 232
mind-body split, 2, 47–50
Mintz, Sydney, 30
Mitchell, Jon, 82–83
moonshine. See *kasippu*
motor control, 46–47
Muslims, 9, 91, 106, 117

National Authority on Tobacco and Alcohol,
    26, 39–41, 233
National Dangerous Drugs Control
    Board, 40
networks, 4, 69, 75, 79, 82, 86, 91, 99,
    117–18, 124
New Year holiday, 9, 21–23, 32–33, 89–91,
    102, 195
nirvana, 51
Noble Eightfold Path, 27, 153
non-governmental organizations (NGO),
    12, 211–12
normal drinking, 5–6, 49, 177, 182

Pali, 27–28, 85, 219
Pallekale Open Prison Camp, 215–17
pansil, 26, 215
Peebles, Patrick, 5, 29–30
peer pressure, 19, 95, 116, 203–4, 213, 226
Peiris, Pushpalatha, 169–70, 173

Perez, Joseph, 127, 178, 185, 188–89
Pernanen, Kai, 14, 46–48, 64–65, 107, 118–20, 126, 166
personhood, 6, 46, 54n
pin, 153
pirith, 22, 92, 96, 152, 168, 195, 218–19
Plant, Martin, 176, 180–81, 230
plantations, 30–32, 71, 118, 132, 147n
Poisons, Opium and Dangerous Drugs Ordinance, 38
Police Narcotics Bureau, 132, 145, 149
political economics, 4–5, 24, 30, 131–34, 188, 229
politicians, 4, 39, 44, 90, 110, 114, 146, 150–52
Popp, Sharon, 75
Poya Days, 91, 159, 215–16
Prevention of Substance Abuse and Rehabilitation (Sarvodaya Samodaya Sewa) program, 214–15
problem drinkers, 5–7, 51, 128, 180–99, 204–6, 209, 229–30
production of alcohol, 27–31, 35–36, 42, 133–38, 147–48, 232
pseudointoxication, 65, 167–68

quarter (bottle), 17, 56–58, 139, 198n,
Quintero, Gilbert, 17–18, 34, 59

Ramadan, 117
rational economic man, 50–51
rational social man, 49, 51–54, 59–60, 67, 184–89
reciprocation. *See* syndication
rehabilitation, 40, 44, 196, 200, 211–17, 226–27
reincarnation, 51, 81
religious prohibition, 26–28, 43–44, 71
retailers, 101–4, 132, 136, 138–46, 148–50, 154, 202
revenue from alcohol, 5, 25, 29, 36–39, 42, 132
Right Livelihood, 26–27
rituals, 22, 26, 47, 60, 67, 88, 97, 105, 221–25
RoDii, 33
Rogers, John, 26, 29–31, 92
Room, Robin, 13–14, 36, 65, 67, 82, 156, 166–68, 176, 179
Rosovsky, Haydee, 37, 42–43, 82, 84–85, 181
Royce, James, 50, 165–66, 173, 177–78, 181, 185–86

Samarasinghe, Diyanath, 15–19, 31–32, 42, 62, 64, 71, 75–78, 92, 100, 105, 112–13, 126
Saudi Arabia, 5, 114, 116–18
Scratchley, David, 50, 165–66, 173, 177–78, 181, 185–86
Sedgwick, Eve Kosofsky, 48, 50
self-control, 49, 51, 54–60, 63, 116, 180, 205
sellers. *See* retailers
Senchak, Marilyn, 118–19
sexism. *See* gender roles
sihiya naetuwa, 24, 49, 51–54, 56–57, 59–60, 65, 67, 161, 176. *See also* intoxication
siitu, 158–59
sil, 215–16
Singer, Merrill, 5, 110, 112, 182, 188, 230, 232–33
Single, Eric, 41–42, 60, 164
Sinhalas, 9, 11, 31–34, 51–52, 55–58, 73, 153, 231
Sinhalese Buddhism. *See* Buddhism
Sobell, Linda, 205
social norms
    acceptance of drinking, 132, 134, 150
    conduct, 59–61, 64–65, 107, 173
    drunken comportment, 6, 47, 60, 64, 156–62, 166–69, 172–73, 202
    dry vs. wet societies, 82–83
    effect on ceremonies, 4, 60, 88, 91, 94–95
    enabling, 127, 129, 184, 195, 200, 213, 233
    enjoyment, 43, 71
    extreme intoxication, 160–66
    fighting, 23, 61, 110, 118–27, 166–69
    hooting, 161–62, 174, 202
    networks, 4, 69, 75, 79, 82, 86, 91, 99, 117–18, 124
    peer pressure, 19, 95, 116, 203–4, 213, 226
    relationships, 3, 11, 28, 77, 82, 99, 117–18, 152
    rituals, 22, 26, 47, 60, 67, 88, 97, 105, 221–25
    rules, 47, 64–66, 68, 107, 126, 170, 174
    status, 60–61, 64, 76–77, 94–95
    stigma, 60–61, 63, 129, 183
    suicides, 128, 169–71, 175, 191
    "time out" behavior, 47, 60, 156–62, 168
    See also gender roles
somiya, 55, 89
sorghum, 18, 77, 88
Spicer, Paul, 4–5, 79–80
Sri Lanka Bureau of Foreign Employment, 114

stages of intoxication, 55–62
statistical data
    addiction, 17
    consumption, 15, 20–21, 35–36, 71,
        177, 240–42
    cure rates, 209
    expenditures on alcohol, 78,
        111–12, 195–96
    household expenditures, 112
    kasippu production, 134–36
    labor force, 114–15
    literacy, 9
    revenue from alcohol, 25, 33–39
    suicides, 169
stigma, 60–61, 63, 129, 183
Structural Adjustment Programs, 9,
    230, 232
Strunin, Lee, 72
Suggs, David, 18, 70, 77, 87–88, 113, 230
suicides, 128, 169–71, 175, 191
Sumithrayo Drug Demand Reduction
    Programme, 212–14
syndication, 77–79, 106, 117, 183

taanhaawa, 51
Tamils, 9, 21, 32–33, 89–91, 102, 195, 223
taverns, 7, 35, 88, 99–107, 136, 141–44,
    147, 149–50
taxes, 37–40, 42, 132, 147
temperance, 25, 31–32, 36, 45, 214, 231
Theravada Buddhism. *See* Buddhism
Thornton, Mary, 87
"time out" behavior, 47, 60, 156–62, 168
tourism, 35, 40, 71, 83, 93, 100, 134,
    211, 230
Travel Lanka, 35–36
treatments
    charmings, 218–20
    community-administered
        correctives, 201–4
    educational programs, 84–86, 208,
        216, 226
    facilities shortages, 211
    imprisonment, 145, 203–4, 215–17

indigenous (Ayurvedic) methods, 206,
    210–11, 214, 217, 219
    medical intervention, 205–11
    rehabilitation, 40, 44, 196, 200,
        211–17, 226–27
    role of families, 213
    social pressure as deterrent, 203–4,
        213, 226
    spiritual resources, 217–26
    vows, 220–26, 234
    western (allopathic) methods,
        206–10, 217
tricksters (drinkers), 158–59, 162
trishaws, 138, 222, 225
tsunami. *See* Indian Ocean tsunami (2004)

unemployment, 9, 11, 44, 112–13, 116
United National Party (UNP),
    106–7, 151–52
United States, 8, 56, 82–85, 89, 128, 169,
    177, 179–80, 184, 193, 217

Valverde, Mariana, 6, 37, 50, 59, 67, 70, 75,
    179–80, 231
van der Hoek, Wim, 169–70, 173
Veddas, 33–34
vedamahattayaa, 32–33, 43, 147
Very Special Old Arrack (VSOA), 35
Vesak, 23, 91, 159
violence, 20, 53, 61, 120, 126, 166–69
vows, 220–26, 234

weddings, 11–12, 61, 92–96, 98–99, 161, 194
Wilcox, Danny, 18, 49, 116, 177, 193, 217–18
Williams, Raymond, 69
Wilson, Thomas, 3–4, 75, 91
withdrawal, 54, 62, 178, 181, 192, 195, 205,
    209, 211, 214
within-limits drinking, 60, 64, 156–57, 201
World Health Organization (WHO), 15, 17,
    36, 109, 118–19, 162, 177, 240, 242
Wright, Linda, 84–85

Zakat, 117